CW00326884

Amsterdam
and the Randstad

22nd 23rd

Dialling code: 153
0031 20 7 digit

Cadogan Guides
West End House (3rd Floor), 11 Hills Place,
London W1R 1AG, UK
becky.kendall@morrispub.co.uk

The Globe Pequot Press
246 Goose Lane
PO Box 480, Guilford
Connecticut 06437–0480

Chapter title pages taken from photographs
    by Gerard van Vuuren and Kate Paice

Book and cover design by Animage
Cover photographs: front: Kicca Tommasi
                back: Kicca Tommasi
Maps © Cadogan Guides, drawn by Map Creation Ltd

Editorial Director: Vicki Ingle
Series Editor: Linda McQueen

Editor: Matthew Tanner
Indexing: Isobel McLean
Production: Book Production Services

A catalogue record for this book is available from the British Library
ISBN 1–86011–941–7

Printed and bound in Great Britain by Cambridge University Press.

About the Author

Rodney Bolt is seldom happier than when rattling along the canals of Amsterdam on his Miss Marple Dutch bicycle, or burrowing through papers in the Municipal Archive. Having lived in Greece, South Africa, Britain and Germany, he arrived in Amsterdam in 1991, and now nothing can convince him to leave. He has also written Cadogan Guides to Germany, Bavaria and Madeira, as well as other books and numerous articles on the Netherlands. In 1994 he won the German National Tourist Office's 'Travel Writer of the Year' award.

Please help us to keep this guide up to date

We have done our best to ensure that the information in this guide is correct at the time of going to press. But places and facilities are constantly changing, and standards and prices in hotels and restaurants fluctuate. We would be delighted to receive any comments concerning existing entries or omissions. Authors of the best letters will receive a copy of the Cadogan Guide of their choice.

Contents

A Guide to the Guide

This guide begins its journey before you do, with **Travel** and **Practical A–Z** chapters packed with information to help you plan your trip; while **History** and **Art and Architecture** fill in the background to what you will see when you arrive.

Many visitors to Holland start with **Amsterdam,** and for many this is their only experience of the country. The city therefore has a chapter to itself, with practical information at the beginning and listings of hotels, restaurants, shopping, entertainment and gay life at the end of the chapter. This is followed by a number of **Day Trips** from Amsterdam, all of which are close enough to get back in time for an evening drink, but far enough away to be different.

The urban sprawl around Amsterdam on the western coast of the country is known as the **Randstad.** Within this region are a number of destinations which deserve their own chapter: the bustling port of **Rotterdam**; Rembrandt's birthplace, **Leiden;** the tranquil refinement of **The Hague and Delft** and **Utrecht** which, according to the Dutch, was built by 'God himself'. Finally, the **Language** section offers a selection of words and phrases to help you get around, a menu reader and a list of Dutch culinary treats for you to try.

Introduction

We had a pleasant time in Holland. They have reduced work to a minimum there. They seem to be simple, polite and dignified folk. Well set up men and girls and women who laughed all the time.

James Joyce, 1927

Amsterdam, The Hague and Rotterdam—and their surrounding towns—have moved so close together over the centuries that they now almost form a single giant metropolis. Utrecht, though not officially in the Randstad, is so close that is has become an honourary member. The Dutch even give this conurbation a name: the Randstad—which translates literally as 'Edge City', or 'Border City'. The towns form a rough line along the coast and rivers that marked the traditional boundaries of the State of Holland.

Yet there are patches of green in-between each urban sprawl—patches of red, yellow and mauve too, if you happen to be travelling in early spring, when the bulb fields are in bloom. And the cities preserve their particular styles and atmospheres so determinedly that they could be on far sides of the country. The Hague, graceful and sedate, is the age-old rival of rough, quirky Amsterdam. Rotterdam, an architecturally edgy phoenix that pushed its way out of the ashes left by the Second World War, is perhaps the one place in the Netherlands that actually feels like a city, rather than a grown-up village. Haarlem and Leiden recline and revel with university-town abandon, and Delft quietly preserves its historical air.

Travel

Getting There

By Air

The Netherlands' major international airport, **Amsterdam Airport Schiphol**, enjoys a reputation as one of the world's sleekest and most user-friendly airports. It serves direct flights from London, Manchester, New York, Los Angeles, Toronto, Vancouver and Sydney as well as many other airports around the UK and Americas. There is also a smaller airport at **Rotterdam**, which receives some international flights, mainly from continental Europe.

Flights from London take about 45 minutes, from New York about 8 hours. Several carriers operate the London–Amsterdam route (see list below), so competition is strong. A browse through the travel ads in the British press (such as *Time Out* or the *London Evening Standard* will divulge any number of return flights priced below £100, even on scheduled airlines.

From **Ireland**, Aer Lingus has four flights daily from Dublin to Amsterdam, and daily flights from Cork; prices start at around IR£142 return. From **North America**, KLM, the Dutch national airline, operates in partnership with the American company Northwest Airlines. Together they offer a service that takes in most major US cities, including daily flights from New York, Baltimore, Los Angeles and Miami. KLM also flies daily to a number of Canadian cities, including Vancouver, Toronto and Montreal. Delta operates daily nonstop from New York, and Martinair, a Dutch airline, flies from many US cities and from Toronto. Prices direct from New York start at about $308 for special deals and go up to around $799 for more conventional fares. American travellers thinking of stopping over in London might find it cheaper to buy a ticket to Amsterdam in the UK.

transport from the airport

Schiphol airport is well served by road and rail connections—you can get almost anywhere in the country in an hour or two. Most people head first for Amsterdam (for connection details *see* p.60).

discount and student fares

UK

Europe Student Travel, 6 Campden Street, London W8, ✆ (020) 7727 7647, catering to non-students as well.

STA Travel, 6 Wright's Lane, London W8 6TA, or 85 Shaftesbury Avenue, London W1V 7AD, ✆ (020) 7361 6161/6262; Bristol, ✆ (0117) 929 4399; Leeds, ✆ (0113) 244 9212; Manchester, ✆ (0161) 834 0668; Oxford, ✆ (01865) 792800; Cambridge, ✆ (01223) 366966 and many other branches in the UK.

Trailfinders, 194 Kensington High St, London W8 7RG, ✆ (020) 7938 3939 (for non-students as well).

Travel Cuts, 295a Regent St, London W1R 7YA, ✆ (020) 7255 1944.

USIT Campus Travel, 52 Grosvenor Gardens, SW1W OAG, or 174 Kensington High Street, London W8 7RG, ✆ (020) 7730 3402 with branches at most UK universities, including Bristol, ✆ (0117) 929 2494; Manchester, ✆ (0161) 833 2046; Edinburgh, ✆ (0131) 668 3303; Birmingham, ✆ (0121) 414 1848; Oxford, ✆ (01865) 242 067; Cambridge, ✆ (01223) 324283, or see their website at *www.usitcampus.co.uk.*

Airline Numbers

Schiphol Airport (info)		✆ (0900) 0141
Air Exel	UK	✆ (020) 8750 9002
Aer Lingus	UK	✆ (020) 8899 4747
	Dublin	✆ (01) 886 8888
	Amsterdam	✆ (020) 520 5288
American Airlines		
	USA	✆ (800) 433 7300
	Amsterdam	✆ (06) 022 7844
British Airways	UK	✆ (0345) 222 111
	Amsterdam	✆ (020) 346 9559
British Midland	UK	✆ (0345) 554 554
	Amsterdam	✆ (06) 601 2301
Canadian Airlines		
(Toronto)	Canada	✆ (800) 665 1177
	UK	✆ (020) 7745 5000
	Rotterdam	✆ (0800) 022 8270
Delta	USA	✆ (800) 241 4141
	Amsterdam	✆ (06) 504 0606
easyJet	UK	✆ (0870) 6000 000
	Amsterdam	✆ (023) 568 4880
	www.easyjet.com	

KLM	UK	✆ (0990) 750 900
	USA	✆ (800) 3 747 747
	Amsterdam	✆ (020) 474 7747
	www.klm.com	

(direct flights to Amsterdam from New York, LA, Vancouver, Toronto, Belfast, Bristol, Birmingham, Cardiff, London Heathrow, Southampton)

KLM uk	UK	✆ (0990) 074 074
	Amsterdam	✆ (020) 474 7747

(flights to Amsterdam from Aberdeen, Edinburgh, Glasgow, Leeds and Newcastle)

KLM Cityhopper	UK	✆ (020) 8750 9002

(flights from London Heathrow to Rotterdam)

Martinair	USA	✆ (800) 627 8462
	Amsterdam	✆ (020) 601 1767
TWA	USA	✆ (800) 892 4141
	Holland	✆ (023) 548 3777
	UK	✆ (0845) 733 3333
VLM	UK	✆ (020) 7476 6677

(flights from London City Airport to Rotterdam)

Ireland

Budget Travel, 134 Lower Baggot St, Dublin 2, ✆ (01) 661 1866.

United Travel, Stillorgan Bowl, Stillorgan, County Dublin, ✆ (01) 288 4346/7.

USA and Canada

It's worth sifting through the small ads in newspaper travel pages (e.g. the *New York Times, Chicago Tribune, Toronto Globe & Mail*) before contacting travel clubs and agencies, some of whom may require an annual membership fee.

Airhitch, 2472 Broadway Suite 200, New York, NY 10025, ✆ (212) 864 2000.

Council Travel, 205 E 42nd St, New York, NY 10017, ✆ (800) 743 1823.

Last Minute Travel Club, 132 Brookline Avenue, Boston, MA 02215, ✆ (800) 527 8646.

STA Travel, 10 Downing St, New York, NY 10014, ✆ (212) 627 3111 or (800) 777 0112; 51 Grant Avenue, San Francisco, CA 94108, ✆ (415) 391 8407.

Travel Cuts, 49 Front St East, Toronto, ON M5E 1B3, ✆ (416) 365 0545.

Internet

Some of the tastiest bargains of all are posted on the **Internet**. Check out *www.last-minute.com* or *www.travelocity.com*.

A direct **Eurostar** service from London Waterloo to Amsterdam through the Channel Tunnel is scheduled to go into operation one day. Until it does, you have to catch the train through the tunnel and make a simple platform change at Brussels. It is possible to book a through-ticket, which costs £75–105 return if you stay for a minimum of three nights, one of which must be a Saturday, otherwise up to £270 for a standard return. There are frequent special offers that can bring the price down even further. The journey time is 2hrs 40mins to Brussels, involving a wait between trains of approximately 25–30 minutes, and a 3 hour journey on from Brussels to Amsterdam Centraal Station (new high-speed rail links in Holland should speed up the journey considerably by 2003). Note that you absolutely must check in 20mins before the train departure time from Waterlooo or you will not be allowed to board. For information and bookings call ✆ (0990) 186 186.

If you are travelling from Scotland or the north of England, especially Edinburgh, Glasgow, Newcastle, Manchester, York or Birmingham, ask Eurostar when you book about special subsidized national train fares to London.

Stena Line, ✆ (08705) 70 70 70, *www.stenaline.co.uk,* offers combined rail and ferry tickets from London to Amsterdam, departing from Liverpool Street via Harwich and the Hook of Holland. The total journey time is about 7hrs, and standard fares start at about £80 return, although there are often promotional fares like the 3-day Apex return which can bring the price down to a mere £49.

There's a talking **timetable** for Amsterdam on ✆ (0891) 888 731. Centraal Station's European enquiries number is ✆ (0900) 9296.

This is the cheapest way to go, but it can also be the nastiest. Overnight journeys, in particular, seem maliciously planned so that you're woken at a border crossing every few hours. **National Express/Eurolines** (✆ (0990) 80 80 80/✆ (01582) 404 511) offer two options from London Victoria daily. On the morning departure you cross the Channel by Hovercraft; the overnight trip involves the ferry and takes 2hrs longer. The current return price for either choice is £44 (or £31 single), under-26/over-60 £39 (or £28 single).

To bring your car into the Netherlands you'll need a valid insurance document (such as the EU 'green card'), current registration and road safety test certificates, an international identification disc and an EU or international driving licence. The shortest **ferry crossing** (6½hrs by day or 8hrs by night) is Harwich–Hook of Holland (Stena Line, ✆ (0990) 707 070)—though, depending on where you're setting off from, you might find other lines more convenient: P&O North Sea Ferries (Hull–Rotterdam, ✆ (01482) 377177, 13½hrs) or Scandinavian Seaways (Newcastle–IJmuiden–Amsterdam, ✆ (01255) 240 240).

You can also take your car through the Channel Tunnel with **Eurotunnel,** ✆ (0990) 35 35 35. You enter the tunnel at Folkestone (take Junction 11a off the M20), and exit south of Calais on the French A16. You do not have to book ahead to use the tunnel, but it will be faster if you have.

passports and visas

EU nationals and citizens of Australia, Canada, New Zealand and the USA need only a valid passport to visit the Netherlands if their stay is for less than three months. If you intend to stay for longer than three months you should get your passport stamped on entry, and will need a **resident's permit**.

Dutch Embassies and Consulates Abroad

Australia, 120 Empire Circuit, Yarralumla, Canberra ACT 2600, ☏ (02) 6273 3111.

Canada, 350 Albert St, Ottowa, Ontario K1R 1A4, ☏ (613) 237 5030.

New Zealand, Investment House, Tenth Floor, Ballance St, Wellington, ☏ (04) 471 6390.

UK, 38 Hyde Park Gate, London SW7 5DP, ☏ (020) 7590 3200.

US, 4200 Linnean Ave NW, Washington DC, 20008, ☏ (202) 244 5300.

customs

People travelling within the European Union are no longer allowed to buy **duty free**, but if you are coming from outside the EU and are over 17, you can enter the Netherlands with 200 cigarettes (or 50 cigars or 250g/8.82oz of tobacco), 1 litre of spirits (or 2 litres of fortified wine) and 2 litres of non-sparkling wine, 50g/1.76oz of perfume and ƒ300 worth of gifts. If you've bought goods tax-paid within the EU then there are no restrictions, within reasonable limits. You should leave any meat, fruit, plants, flowers, radio transmitters and offensive weapons at home. If you bring in your **dog or cat** it must be accompanied by a certificate stating that it's been inoculated against rabies.

The exporting of **flower bulbs** is permitted to the UK, but you need an inoculation certificate for the USA. It's best to have bulbs posted home to avoid border hassles. Most reputable dealers will do this, and all the necessary paperwork, for you.

Tour Operators and Special-interest Holidays

It can work out cheaper to get to Holland with a package tour, especially if you will be spending much of your time in Amsterdam. Tour operators can also arrange specialist holidays, cycling tour and trips that include Belgium and Luxembourg as well as the Netherlands. Try these suggestions below.

in the UK

Amsterdam Travel Service, Bridge House, 55–59 High Road, Broxbourne, Hertfordshire EN10 7DT, ☏ (01992) 456 056, *www.amsterdamtravel.co.uk*. Offers a comprehensive range of holidays in Holland, from accommodation only (1–5-star hotels), to excursions to Rotterdam, Haarlem, Delft and Utrecht.

Bridge Travel Service, Bridge House, 55–59 High Rd, Broxbourne, Herts EN10 7DT, ☏ (01992) 456 654. Self-drive holidays throughout Holland.

Cresta Holidays, Tabley Court, Victoria Street, Altrincham, Cheshire WA14 1EZ, ☏ (0161) 927 7000, *www.crestaholidays.co.uk*. City breaks in Amsterdam, The Hague and Delft staying in 2–4-star hotels, also a wide range of themed excursions.

Crystal Holidays, Crystal House, The Courtyard, Arlington Road, Surbiton, Surrey KT6 6BW, ✆ (020) 8390 9900. Tailor-made excursions throughout Holland.

DFDS Seaways, Scandinavia House, Parkeston, Harwich, Essex CO12 4QG, ✆ (08705) 333 111, *www.dfdsseaways.co.uk*. Two-night cruise breaks visiting the bulb fields of Holland from £54.

Eurobreak, 10–18 Putney Hill, London SW15 6AX, ✆ (020) 8780 7700. Short breaks/weekend breaks in Amsterdam.

Kirker Holidays, 3 New Concordia Wharf, Mill St, London SE1 2BB, ✆ (020) 7231 3333. Tailor-made weekend breaks in Amsterdam.

Osprey Holidays, Broughton Market, Edinburgh, Scotland EH3 6NU, ✆ (0131) 557 1555. More weekend breaks in Amsterdam.

Stena Line Holidays, Charter House, Park St, Ashford, Kent TN24 8EX, ✆ (01233) 647022/✆ (08705) 747474. City breaks in Amsterdam, The Hague and Rotterdam.

Thomson Breakaway, Centenary House, 3 Water Lane, Richmond, Surrey TW9 1TJ, ✆ (020) 8210 4210. City breaks and package tours in Amsterdam.

Time Off, 1 Elmfield Park, Bromley, Kent BR1 1LU, ✆ (0990) 846 3633. City breaks in Amsterdam.

Travelscene, Travelscene House, 11–15 St Annes Road, Harrow, Middlesex HA1 1LQ, ✆ (020) 8427 8800, *www.travelscene.co.uk*. City breaks and driving holidays.

in the USA

Abercrombie & Kent, 1520 Kensington Road, Oakbrook, IL 60523, ✆ (800) 323 7308/ (630) 954 2944, *www.abercrombiekent.com*. Six-day tulip cruises on the *Princesse Royale* through Holland.

BA Holidays, ✆ (800) 359 8722. Package tours to Amsterdam.

First Cultural Tours, 225 West 34th, New York, NY 10122, ✆ (212) 563 1202; *istny@aol.com*. Organizes weekly barge trips from Amsterdam to Brussels.

Grand Travel, 6900 Wisconsin Avenue, Suite 706m Chevy Chase, Maryland, MC 20815, ✆ (800) 247 7651; *www.grandtrvl.com*. Fully escorted summer tours specially designed for grandparents travelling with grandchildren.

Hibiscus Tours, 885 3rd Ave, 29th floor, New York, NY 10022, ✆ (800) 653 0802, ✆ (212) 759 9087, *www.hibiscustours.com*. Garden, art and Jewish Heritage escorted tours.

Hilliard and Olander, 608 2nd Ave S, Suite 181, Minneapolis, ✆ (800) 229 8407. Package and driving tours all over Holland, de luxe accommodation.

Holland Bicycling Tours, PO Box 6068, Huntington Beach, CA 92615, ✆ (800) 852 3258, *faygrassi@earthlink.net*. Escorted bicycling tours in Northern and Southern Holland.

KLM/Northwest World Vacations, ✆ (800) 800 1504. City breaks in Amsterdam.

Mayflower Tours, PO Box 490, 1225 Warren Avenue, Downers Grove, Illinois 60515, ✆ (800) 323 7604. Nine-day horticultural tours in spring through the Netherlands.

Maupintours, 1421 Research Park Drive, Suite 300, Laurence, Kansas 66049, ✆ (800) 255 4266. Two tours in April: 'Holland in Bloom' and 'Gardens and Treasures of Holland.'

Saga International, ✆ (800) 952 9560. City breaks in Amsterdam.

*A telephone call to the national travel information service ☎ (0900) 9292 will put you in touch with someone who can give you **information** in English on all forms of public transport (including trains) nationwide.*

*See the **Language** chapter, pp.207–10, for some basic travelling vocabulary.*

By Train

Travelling around the Randstad by rail is cheap and easy. You don't have to book, as services are extremely frequent and efficient, and you can hop off a train to explore towns en route to your destination without paying extra. Holland is a small country, and nowhere is more than about three hours' journey time from Amsterdam, which is the hub of most national travel. Fares are calculated by distance in a fair and systematic way, so there shouldn't be any surprises. The table below should give you a rough idea of average fares.

Return fare Amsterdam to:	
Gouda	ƒ29.25
Haarlem	ƒ10.75
The Hague	ƒ29.25
Leiden	ƒ22.00
Rotterdam	ƒ39.25

Tickets and Passes

Domestic as well as international rail tickets, passes and timetables can all be purchased in advance (though slightly more expensively) from **Holland Rail**, Chase House, Gilbert Street, Ropley, Hants SO24 OBY, ☎ (01962) 773646, *www.hollandrail.com*. A free brochure called *Exploring Holland By Train* is available from Holland Rail or Netherlands Tourist Board offices, and the NTB *www.holland.com/uk* also includes full details of international train travel timetables.The information desk at most stations will give you details of all the various tickets and passes offered by the network—as well as a condensed version of the national rail timetable costing ƒ2.

Senior citizens in the UK should also consider buying a **Rail Europe Senior Card** which gives holders 30% reductions on all international travel (details available from UK stations).

Many rail stations in Holland also include a bike depot, and will hire out **bikes** at specially reduced rates for rail passengers (these can even be reserved in advance via Holland Rail). In smaller stations that are poorly served by other forms of public transport, you'll find **Trein Taxis**. Available at most railway stations, these communal taxis will take you to any address in the town or village for a flat fare of ƒ7/£3 (tickets available from the ticket office or ticket machine in the station hall).

By City Public Transport

Public transport in the Netherlands is safe and relatively inexpensive. Most larger cities have tram as well as bus networks. Rotterdam and Amsterdam have small metro systems.

Although you can buy single tickets on boarding trams and buses, it's much cheaper and easier to buy a **strip ticket** (*strippenkaart, f* 11.75). This is valid on the Amsterdam and Rotterdam metros, and on all buses and trams throughout the Randstad. The *strippenkaart* is divided into 2, 3, 8 or 15 units. Each time you make a journey allow 1 unit for 'boarding', then one more for each zone you travel through: a journey in one zone needs 2 units, through two zones 3 units, and so on. You can buy them from stations, newsagents, supermarkets, and the GVB (Amsterdam Muncipal Transport Authority, Stationsplein 15, opposite Centraal Station, Amsterdam). Available in summer only, the slightly more expensive *zomerzwerfkaart* (*f* 16) gives open access to all bus routes for 24 hours.

By Bicycle

Bicycles are the quintessential Dutch mode of transport. Cities generally have safe, separate cycle paths, and there are marked routes all over the countryside (ask local tourist offices or the ANWB motoring organization for maps and booklets). You can weave around as blithely as you like, secure in the knowledge that Dutch law holds that in an accident between a motorist and a cyclist, the cyclist is always right, whatever the circumstances.

Most main railway stations will have a bicycle storage depot with **bikes for hire**, and you'll find hire shops in nearly every town. Bike renting is cheap (seldom more than *f* 10 a day). You'll need to take your passport, and a deposit. This ranges from *f* 50 to *f* 200, but you can usually get around it by leaving an imprint of your credit card. **Bicycle theft** is endemic, especially in Amsterdam. Never leave your bike unlocked. It's a good idea, when you're hiring a bike, to check your liabilities under the rental firm's terms of insurance.

By Car

An EU or international **driving licence** is valid. Speed limits are 50kph (31mph) in built-up areas, 80kph (50mph) on the open road, and 100kph (75mph) on motorways. Drive on the right, and give way to traffic approaching from the right, except where you have clear right of way. Be wary of sightseeing pedestrians, give way to cyclists and remember that trams give way to no one. Finding **parking** can be a nightmare, especially in Amsterdam. The national **emergency car-repair** service is ANWB Wegenwacht (℡ (0900) 0888; open 24 hours daily). ANWB shops in larger cities are useful sources of maps and route planners.

car hire

Most major **car hire** companies have offices at Schiphol airport and in the larger cities. You'll need your driving licence, passport and a credit card (to pay a deposit).

Avis ℡ (020) 655 6050 or ℡ (020) 430 9609
Budget ℡ (0800) 0537 or ℡ (070) 384 4385
Cars for Less ℡ (020) 7287 2625—up to 80% off local rates in Holland
Europcar ℡ (020) 683 2123 or ℡ (020) 316 4190
Hertz ℡ (0800) 23 54 37 89 or ℡ (020) 504 0554

Practical A–Z

Addresses

The Dutch write the house number after the street name, and follow it by Roman numerals indicating the storey: Bloemstraat 56 II would be an apartment two floors above street level at No.56 Bloemstraat. An apartment at street level is shown by the letters 'hs' (*huis*, house). Postcodes are written before the name of the city. (Postcode directories are available in all of the post offices.)

Addresses in Amsterdam are discussed in the **Amsterdam** chapter, *see* p.64.

Climate and Packing

The songs, and all the clichés, about tulips and the **spring** are right: it's a heady time to be in Holland, especially Amsterdam. Café owners tentatively put out a few tables and chairs to catch the new sun, there are flowers everywhere and everyone seems to be in a good mood. In **summer** the atmosphere becomes almost feverish. Tourists crowd the streets and bars, the air gets heavy and humid and mosquitoes breed abundantly on the canals. But it's a great time for countryside cycle jaunts. Gable-spotters enjoy **autumn** and early **winter**, as long lines of houses reappear from behind the summer foliage. Brick, cobblestone and leaves mingle in a subtle spectrum of browns. **January** and **February** can be punishing. As you teeter along the slippery pavements, you're assassinated by the icy blasts of wind that howl down the narrow streets and lash around corners. But as the door bangs behind you in a warm café, you'll discover the true meaning of the Dutch word '*gezelligheid*' ('convivial' or 'cosy'). The one thing common to all seasons is rain—sudden showers more than the monotonous drenching sort. It's a good idea to pack an umbrella at any time of the year. The temperature can drop rather suddenly, even in summer, so a few warm clothes are a wise precaution.

The Dutch are not ostentatious dressers. The dress code seems to be that if it feels good, it looks good.

English-language books are readily available, though expensive, so it's better to buy your holiday reading before you go.

Consulates and Embassies

Australia	Carnegielaan 4, 2517 KH, The Hague, ✆ (070) 310 8200.
Britain	Koningslaan 44, 1075 AE, Amsterdam, ✆ (020) 676 4343.
Canada	Sophialaan 7, 2514 JP, The Hague, ✆ (070) 311 1600.
Ireland	Dr Kuyperstraat 9, 2514 BA, The Hague, ✆ (070) 363 0993.
New Zealand	Carnegielaan 10, 2517 KH, The Hague, ✆ (070) 346 9324.
USA	Lange Voorhout 102, 2514 EJ, The Hague, ✆ (070) 310 9209.

Crime and Drugs

Police ✆ 112

Holland is comfortably safe. Even in larger cities you need have little fear of serious street crime at any time of day or night (though women walking alone would be well advised to avoid red-light districts after midnight).

Contrary to received opinion, soft drugs are not legal in Holland, though an official blind eye is turned to the possession of under 28g (1oz) of cannabis. The tolerance goes as far as allowing some coffeeshops to sell cannabis over the counter; here people smoke marijuana on the premises. But this is not true of all coffeeshops and cafés, and anyone found in possession of hard drugs, such as heroin or cocaine, can expect swift prosecution.

Bicycle theft, theft from cars and pickpocketing are something of a problem. You'll often see quite abusive signs on car windows informing all who might be tempted that there is nothing at all inside to steal. The Dutch sometimes spend more on a lock than on their bicycle ('And I'd just bought a new lock!' is a common wail after a bike has been stolen). A favourite trick of pickpockets is to sidle up close and offer to sell you something illicit. In your annoyed efforts to get rid of them (or keenness to see what they've got) you don't notice that your wallet is being gently removed. Sensible vigilance is the only way to avoid these petty crimes: don't leave valuables in your car, always lock your bike securely and don't carry a wallet in your back pocket or leave it on top of a shop counter when paying. Keep traveller's cheques and stubs separate and don't carry large amounts of money in one pocket.

The Dutch police generally keep a low profile and are a relaxed and sympathetic lot.

Disabled Travellers

Cobbled streets and tiny houses with narrow doorways and steep stairs can pose problems for those with limited mobility. Older trams have high steps, and are not accessible at all, though newer models are more wheelchair-friendly. In Amsterdam, however, there is a special taxi service for wheelchair-users (✆ (020) 613 4134) and the metro is accessible. The Netherlands Railways publishes timetables in Braille and a leaflet on *Rail Travel for the Disabled*, available at larger stations, or through their London office (✆ (01962) 773646, ✉ 773625, *www.hollandrail.com*).

The Dutch government takes an enlightened and constructive view of the problems faced by disabled people. They have, for example, introduced banknotes with raised shapes in the corner that indicate their value to the visually impaired. You'll find that nearly all museums, cinemas and churches have wheelchair access and many have facilities for the visually impaired and hard of hearing. Local tourist offices or the London branch of the **Netherlands Board of Tourism** (PO Box 523, London SW1E 6NYT, ✆ (020) 7828 7900) will have lists of accommodation, restaurants, museums and tourist attractions with facilities for the disabled. For information on specialized holidays contact:

RADAR, 12 City Forum, 250 City Rd, London EC1V 8AF, ✆ (020) 7250 3222, minicom ✆ (020) 7637 5315.

Disability Action Group, 2 Annedale Ave, Belfast BT7 3JH, ✆ (01232) 91011.

SATH (Society for the Advancement of Travel for the Handicapped), 347 Fifth Avenue, New York, NY 10016, ✆ (212) 447 7284.

Mobility International USA, PO Box 3551, Eugene, OR 97403, ✆ (503) 343 1284.

Wheelchair Hire in Amsterdam, Beumer de Jong, Haarlemmerstraat 49–53, 1058 JP Amsterdam, ✆ (020) 615 7188. Wheelchair hire from ƒ40/week; book in advance, especially in the summer.

Electricity

The voltage in the Netherlands is 220 AC, which is compatible with the UK, but you'll need a transformer if you are bringing American electrical equipment. Wall sockets take rather flimsy two-pronged plugs.

Emergencies

Police, ambulance, fire brigade, ✆ 112. The operators speak English.

For medical emergencies, see 'Health' below. Lost or stolen credit cards can be reported on the following numbers: American Express, stolen cheques ✆ (0800) 022 0100, stolen cards ✆ (020) 504 8000/504 8666 after 6pm; Diners Club ✆ (020) 557 3407; Mastercard/Access ✆ (0800) 022 5821; Visa ✆ (020) 660 0611.

Entertainment

Film

The Dutch are avid movie-goers. Most cafés and some restaurants and takeaways have a list of the week's films pinned up on the wall. Home-grown products haven't, however, made much of an impact on the international movie scene—although director **Paul Verhoeven** is known for the action movies *Robocop* and *Total Recall*, a Dutch film, *Antonia*, picked up the 1996 Oscar for Best Foreign Film, and the British director **Peter Greenaway** operates largely with Dutch funding.

Cinema prices in Holland range from ƒ10 to ƒ15 and there are often discounts on week nights. In the rare cases where an English film has been dubbed over you'll see '*Nederlands Gesproken*' on the publicity material. For real film buffs, the internationally important **Rotterdam Film Festival** is held in January/February. Information on this is available from any Dutch tourist office.

Theatre

Like England, the Netherlands experienced a 17th-century **Golden Age** of the theatre. Playwrights of that era, such as Vondel, Hooft and Bredero, are still performed in Holland. The 18th and 19th centuries saw the growth of extravagant stage spectacles. (On the nights they went to the theatre, wealthy families would send their maids and cooks on ahead to swell the ranks of the extras.) By the end of the 19th century, theatre had ossified from a popular into an élitist form. The '**Tomato Action**' of 1968 put an end to that. A disgruntled new generation of actors began throwing tomatoes at their older colleagues during performances and sparked off a theatrical revolution. In the decade that followed, Amsterdam theatres like the **Mickery** and the **Shaffy** earned a worldwide reputation for high quality avant-garde work. Government cuts and changing tastes have curtailed much of the mud-wading and body-painting, but there is still a strong tradition of excellent, highly visual theatre (in particular look out for work by Orkater theatre company and spectacular outdoor romps by the Dogtroep). There is no national theatre company; the chief mainstream company is the rather stolid Toneelgroep Amsterdam, resident at the Westergasfabriek in Amsterdam.

Dance

Until recently, Dutch dance was sagging sadly, propped up by a rather unvivacious Nationale Ballet in Amsterdam and the practically moribund Scapio Ballet in Rotterdam. Only The Hague's **Nederlands Dans Theater** had the verve and energy to prevent complete artistic prolapse. But at the moment the Netherlands is rising towards the crest of a new wave of dance, inspired perhaps by the big stage at Amsterdam's **Muziektheater**, an influx of foreign dancers and traditional rhythms from the former colonies. The **Nationale Ballet** has imported Canadian Wayne Eagling to be its Artistic Director, has expanded its repertoire, and is benefiting from the visits of touring companies who, at the Muziektheater, now have a suitable Amsterdam venue. Likewise, the **Scapio** is dusting off the cobwebs and under new artistic direction has appointed Ed Wubbe as their daring new choreographer; the Nederlands Dans Theater keeps up a salvo of fine ballet and modern dance. Look out also for work by **Djazzex** (jazz dance) and **Dansgroep Krisztina de Chatel** (vivid, fairly theatrical style).

Classical Music

After a lull during the 1980s, when government cuts guillotined five of the Netherlands' thirteen major orchestras and public interest began to wane, Dutch music seems to be undergoing a renaissance. Baroque and period instrument orchestras are reaching particularly high standards (try to catch the **Amsterdam Baroque Orchestra** or the **Orchestra of the 18th Century** when they are not on tour). The **Nederlandse Opera** (also based in Amsterdam) repeatedly comes up with sharp, adventurous productions, often of 20th-century works, and the contemporary music scene is very lively (look out for pieces by **Louis Andriessen** and performances by the refreshingly unorthodox **Ricciotti Ensemble**). The famed **Royal Concertgebouw Orchestra** first established its reputation before the Second World War under the baton of Willem Mengelberg. He built up a close working relationship with Mahler and Richard Strauss and devoted 50 years to establishing his orchestra as one of the greatest in the world, only to be sacked after the war for pro-German sympathies. In the 1960s the orchestra was propelled to even greater heights by Bernard Haitink. It too has been through a dry patch, but conductor Riccardo Chailly is giving it new life.

Tickets

Tickets for opera, ballet and concerts will seem cheap if you're used to London or New York prices, but they sell out quickly. You can try for returns half an hour before a performance, but there are no last-minute discounts and systems of selling return tickets can be disorganized. Churches are favourite venues for concerts and recitals.

Rock Music

Chart-busters and rock and pop stadium-packers like Madonna and Prince used to give Amsterdam a miss and head for the larger venues such as the **Rotterdam Ahoy**. But in 1996 Amsterdam gained a state-of-the-art sports and entertainment stadium. The **Amsterdam ArenA** looks like a giant spaceship, hovering on the southeast outskirts of the city. It opened with concerts by Tina Turner and Michael Jackson, and has been packing in the audiences ever since. Keep an eye out also for Dutch stars who have made it internationally—such as Mathilde Santing, Eton Crop and the not so gently ageing Golden Earring—who have a loyalty to the old country and come back for a gig every year or two. Young British bands are often the best bet if you're looking for good rock. Many of these head for Paradiso or De Melkweg in Amsterdam. The Netherlands' large Indonesian and Surinamese populations swell many a bar with pulsating ethnic rhythms—the Latin and South American music scene is especially lively. Summer is the time for lively music festivals (*see* individual festival listings under: Amsterdam, pp.65–6; Rotterdam, p.165; Leiden, p.177; The Hague, p.187, and Utrecht, p.203).

Jazz

The mellow tones of jazz seem to suit the atmosphere of Dutch 'brown cafés', and many will have a live band on a Saturday night or Sunday afternoon. But the excellent **North Sea Jazz Festival** in The Hague (*see* p.187) is the jazz gig of the year. Surinamese and other South American immigrants crowd out a number of vibrant drinking and dancing venues—the music is great, and often live. Bars and cafés with live music often don't charge entrance, but have more expensive drinks.

Clubs

Dutch clubbers don't suffer the fashion neuroses of their London or New York counterparts. You can dress up, down, wild or straight: there's seldom any need to shock or impress some cool doorman before you're let in. The mood is carefree and unpretentious—late-night clubbing seems just an extension of early evening café life. Club nights on the beach at **Zandvoort** are the current focus of the summer dance scene.

Festivals and Events

Details of smaller local festivals and market days are given in the relevant chapters.

Feb: Though it is more of a southern, Roman Catholic tradition, Amsterdammers (always in the market for a party) have also taken to the traditional dressing up and last-minute boozing before Lent.

Mar/ April: The best time to drive through the bulb fields or visit flower-filled gardens is in late March and early April.

National Museum Weekend is usually held on the third weekend in April. All museums are free—and crammed to capacity. A date to avoid unless you are particularly hard up.

Queen's Day, the Dutch monarch's official birthday, is held on 30 April, and celebrated right across the country with street parties and a 'Free Market', which means that anyone can sell just about anything anywhere. Amsterdam used to be the best place to be, but during the late 1990s mayor Patijn introduced more strictures on the fun with each passing year, and current gossip has it that Utrecht is now the better place to be, especially on the night of 29 April, when things hardly get going until around midnight and don't stop all night.

The **World Press Photo Exhibition** is a show of the winning and finalists' pictures from the world's top annual photo-journalism competition. The award ceremony and opening exhibition are always held in Amsterdam in mid-April/early May.

May: **Dodenherdenking** (Remembrance Day) on 4 May is a sober, low-key occasion during which people lay flowers at monuments and places of significance (such as points from which Jews were deported). There is a genuine, nationwide two-minute silence at 8pm. The next day, **Bevrijdingsdag** (Liberation Day) is usually celebrated in much the same manner as Queen's Day, though these days it is generally declared a public holiday only once every five years.

On **Nationale Molendag** (National Windmill Day, usually the second Saturday in May) about 600 of the country's 1,000 or so windmills are in full sail and open to the public. The same day is also declared **National Bicycle Day**, which doesn't mean much except that everyone cycles out to see the windmills.

June: The **Holland Festival** runs for the whole month of June and is the country's leading arts event and attracts world names in music, opera, dance and theatre. Emphasis has been mainly on music, but in recent years focus has changed to performance of a more avant-garde nature. On the 2nd Sunday in June 5,000 people go for a jog around the canals in the **Grachtenloop** ('canal run').

In the second half of June, The Hague's substantial Indonesian community get together for the **Pasar Malam Besar**, a bonanza of music and dance, traditional puppet shows and cookery demonstrations, all centred on a large and colourful market on the Malieveld.

July: The famous **North Sea Jazz Festival** is held for three days in mid-July in The Hague, attracting top-drawer performers from around the world.

Not to be outdone, Rotterdam responds with a **Summer Carnival** on the last Saturday in the month. This is carnival very much in the Caribbean mode. Amsterdam has its own Summer Festival—a which is showtime for the avant-garde and goes on all over town (often in the strangest places).

Aug: Culture vultures can dip their beaks in a variety of fare during the two-day-long **Uitmarkt** in Amsterdam at the end of August. The country's leading dance and theatre troupes, orchestras, and opera companies—and just about everybody else in the arts too—give a flavour of their programme for the forthcoming season, at (mostly free and open-air) venues all over Amsterdam. For most of the month in Amsterdam Martin Luther King Park beside the Amstel on the southern outskirts of town is the scene of De Parade, a 'theatre funfair' with various theatre groups and performers arranging bright show booths.

Sept: On **Monumentendag** (Monument Day, second Saturday) historical buildings all over the country that are not usually open to the public throw open their doors. Queues can be long, but you get a fascinating glimpse of interiors that are usually hidden from view.

Prinsjesdag (third Tuesday) is the official opening of the Dutch parliament. Queen Beatrix whisks through The Hague in a golden coach to make a speech in the Ridderzaal.

The **Bloemencorso** (Flower Parade) is a parade of floats smothered in flowers from the Aalsmeer (site of the Netherlands' main flower auction houses) to Amsterdam, on the first Saturday of the month.

Nov: In mid-month **Sinterklaas** (St Nicholas) arrives, usually by steamboat and with an uncanny ability to appear in many places at once, all over the country. He then rides his dappled horse through town. He is accompanied by his servant Zwarte Piet (Black Pete), who to most outsiders appears a grotesque racist caricature (he's invariably a blacked-up white person with thick red lips and a fuzzy wig). Even liberal-minded Dutch people go into angry denial mode if you point this out.

Dec: The high point of the Sinterklaas festivities, which continue throughout November and early December, is **Sinterklaasavond** (a.k.a. Pakjesavond) on 6 December, very much an at-home affair at which families swap small gifts, often accompanied by mildly insulting doggerel about the recipients' various foibles. **Pakjesavond** ('parcel evening') on December 5 is the traditional Dutch time to give presents (rather than Christmas Day). The country is awfully quiet at this time.

Oudejaarsavond (31 December) is celebrated with gusto. Vast numbers of *oliebollen* (literally 'oil-balls', and that's what they are—deep-fried lumps of dough) are consumed, and fire crackers are let off everywhere, with apparent complete disregard for safety. You need nerves (and sometimes limbs and other organs) of steel to survive.

Erasmus, the great 16th-century Dutch humanist and man of letters, was pleased to note that his fellow countrymen were not given to much wild or ferocious behaviour, treachery or deceit, indeed were 'not prone to any serious vices except, that is, a little given to pleasure, especially to feasting'. Two centuries later the national ability to tuck in and drink up was still impressive enough to shock the British—themselves no mean feasters. In 1703 the seven or so deacons of the Arnhem guild of surgeons dispatched, at one sitting, 14lb of beef, 8lb of veal, six fowl, stuffed cabbages, apples, pears, bread, pretzels, assorted nuts, 20 bottles of red wine, 12 bottles of white wine and some jugs of coffee. Today, eating is still a supreme Dutch enthusiasm.

Paradoxically, **native Dutch cuisine** is not all that inspiring. The Dutch culinary clichés are *hutspot* ('hotchpotch'), a well-boiled stew that was much appreciated by starving citizens after the siege of Leiden and still requires a similar state of ravenousness before it can really be enjoyed; and *erwtensoep*, a porridgy pea soup which comes (vegetarians beware) with bits of sausage floating in it and a side dish of bread and raw bacon. The quality of *erwtensoep* is judged by testing whether or not your spoon will stand up on its own in the middle of the bowl. These are the staples of many a 'tourist menu', but (like the English) the Dutch have recently begun to explore more exciting avenues in their local cuisine—with game and fish especially. Other palatable traditional foods include *pannekoeken* (pancakes) which come with sweet or savoury fillings and *haring* (herring) eaten raw by tossing your head back and dropping a whole fillet down your throat, holding it by the tail. (If you can stomach it, this is a marvellous cure for a hangover.) *Belegde broodjes* are crusty rolls filled with a delicious variety of fillings—travellers' tales of sliced beef layered on buttered bread predated anecdotes about Lord Sandwich's invention by about a century. Waffles, dripping with syrup or smothered with fruit and cream, are sold on the streets. Cones of *frites* (potato chips), usually with a large dollop of mayonnaise,)are ubiquitous. They're normally cooked with good-quality potatoes in clean oil. (*See* **Language**, p.210, for a selection of Dutch food terms.)

In the absence of a stimulating local tradition, Dutch chefs have looked further afield. **French cuisine** first came into fashion during the Napoleonic occupation, and remains the cornerstone of many of the best kitchens. Nowadays most menus are tantalizingly eclectic, showing influences from Japan, Indonesia, Surinam and Turkey. Don't be surprised to find peanut sauce, saffron pasta and oysters on the same menu. The Dutch were enjoying '**fusion cuisine**' years before trendy London and New York chefs could distinguish lemongrass from lime leaves.

Specialist **ethnic restaurants** abound. Reasonable Indian and Italian food is to be had all over town, though the increasingly popular Thai and Japanese restaurants make a more exciting alternative. It's the culinary heritage of Holland's imperial past, however, that makes for the best ethnic binge. Treat yourself to an **Indonesian *rijsttafel***—a personal banquet of rice or noodles with a myriad spicy side dishes.

Vegetarians will have a difficult time in the Netherlands. The Dutch are great carnivores. Fish doesn't seem to count as meat, so if you enquire about vegetarian dishes you're often offered *kabeljauw* (cod). However, in the 1970s the tastes of the hippies spawned a few vegetarian restaurants and more have opened recently. Chefs in better kitchens are beginning to be more imaginative with their vegetarian options, and most restaurants will have at least one vegetarian meal on the menu.

Restaurants and Eating Out

Ingredients are usually market-fresh and microwave cookers are pleasingly thin on the ground. Food is cooked to order in most restaurants, so expect an unhurried meal. The Dutch **eat early** in the evening—between 7 and 9pm—and many kitchens are closed by 10 or 11pm. You may well find Dutch restaurants, bars and cafés **smoky**—the non-smoking revolution has not hit Holland by any means, and no amount of huffing and menu-flapping will even be understood let alone complied with. As in France, cafés and even some restaurants allow dogs in with their owners.

Budget eating is easy, and needn't be boring. Many restaurants offer a three-course 'Tourist Menu' for under ƒ30, but you're generally better off looking out for signs advertising a *dagschotel* (dish of the day). You usually end up with an oversized white plate with some well-prepared meat and a constellation of pickles and salads. Many cafés serve food—menus change daily and often offer the best value of all.

Takeaway foodstalls punctuate markets and shopping streets all over the country. As well as *frites, haring* and waffles you can sample all sorts of foreign delights: Turkish kebabs, Israeli falafel, Japanese sushi and spicy nibbles from Surinam and Indonesia. Under signs flashing '**Automatiek**' you can select a deep-fried croquette from a row of tiny windows displaying this and similar wares: drop in your ƒ1.50, pull a lever and collect your reward. 'Snack' was originally a Dutch word. Snack bars are the Dutch equivalent of street food. At worst they sell pre-prepared mushy croquettes, but at best they are tiny family-run establishments that hover in the middle ground between restaurant and takeaway.

Note that many smaller restaurants **don't accept credit cards**, and there's an air of reluctance about those that do. Even some of the larger establishments don't like plastic—so it's always a good idea to check in advance. Most good restaurants fill up pretty quickly, so it's wise to **reserve** a table by telephone. The restaurants in the guide are all graded according to the approximate price of a three-course meal, without wine.

Restaurant price ranges (for a 3-course meal)

expensive	over ƒ80 (though seldom more than ƒ175)
moderate	ƒ55–ƒ80
cheap	under ƒ55

The bill will include tax and a 15% service charge—though if you feel you've been well looked after you can leave extra. It's usual to leave small change (or round up larger bills to the nearest ƒ5). It's worth checking out expensive restaurants, even if they seem above your budget, as many offer special three- or four-course meals for between ƒ45 and ƒ75.

Cafés and Coffeeshops

The term 'café' covers a wide range of establishments. At one end of the spectrum are the poky bars, where you go to knock back a few beers (with a *jenever* chaser); you might also be able to buy bread rolls, *tostis* (pale toasted sandwiches) or *bitterballen* (balls of meat purée, coated in breadcrumbs and deep-fried). At the other end you'll find airy **grand cafés** and places that offer such sumptuous fare that they're really indistinguishable from small restaurants. These often call themselves *eetcafés* (literally 'eating cafés') or even *petit restaurant cafés*.

Most Dutch drink beer. Ordering *een Pils* at the bar will get you a small glass of lager topped with a finger or two of froth. Or you might prefer a *jenever* (Dutch gin—oilier and weaker than its British counterpart, with a whiff of juniper berries). In this case ask for a *borrel*. You can have either *oud* (old—more mellow) or *jong* (young—sharper). *Jenever* may also be flavoured: *citroenjenever* (lemon) or *besenjenever* (blackberry) are popular. Ask for a *kamelenrug* (camel's back) and your glass will be filled to the rim. Traditionally, you knock back all of your *jenever* with a single gulp. Should you require both beer and gin simultaneously, request a *kopstoot* (literally: 'knock on the head'). On freezing winter days a quick visit to a **proeflokaal** will warm your blood. These were once free tasting houses attached to spirit-merchants and taphouses. These days you have to pay, but the procedure is much the same: walk in, drink up, walk out.

Coffeeshops serve tea, coffee and wonderful cakes and pastries. Sometimes they serve snacks and fuller meals, but never alcohol. Tea is seldom served with milk, unless you specifically ask for it. Coffee will come black or with strange processed *koffiemelk*, unless you order *koffieverkeerd* (literally 'coffee wrong'), in which case you'll get a delicious 50:50 mixture with fresh milk. Since the 1970s some coffeeshops (the so-called **smoking coffeeshops**) have openly sold marijuana. These are easily distinguishable at first glance/sniff. They are painted psychedelic colours, often have leaf designs on the windows and emit loud music and fazed customers.

Health and Insurance

Ambulance, © 112

It is always advisable to take out travel insurance before any trip abroad—and to do so as soon as you buy your tickets. Specially tailored travel insurance packages cover medical expenses, lost luggage and theft, and also offer compensation for cancellation and delayed departure. The cost of travel insurance is steadily rising, but is still insignificant when compared with the potential costs of a serious emergency, or even the value of your tickets should you have to cancel your trip. Consult your insurance broker or travel agent. In the event of needing to make a claim, be sure to check the small print of your policy to see what documentation (police report, medical forms, invoices, etc.) is required by the insurance company.

That said, EU nations are entitled to receive free or reduced-charge medical treatment in the Netherlands: British visitors will need a form E111 (fill in application form SA30, available from DSS branches or post offices). Theoretically you should organize this two weeks before you leave, though you can usually do it over the counter in one visit. The E111 does not insure personal belongings.

Money

For lost credit cards, see 'Emergencies'.

The unit of Dutch **currency** is the guilder, which is abbreviated as *f*, f, fl (for the old Dutch term florin) or NLG (in business and banking contexts). On price tags, 'guilders' is often written as /–. A guilder is divided into 100 cents (shortened to 'c'). There are around *f*2.5 to the pound sterling, and about *f*1.66 to the US dollar. The notes are said to be the prettiest in Europe, and come in *f*10, *f*25, *f*50, *f*100, *f*250, *f*500 and *f*1000 denominations (though you seldom see notes above *f*100, and may have trouble finding shops that accept larger denominations). There are six types of coin: a *stuiver* (5c, copper); the *dubbeltje* (10c), *kwartje*

(25c), *f*1 and *rijksdaalder* (*f*2.50)—all silver-coloured; and the *f*5 (gold-coloured). All prices are rounded up to multiples of five. Once you've got used to counting in 25s and 2.5s, it's pretty straightforward.

Credit cards are not as widely accepted as you might expect—the Dutch generally prefer cash in shops, restaurants and even hotels. It's always a good policy to double-check. The small commission that banks charge businesses on credit card payments seems to sit uncomfortably with the Dutch sense of financial prudence. A number of shops will charge you extra if you pay by credit card. Eurocheques and traveller's cheques are a better idea. If you have appropriate identification, many establishments will accept them direct. Nowadays hole-in-the-wall cash dispensers are the most convenient way of getting money. Check before you leave that your bank card is programmed for overseas withdrawals, and that your bank doesn't make any outrageous charges for the service. You can usually withdraw up to *f*300 a day.

Banks are open 9–4/5 Mon–Fri (some stay open until 7 on Thursdays).

Head offices of the main Dutch banks in Amsterdam

ABNAMRO, Vijzelgracht 32, ✆ (020) 629 9111.
ING, Bijlmerplein 888, ✆ (020) 563 9111.
Rabobank, Wilhelminaplantsoen 124, ✆ (020) 495 0950.
VSB Bank, Singel 548, ✆ (020) 624 9340.

Some foreign bank head offices

Barclays Bank, World Trade Center, Stravinskylaan 3051, ✆ (020) 301 2364.
Citibank NA, Hoogoorddreef 541B, ✆ (020) 651 4211.

The **Postbank** (at post offices) and **GWK** (Grens Wissel Kantoor—official *bureaux de change*) are the best places to change your money. ***Bureaux de change*** often offer the same rates as banks, but take more commission; however, the GWK exchanges at Amsterdam's Centraal Station and Schiphol (both open 24 hours daily) are a better bet than the deals offered by hotel receptions, and even many banks.

If you exchange traveller's cheques at a company branch, you don't have to pay commission at all. In Amsterdam, you'll find offices of American Express at Amsteldijk 166, Damrak 66 (with 24-hour cash dispenser for cardholders and automatic traveller's cheque refund service) and Van Baerlestraat 39; and Thomas Cook at Dam 23–25, Damrak 1–5 (open Mon–Sat 8–8 and Sun 9–8), and Leidseplein 31a.

Museum Admissions and Discount Cards

In the text of this book, you will see 'adm' after the opening hours if there is an admission charge, and 'adm exp' if the charge is more than f15.

Museums in the Netherlands are seldom free, but for *f*55 (*f*25 for under-24s and *f*45 for over-55s) you can buy an **Annual Museum Card** (*Museumjaarkaart*/**MJK**) which gets you into most museums in Holland for nothing, or at a substantial discount. Buy one at the museum ticket office, and ask for the booklet listing the 300–400 museums the discount applies to.

If you're under 26 the **CJP** (*Cultureel Jongeren Passport*) entitles you to discount at museums, theatres and cultural events. It's available from tourist offices, many theatres, and some libraries and other cultural institutions for f20.

You will need a photograph for all these discount cards, and proof of age for the CJP.

Post Offices

The Dutch postal service logo is a white **ptt post** on a red background. Post offices are generally open Mon–Fri 8.30–5. Larger branches may also open Sat 9–12 noon. Here you can buy stamps, and send letters, express letters and telegrams (make sure you're in the right queue—sometimes counters are labelled for certain functions only). Stamps (*postzegels*) can also be bought from tobacconists. At the time of writing it costs f1 to send a postcard to the UK, f1 to send an airmail letter to the UK or a postcard to the USA and f1.30 to send an airmail letter to the USA (prices for letters under 20g). The slot for overseas mail on post boxes is marked 'Overige'. A poste restante service is available. Letters should be addressed to: Poste Restante, Hoofdpostkantoor PTT, Singel 250, 1016 AB Amsterdam. You'll need a passport to claim your mail.

Public Holidays

New Year's Day, Good Friday, Easter Sunday and Monday, Queen's Day (30 April), Ascension Day, Whit Sunday and Monday, Christmas Day and Boxing Day. On public holidays most things close, and towns can be very quiet indeed.

Shopping

Weekday opening hours are generally 9–6. On Saturdays shops close around 5pm, and some do not open on Monday mornings either. Some shops in larger city centres now open from noon to 6pm on Sundays. Many of the smaller shops can be quite idiosyncratic about when they open, but all will have a little black and yellow timetable of opening hours posted on an outside window. Most neighbourhoods have one or two shops that open around 5pm and stay open until between 11pm and 1am. Here you can buy, at a suitably inflated price, emergency bottles of wine, groceries and gooey cakes for late-night munchies. Some of the more upmarket establishments sell gourmet meals and chocolates to bring tears to your eyes. Look out for signs reading 'Avondverkoop' or 'Nightshop'.

Dutch sales tax (BTW—17.5% on most goods) is included in the marked price, though many stores offer tax-free shopping for the benefit of non-EU tourists. They'll also help with the paperwork.

Telephones, E-mail and the Internet

Dutch telephone boxes are green, with a white ptt telecom logo. Payphones take 25c, f1, f2.50 and coins. Increasingly, cardphones are taking the place of payphones. Many accept credit cards, and all operate with phonecards, which you can buy at post offices, railway stations and newsagents. Instructions in phone boxes are clear, but don't be confused by the local ringing tone, a long continuous sound rather like the British 'engaged' signal. A busy line in Holland is indicated by rapid tones. Another confusing surprise is the dalek voice you get when phoning popular numbers such as airports or taxis. You're told: '*Er zijn nog drie (three)/twee (two)/een (one) wachtenden voor u*'—an indication of how many people are patiently waiting ahead of you in an electronic queue.

Numbers preceded by 0800 are free; those beginning 0900 are charged at a special rate, usually between 50c and *f* 1 a minute (for these calls a recorded voice will tell you how much you are having to fork out).

> Directory Enquiries: ✆ (0900) 8008
> International Operator (also for collect calls): ✆ (0800) 0410
> International Directory Enquiries: ✆ (0900) 8418
> International direct dialling codes:
>> From Holland to USA: ✆ (00 1)—area code without the first 0
>> From USA to Holland: ✆ (011 31)—area code without the first 0
>> From Holland to UK: ✆ (00 44)—area code without 0
>> From UK to Holland: ✆ (00 31)—area code without 0

International calls are cheaper between 8pm and 8am, but calls to other European countries don't count as international.

Most cities now have an abundance of Internet cafés and, uniquely, Amsterdam has Internet booths on street corners. These look just like telephone booths, but are marked with an @. A normal telephone card gives you access to the Net and e-mail facilities.

Time

The Netherlands is 2 hours ahead of Greenwich Mean Time in the spring and summer, and 1 hour ahead in winter and autumn. It is 6 hours ahead of Eastern Standard Time and 9 hours ahead of Pacific Standard Time.

Tipping, Etiquette and Service

Restaurant and bar bills in Holland are inclusive of tax and service, so a tip isn't really necessary. It's customary, though, to round the amount up to the nearest guilder (or *f* 5 for a big bill). If the service has been exceptional, it's quite acceptable to add a little more. Taxi drivers expect 10 per cent—especially if they've helped with luggage.

Queuing at supermarket delicatessens, some banks and public institutions is controlled by an electronic ticketing system. You tear off a ticket as you enter and wait for your number to flash up on a screen. At cash machines and bank and post office counters, the rest of the queue keeps a polite metre or so's distance from the person transacting business. Sometimes there's a boundary line painted on the floor. Step over this mark (visible or otherwise) and the atmosphere turns icy.

English is spoken almost as a second mother tongue in Amsterdam. Some Hollanders seem to resent this, but many seem insulted if you ask 'Do you speak English?' One way round this is to open with a cheery dag! ('darhg'—good day) and then speak English. 'Dag'—called out with a friendly upward lilt in the voice—is used at all times of day or night, entering and leaving shops, when speaking to barmen, policemen, cabbies and tram drivers. When you meet a Dutch person for the first time, it's polite to shake hands and say your name clearly.

If you are used to slick New York **service**, or even to the slightly less brisk British style, then you are in for a sad surprise when you visit Amsterdam. Bring a bottle of Valium to help keep calm and a pack of cards to while away the time, or you will find your holiday intensely frustrating. It is not unknown for customers to sit for twenty minutes to half an hour in a café before there is even a whiff of a waiter, though when they do come they are so full of shiny-eyed friendliness that it is difficult to be angry. Expect to wait at least half an hour to forty minutes for your dinner to arrive once you have ordered it.

Toilets

Apart from those at railway stations and the odd foul-smelling urinoir, there are few public toilets in the Netherlands. The best option is to duck into a café. This is perfectly acceptable practice, though bars in some of the busier tourist areas discourage it. The better hotel foyers provide classier options, but this takes a certain amount of poise, as you have to stroll through the lobby as if you're a resident, all the time darting your eyes about for the relevant sign—not easy if you're caught in a last-minute dash. Station loos—and sometimes those in larger cafés—are guarded by fierce women, who require you to drop at least 25c into a saucer before passing.

Tourist Information

There is a nationwide tourist office at Schiphol airport, Holland Tourist Information (HTI, Schiphol Plaza, Mon–Sun 7am–10pm). You can get information on the Internet at the official website: *www.holland.com*. The Netherlands Board of Tourism (NBT) offices abroad can give you details of hotels and events:

UK   PO Box 523, London SW1E 6LB, information line © (0906) 871 7777 (charged at premium rate), (recorded info) © (0891) 717 777, *www.holland.com/uk.*

USA   355 Lexington Av, 19th Floor, New York, NY 10017, © (212) 370 7360, or toll free (1 888) GO HOLLAND, *www.goholland.com*, *info@goholland.com.*

Canada   25 Adelaide Street E., Suite 710, Toronto, Ontario, M5C 1Y2, © (1 888) GO HOLLAND, or, for French speakers, (1 888) PAYS BAS, *www.goholland.com*, *info@goholland.com.*

VVVs

Most towns and villages in Holland have a local tourist office or **VVV** (look out for the eye-catching blue triangle sign containing the letters VVV in white) which will be able to advise you on accommodation, opening times and local sights etc. They should also have a wide range of motoring, cycling and tourist maps for sale. You can write directly to a VVV from abroad by addressing your letter to VVV followed by the name of the town you are visiting.

Where to Stay

All sorts of old houses—poky, grand and resonantly historical, beside canals and in the middle of forests—have been given new life as hotels in the Netherlands. Many of these are privately owned and have been lovingly turned into little havens of *gezelligheid* (cosiness) or store-houses of antiques. These are the best places of all to stay—but most have built up a dedicated clientele and require booking some time in advance. Rooms in the same house will vary enormously in size and en suite bathrooms tend to have showers only. If you hear of a particularly desirable room, try to book it specifically by number. If you cannot book in advance try calling the hotel just before noon and try your luck.

Reservations

Reservations can be made direct to the hotel or, once you're in the country, through local tourist offices or VVV (phone the Netherlands Tourist Board on ✆ (070) 419 5544 for their details). VVVs charge around ƒ5 booking fee and a ƒ10 room deposit which is later deducted from your bill. The Netherlands Board of Tourism in your home country can give you a list of hotels, but can't make bookings. If you need to book in advance the **Netherlands Reservation Centre** (NRC) offers a broad choice from budget to 5-star on ✆ 0031 (0)70 419 55 44, *www.hotelres.nl*, *info@hotelres.nl*.

Because accommodation is at such a premium, you'll find that most hotels will ask for a deposit or the security of a credit card number.

Accommodation Categories

Standards of cleanliness and service are high and, unless you're scraping along at the very bottom of the price range, you're unlikely to find yourself sharing your room with local fauna, thumping faulty electrical equipment or speculating about the origins of the hairs on the sheets. Facilities can be quite spartan, however, and a lot of the smaller hotels offer rooms of the bed/bedside table/wardrobe-only variety. Yet even these are usually tastefully done up and almost invariably impeccably clean.

Hotels are graded by the Benelux star system (one to five stars), though this isn't a particularly useful guide as it is based on an inventory of facilities and tells you nothing about location, service or ambience. Facilities vary in direct relation to price—you get what you pay for. Around the top end of the 'moderate' range (ƒ220–ƒ280) you should be assured of a TV and telephone in your room. Beyond that lies the world of mini-bars, en suite jacuzzis and telephones in the loo.

The hotels in the 'expensive' range tend to be business hotels. Here you're paying for facilities like fax machines and meeting rooms. Such places are briskly efficient, but are often soulless and used to expense-account customers. You can be just as comfortable, and probably far happier, in a more idiosyncratic hotel from the top of the 'moderate' range. Price ranges given in this guide are as follows:

Hotel price ranges used in this guide	
luxury	ƒ450 and over
expensive	ƒ280–ƒ450
moderate	ƒ180–ƒ280
inexpensive	ƒ100–180
cheap	under ƒ100

These prices are for a double room with bath or shower en suite in season, and include services and taxes and (unless otherwise stated) Dutch breakfast. For prices of single rooms deduct 15–20 per cent.

Self-catering

Amsterdam Apartments, Kromme Waal, 1011 BV, ✆ (020) 626 5930, ✉ 626 9544. Privately owned flats around town—usually flats let by Amsterdammers away on holiday—*from f700 per week.*

GIS Apartments, Keizersgracht 33, 1015 CD; ✆ (020) 625 0071, ✉ 638 0475. From simple to luxurious. *From f2,000 per month, minimum 3 months.*

Global Home Network, Suite 205, 110-D Elden Street, Herndon, Virginia, USA; ✆ +1 703 318 7081, ✉ + 1 703 318 7086 have a number of canalside apartments on their books, for short- and medium-term lease. *Prices on application.*

Bed & Breakfast

Bed & Breakfast Holland, T. de Bockstraat 3, 1058 TV Amsterdam, ✆ (020) 615 7527, ✉ 669 1573.

Bed & Breakfast in Holland & Amsterdam Information, Kraneweg 86a, 9718 JW Groningen, ✆ (050) 313 2424, *www.holidaylink.com, b&b@holidaylink.com.*

History

Watery Beginnings

As long ago as 150,000 BC there were nut-nibblers and hewers of flint tools near Utrecht. The Ice Age did for them. Next came hungry hunters and nomads, most of whom were flooded out by the fickle North Sea. It wasn't until about 6000 BC that farmers began to settle on what high muddy banks they could find, and it was only around 750 BC that they began to build their own mounds to protect farmsteads from the floods.

By the time written records began, in 57 BC, most of the territory was occupied by **Germanic tribes**, whom the Roman writer Tacitus dismissed as 'proud, touchy and warlike'. It was around this time that the Romans pushed their way in, conquering all but the Frisians in the very north of the land. But the North Sea again intervened, turning most of the west of the country to bog (Pliny was miserable near Leiden in AD 50). Disheartened, and with their empire crumbling behind them anyway, the Romans eventually withdrew. The end of Roman rule in the area is generally set at AD 406, when the Romans surrendered their forts along the Rhine.

Tribal Gatherings

Gradually, the remaining Germanic folk formed themselves into larger groups—the Saxons in the east, the Franks to the south of the great rivers (the Rhine and the Maas), and the plucky Frisians on their mounds in the north. At the beginning of the 6th century the Frankish **King Clovis I** converted to Christianity in the heat of a battle. That would appear to have been a good move, because not only was he victorious, but the Franks went on to establish a far-reaching empire—this was eventually to develop into the Holy Roman Empire, with the coronation of **Charlemagne** in AD 800.

Officially, the Netherlands was part of the **Holy Roman Empire** until 1648, but in reality power was held (after a brief and violent Viking interlude) by a number of local overlords, who were constantly at each other's throats. During the Middle Ages the most powerful rulers to emerge were the **Counts of Holland**, the **Bishops of Utrecht**, and the **Dukes of Gelderland** and of **Brabant**. No one ever really managed overall domination over the rebellious Frisians, who fought among themselves for most of the 14th and 15th centuries.

A Measure of Independence

By 1350, most of the future regions of the Netherlands had established themselves as **independent states**. Wars between local nobles continued to rage, with two main factions forming—the 'Hoeksen' (Hooks) and the 'Kabeljauwsen' (Cods), who fought for succession in the counties of Holland, Zeeland and Hainault. At the same time a power struggle developed between increasingly wealthy cities and the landed aristocracy.

As early as the 11th century, once the Vikings had stopped raiding and the weather had improved, the occupants of the Low Countries had begun to get the hang of reclaiming marshland and building **dykes** against the incursions of the sea. Soon they formed **water boards** (to regulate water levels in low-lying parts of the countryside) and constructed inland waterways. Trade along these routes flourished, and wealthy towns began to grow up. Some of these towns joined the powerful Baltic trade organization, the **Hanseatic League**.

Town councils were well organized, and enjoyed considerable freedom. Town charters were granted to these wealthy merchant strongholds, guaranteeing their privileges in return for financial support for the local lord's war. One of the first towns to gain such a charter was 's

Hertogenbosch (Den Bosch) in 1185. Similar privileges were granted to **Haarlem** by Count William II of Holland in 1245 and, after a struggle involving the Lord of the Amstel, the Count of Holland and the Bishop of Utrecht (*see* p.55), **Amsterdam** emerged as a powerful force, gaining its charter in 1300.

Part of Burgundy

Meanwhile, machinations in the upper realms of European royal courts were beginning to have an effect back down on the ground. In 1363 the King of France had given the Duchy of Burgundy to his son **Philip the Bold** (1342–1404). Philip married **Margaret of Flanders**, and subsequent clever unions and fortuitous inheritances meant that Burgundian influence spread ever northwards. By the middle of the 15th century, Philip's grandson **Philip the Good** (1396–1467) managed to unite a large chunk of what we now known as the Netherlands, together with Flanders and Luxembourg, under **Burgundian rule**. The Frisians, of course, held out, as did their neighbours in Groningen and Gelderland.

Burgundian expansion continued under **Charles the Rash** (1433–77), and links with the Hapsburgs were made when his daughter Mary married Emperor Maximilian I of Austria. Their son **Philip the Fair** (1478–1506) married Joanna of Castile and Aragon, thus adding her lands to the empire. Their heir **Charles** (1500–58) inherited the Austrian States from his grandfather Maximilian, and canoodled his way into being declared Holy Roman Emperor.

A Country Forms

By the time Philip the Fair died in 1506, the counties and duchies around the county of Holland were already being termed 'the Netherlands'. By the mid-16th century, Friesland, Groningen and Gelderland had finally been subsumed into Burgundy, and this northwestern corner of the empire became known as the '**Seventeen United Netherlands**'. Charles appointed his aunt Margaret, dowager Duchess of Savoy, to the post of 'royal governor' over the area. But the increasingly powerful cities were opposed to this Burgundian centralization. As early as 1464 various regional assemblies had convened in Bruges to decide whether Philip the Good should be financed to go on a crusade. This convention, called the '**States-General**', became a permanent and increasingly important feature of regional government.

Growing Prosperity

The blossoming of trade in the Netherlands was principally due to grain, herring and beer. Enormous quantities of grain were needed to feed the growing population in western Europe (bread was still the staple diet). The Netherlands was able to tap rich Baltic and central European supplies through its traditional trading connections. Dordrecht, on the river Rhine, and Amsterdam played a leading role in this activity.

Other towns near Amsterdam, such as Hoorn and Enkhuizen, also prospered. Leiden and Haarlem became busy centres of cloth manufacture. Gouda, Delft and Amersfoort were just three of many **brewing towns**—and as most people drank beer rather than the poisonous local water, merchants did well. Then in 1384 one Willem Beukels hit upon a way of **preserving herring** more efficiently—by gutting them before salting. This meant that ships could stay out at sea longer and travel further afield. At about the same time (as if obeying a cosmic plan) the herring moved their spawning ground from the Baltic to the North Sea, and the industry prospered. It needed salt (from Portugal) and wood for the barrels (from Germany and Scandinavia).

Amsterdam merchants had no qualms, as they moved further into the Baltic, about breaking in on the Hanseatic League's trade and developing new routes. Soon the city's ships were also carrying furs, iron ore, cloth, and wine. Wily merchants began building warehouses all over the city to store goods until the best price could be fetched. Amsterdam became a thriving commercial centre and a nexus for European trade. It fought a bitter trade war with the Hanseatic towns, but by the mid-15th century was indomitable. By 1500 the region around Amsterdam (most of the county of Holland) had taken the lead in the economy. This had a crucial effect on politics in the centuries to come.

Reformation and Revolt

At the beginning of the 16th century Europe was firmly in the grip of the Roman Catholic Church. But on 31 October 1517 a hitherto obscure Augustinian monk called **Martin Luther** calmly walked up to the chapel of Wittenberg Castle and nailed his '95 Theses' to the door. The 'Theses' condemned superstition in the Church and the practice of indulgences. Luther's act marked the beginning of the Reformation—theologians everywhere became braver and more audible in their criticism. In Rotterdam **Erasmus** propounded an idealized man as the pinnacle of creation, rather than the miserable sinner after the Fall. In Geneva **Calvin** appealed to the Age of Reason with his impeccably logical 'Institutes': the State should be separated from the Church, and be in the hands of morally upright citizens. The Catholic Church responded swiftly and thousands were tried for heresy.

Trade routes also served as channels for new ideas. The revolutionary theology caught on quickly in the Netherlands and there were heresy trials, but the Dutch were traditionally tolerant and didn't always carry out sentences they were obliged to impose. In fact Calvin's austere doctrines, and the notion of civic power, rather appealed to a number of wealthy merchant families.

By this time the Netherlands was ruled, as a consequence of marriages made in the stratosphere of the royal courts of Europe, by **Philip II of Spain** (later husband of Mary Tudor). Philip was head of the mighty Austro-Spanish Catholic house of Hapsburg which dominated much of Europe, owned most of South America and even laid claim to the English crown. Unlike his reassuringly named predecessors (Philip the Good, Charles the Bold and Philip the Fair), Philip II was a cruel and fanatical despot. He also took ages to reach decisions, so his subjects spent most of their lives in a terrified limbo. Action was dangerous, no orders came from above and political situations had the habit of deteriorating around the protagonists. This was particularly aggravating in territories as far-flung as the Netherlands. Even Dutch Catholics, outraged by the Inquisition and this distant monarch's cruel repression, became antagonistic. Opposition to Philip began to grow along nationalist as well as religious lines. Philip took a quiet step back, leaving his half-sister, **Margaret of Parma**, to deal with any unpleasantness—though in effect power was wielded by a scheming civil servant Antoine Perrenot, later **Cardinal Granvelle**.

Meanwhile, several leading local nobles had been declared the king's lieutenants—or '*stadhouders*'—in the main provinces. Among these was one **William of Orange**, lord-lieutenant of Holland, Zeeland, West Frisia and Utrecht. Granvelle tried to exclude the *stadhouders* from discussions in the Council of State, but in 1562 dissatisfied court nobles united under William of Orange and demanded Granvelle's dismissal. They were tacitly backed by Margaret of

Palma, who was no friend of the scheming upstart, and in 1564 Granvelle left the Netherlands 'to visit his family', and never returned. Margaret was persuaded to sign the '**Moderation**', which implied some measure of religious tolerance. Protestants from around Europe began to see the Netherlands as the only safe haven outside Germany and Switzerland. Protestant services were permitted outside city walls; during the summer of 1566, hundreds of people left city churches to listen to these open-air 'hedge-sermons'. Meanwhile, a crop failure the previous winter had caused a famine. Southern Flanders, especially, was in the grip of a depression caused by the decline of the cloth trade with England. All this gave an even sharper edge to the religious rancour being stirred up in the polders outside the cities. In August 1566, this erupted in a frenzy of destruction. Puritan iconoclasts smashed church windows and battered or burnt all popish treasures, graven images and artworks.

Persecution and War

Philip II was livid. He sent an army of 10,000 men under the **Duke of Alva**—the 'Iron Duke'—to punish the heretics. Most of the Protestant leaders, sensing what was coming, hastily left the country. When the Duke arrived in Amsterdam, 170 merchants' houses lay empty. A reign of terror began. So many people were executed by the Duke's **Council of Blood** that the city was nicknamed 'Murderdam'.

In 1568, the date taken as the beginning of the **Eighty Years' War** with Spain, the exiled William of Orange attempted a campaign against Alva. (William's previous discretion about his Protestant sympathies had earned him the name 'William the Silent'.) Terrified local Protestants gave him little support and the invasion was a failure. William didn't have enough money to pay his soldiers and had to creep away from them in the night. He wandered around France gathering another army, and by 1572 was meeting with a little more success, capturing Brill, Vlissingen (Flushing) and Veere. He was assisted by the **Sea-beggars**, a rough and ready bunch of quasi-pirates, who proved an embarrassment to their sober general by pillaging churches, massacring clergy, dressing up in desecrated vestments and getting drunk (they were later to form the basis of the Dutch navy).

Most towns (except Amsterdam) now rallied to William's aid. In the town of Dordrecht he was elected overall '*stadhouder*' by the United Provinces, which meant that, technically, he was lord-lieutenant of the King he was rebelling against. As the fighting wore on, this allegiance became a fiction, but initially the intention really was to maintain fealty while demanding that the Netherlands keep control over its own internal policies. In a battle song of the time beginning 'William of Nassau, I am of Dutch blood', William sings, 'I have always honoured the King of Spain.' Curiously, though in the 20th century this song became the Dutch national anthem, the line was not changed, which must make the Netherlands the only country in the world that sings the praises of another land in its national song.

Vengefully, Alva sent troops to punish towns that supported William. But the rebels relieved Alva's **sieges of Alkmaar** (on 8 October 1573) and **Leiden** (3 October 1574)—events still celebrated today. Soon William controlled all the towns around Amsterdam. Meanwhile, the populace was turning against Alva—less as a result of his vicious persecutions than because of the 10th penny tax he had imposed (which diverted 10 per cent of all citizens' income into the Duke's personal coffers). The profligate Alva slipped away one night in 1573, just a few hours before he was due to face a meeting of angry creditors.

In the winter of 1575–6 William laid siege to **Amsterdam**. The town officials were so worried about infiltrators that they banned skating on the canals and even stood guard at important gates themselves. Cattle from the fields were brought within the city walls and stabled in the deserted merchants' houses. Priceless silver was melted down and minted into coins in an attempt to keep business ticking over. The ever-prudent Amsterdam city fathers had only been supporting Philip II because Spain seemed the stronger side. After a long siege, it became clear that William was going to win the war so, in 1578, the city judiciously swapped allegiance and made peace with William. This signalled the virtual end of Spanish dominion over the Netherlands (though they were to retain sovereignty for another 70 years).

In 1579 the southern, Catholic and largely French-speaking provinces signed the **Union of Arras** and declared their allegiance to Spain. This gave Spain a base for attacks on the north (most notably the punishing **Siege of Antwerp** in 1584–5). Seven northern provinces responded with the **Union of Utrecht**, a Protestant military federation with The Hague as the centre of power. The provinces—Holland, Zeeland, Utrecht, Groningen, Gelderland, Friesland and Overijssel—agreed to remain 'in perpetual alliance', united 'as if they were one'. The Union upheld the 'freedom of religious belief'. Each state would decide on religious matters separately, and persecution would end.

In response, Philip II outlawed William, who subsequently advised the States General to elect a new king. By the Act of Abjuration on 22 July 1581, the States General withdrew allegiance from Philip and appointed his brother the **Duke of Anjou** as their monarch. The notion still existed that a state needed a sovereign, though in effect power lay in the hands of William of Orange. But William was assassinated on 10 July 1584. The States General placed the administrative power of the Union in the lap of the Council of State. William's 17-year-old son Prince Maurits was made a member of the Council, and one of his nephews, John of Nassau was elected *stadhouder*. On the death of Anjou a year later, sovereignty was offered to the King of France, who declined, and to Elizabeth of England, who sent along the Earl of Leicester as governor general. Leicester was not popular, and left after two years.

Meanwhile, Philip II was not sitting still. In autumn 1588 he sent along an '**invincible Armada**' to crush the rebellion once and for all—and to teach the English a lesson along the way. And that, as every English schoolchild knows, was a big mistake.

Realizing A Republic

In 1585 **Prince Maurits** was elected *stadhouder* of Holland, largely as the result of the machinations of a senior civil servant **John van Oldenbarneveldt** (1547–1619). It was beginning to dawn on the states that the position of *stadhouder* was really an embodiment of their own power, and that they didn't need to offer allegiance to an external sovereign after all. It was around this time that people began to refer to the northern provinces of the Netherlands as the **Republic of the Seven United Dutch Provinces**. By 1596 both France and England were prepared to acknowledge the United Provinces as an independent power, and to support them against Spain. This was known as the **Triple Alliance**.

With his characteristic knack of avoiding sticky situations, Philip gave the Netherlands to his daughter Isabella as a wedding present in 1598. Van Oldenbarneveldt persuaded her to conclude a truce in 1609. She agreed to acknowledge the sovereignty of the Republic for the duration of the truce. Meanwhile, antagonism grew up between Van Oldenbarneveldt and

Maurits (who was all for continuing the war)—a conflict which eventually resulted in Van Oldenbarneveldt's execution, and in Maurits assuming the *stadhoudership* of the provinces of Groningen and Drenthe, in addition to that of Holland. By the end of the Twelve Years' Truce in 1621, Maurits was the leading power in the land. When he died in 1625, he was succeeded by his half-brother Frederick Henry. The *stadhoudership* was on its way to becoming hereditary.

The *Stadhouders*

Each province of the United Provinces was headed by a *stadhouder* (the title that had traditionally been used for the king's lieutenant in the area). In theory, provinces could choose separate *stadhouders*, but in practice all opted for members of the House of Orange, and gradually this became centred on just one member of the family. Successive generations continued to elect heirs to the House of Orange, so the title became all but hereditary. William's son, Maurits, was styled 'Prince', and soon the family was considered grand enough for a match with an English princess—William II married Mary Stuart, daughter of Charles I, an arrangement that did not please the various city regents, as England was a trade rival.

The *stadhouder* was commander-in-chief of the country's armed forces, and this also brought him into conflict with the regents. Peace was better for business than war, and after the final defeat of the Spanish in 1648 the State of Holland wanted to cut back on military spending. William II of Orange wanted to keep his armies. The traditional unease between Amsterdam and the House of Orange bristled into tension. On 23 June 1650 the *stadhouder* visited Amsterdam and demanded an official reception. The regents refused, and condescendingly invited him for dinner instead. 'If we are to wine and dine together,' sniffed a piqued William, 'then we would have to be better friends than we are at present.'

He left the next day, gathered troops and sent them to take Amsterdam by surprise. Civil war was narrowly averted. The invading army had got lost in a fog and were spotted by a postman on his way over from Hamburg. The city was warned, and William was forced to negotiate. When he died of the pox some months later, it was decided not to appoint another *stadhouder* for the while.

In 1654, as part of the peace negotiations that ended the first Anglo-Dutch War (1652–4), the State of Holland succeeded in passing a law, known as the Act of Seclusion, stating that no member of the House of Orange should ever become *stadhouder* again. This was supported by Cromwell, who feared that the House of Orange might lend support to the deposed English royals. But when the Stuarts returned to the English throne in 1660 they reinforced the position of the Oranges, and when the Act of Seclusion was revoked in 1672 William III was made *stadhouder* of all the provinces (except Friesland), with strengthened powers. His marriage to another Mary Stuart, daughter of James II, was his stepping stone to becoming King of England in 1689, and paved the way to the Grand Alliance, uniting England, the Republic, Spain and parts of Germany against France.

Peace at Last

The war with Spain, which had dragged on since the Union of Utrecht in 1579, was exhausting the coffers of both sides. By the 1640s everyone had had enough. In 1646 delegates of the States General arrived in the German town of Münster to begin talks with Spain, France and the German Emperor. It took two years to argue out a peace plan, but by the 1648 **Treaty of Münster**, the sovereignty of the United Netherlands was finally recognized, marking the end of the Eighty Years' War.

The seven united provinces had the right to vote in the States General. Drenthe had some degree of sovereignty, but the southern states of Brabant, Vlaanderen (Flanders) and Limburg, who had sided with the Spanish, were seen as spoils of war and were not granted independent assemblies or representation in the States-General.

Rather sneakily, the northern Dutch negotiators at the Treaty of Münster had ensured that the Scheldt (the river serving Antwerp, which had been blockaded during the war) was to remain closed. This ensured that the port of Amsterdam had no rival, and it became the hub of international trade—a position that did not appeal to the English. In 1651 England passed the **Navigation Act**, heavily protecting English trade. Two **Anglo-Dutch wars** ensued, the first (1652–4) ending in defeat for the Republic, but the second culminating in one of the Netherlands' most celebrated victories, that of **Admiral Michiel de Ruyter**, who sailed up the Medway and trounced the English fleet in 1667.

The Golden Age (17th Century)

A map worked into the floor of Amsterdam's 17th-century Stadhuis (town hall) places the city at the centre of the universe—and for much of the century that must have seemed true. Goods flowed into the port from around the world, paused for a while in one of the hundreds of brimming warehouses and, as soon as prices went up, were packed off to distant and lucrative markets. Guilds flourished as the abundance of raw materials attracted craftsmen from around Europe, and even the lowliest workers earned nearly twice as much as their English counterparts. The Amsterdam Bourse (Exchange) thronged with merchants from countries as far away as India and Turkey. They conducted a resounding trade in property and shares, and merchandise of all sorts. Isaac le Maire had the idea of trading *in blanco*—dealing on paper with goods he didn't yet own—and the first futures market was begun. In 1609 the city council founded the **Amsterdam Wisselbank** (Bank of Exchange) in the cellar of the town hall. It drew up bank drafts to replace coins (which could be clipped, melted down or stolen), gave quick mortgages and lent at a good rate of interest (an encouraging 3½–4 per cent; England dragged behind at 6 per cent). Amsterdam notes of exchange were accepted throughout the world.

The **arts and intellectual life** flourished. Not only were Rembrandt, Vermeer and Frans Hals kept busy, but lesser painters churned out an estimated 20 million pieces of work during the first part of the century. Even the poorest houses had paintings. Books suppressed elsewhere rolled off Amsterdam's uncensored presses—and if you hung about the right cafés you could bump into Spinoza or Descartes.

The economy was solidly based on the Baltic grain trade (it filled some four-fifths of Amsterdam's warehouses), but the spirit of the Golden Age shines clearest in the romance, daring and glamour of the **trade with the East**. Initially the Dutch hadn't bothered to send ships further than Lisbon, relying on intrepid Portuguese sailors for booty from the Spice Islands. In 1580, however, Philip II conquered Portugal and closed its ports to his arch-enemy. It was clear that the Dutch would have to send their own ships to the East. Jews fleeing the Inquisition brought inside information about trade routes, and in 1595 Jan Huyghens published *Itinerario*, a book which told temptingly of the precariousness of Portuguese government in the colonies. Later that year Cornelis Houtman set off with four ships and 200 men on a voyage of discovery. Only 99 men limped back in battered ships on 23 August 1597, and investors just managed to break even, but the port of Amsterdam buzzed with excitement.

When a second voyage realized a profit of 400 per cent, merchants exploded into action. In 1597 the romantically named 'Compagnie van Verre' (Far Away Company) began direct trade with the East Indies. Everybody wanted to get in on the act. So many new companies were formed that they looked likely to put each other out of business before they'd really started. On 20 March 1602 they all united to form the **Verenigde Oostindische Compagnie (VOC—United East India Company)**. The whole country seemed greedily caught up in the spirit of adventure: domestic servants and seamstresses were among the thousands of early shareholders. The company had the monopoly of Dutch trade from the Cape of Good Hope to Cape Horn, and at the peak of its influence it had over 150 merchant vessels protected by 40 fighting ships and its own army of 10,000 soldiers. It sailed all over the East Indies and also to India, Ceylon, China, the South Pacific Islands and South Africa. For nearly two centuries it was the most powerful trade organization in the world. The VOC could establish colonies, sign treaties and declare war and it became the cutting edge of Dutch colonialism. A contemporary English traveller remarked that it was 'a commonwealth within a commonwealth'.

In 1624 the **West India Company** was formed. It was a copycat venture, smaller and much less prosperous than the VOC, and had the trade monopoly over the seas between Africa and the Americas. It teetered along largely on the profits of the slave trade, but exhausted its coffers waging colonial wars against the Portuguese and Spanish. The company's main claim to fame was that it administered the American colony of New Amsterdam—later captured by the British and renamed New York.

The trading companies' economic clout gave the city of Amsterdam a tremendous sway over the rest of the Netherlands. Eight of the Chamber of Seventeen, the powerful governing body of the VOC, had to be Amsterdam citizens, and managers were appointed by the *burge-meester*. The city itself was ruled by the **Heren (Lords) XLVIII**, a council of four *burgemeesters*, a sheriff, seven jurists and 36 advisers. These 'Regents' often came into conflict with national government.

The Decline

In the first half of the 17th century Germany was battling through the Thirty Years War, the Roundheads and Cavaliers were roughing each other up in England, and France had been left rather limp by the war with Spain. Around 1650 the dust began to settle, and the pugnacious neighbours turned their attention to the prosperous little country in their midst. The conflicts of the late 17th and 18th centuries drained the United Provinces' coffers and gave the warfaring House of Orange a useful step-up back to power.

Squabbles over herring and punitive anti-Dutch import laws led to wars with England in 1652–4 and 1664–7. Rather unwillingly, the Provinces found themselves fighting France in the **War of the Spanish Succession** (1701–14). There was another war in 1780 when England discovered the Dutch had secretly been trading with rebel American colonies. London and Hamburg began to take over as mercantile centres, while Amsterdam's old trade routes were threatened. England's increasing sea power began to erode the East Indies trade, and in 1791, after years of false accounting, the VOC went into liquidation. The river Schelde was reopened as a trade route, putting Antwerp back on the map as an important port. Trade became a less important part of the economy, and while Amsterdam focused its attention on banking, the early industrial revolution passed the country by.

As the money business boomed, the Amsterdam oligarchy became increasingly corrupt and complacent. Children of influential families would be given public posts as christening presents, and they would draw the salary while a menial did the work. The city fathers happily pocketed a large portion of the taxes they collected. The rich got ostentatious, and the poor got angry and subversive. On 24 June 1748 an Amsterdam merchant noticed a 'shameless slut' in the buttermarket who turned her back on a guard and 'several times raised her skirt, smacking her bare buttocks saying, "That's for you."' The guard shot her ('in her bare fundament') and she later died. This was all that was needed to spark off some well-organized street violence. Armed with lists of tax collectors' addresses, a mob stormed the grand canals, sacking houses and destroying anything of value. The **Tax Farmers' Riot** was swiftly suppressed, but the civil guard had to beat drums below the scaffold to drown out the slogans shouted by the ring-leaders as they went to the gallows.

Vociferous, fantastically dressed bands of volunteers, heady with Rousseau's ideas, began to roam the countryside spreading the gospel of democracy. They had the support of some sympathetic patricians, such as Hendrik Hooft (affectionately known as 'Father Hooft'). Soon these **Patriots** had taken over the governments of many smaller towns, and on 27 April 1787 they staged a coup in Amsterdam. The Prince of Orange had had enough. With the armies of his brother-in-law, the King of Prussia, he sent the Patriots packing. Many fled to France, where they were just in time for the Revolution. In 1795 a French Republican army, with the support of exiled Patriots, crossed the frozen Rhine and advanced on Amsterdam. There was, by this time, strong pro-French feeling in the Netherlands. The invading armies were seen as liberators, and the Regents were bloodlessly deposed in what became known as the **Velvet Revolution**. A 'Freedom Tree' was erected on the Dam and Amsterdammers danced around it celebrating the newly declared **Batavian Republic** (the Batavians were the ancient tribe of the Netherlands). But the *liberté*, *égalité* and *fraternité* were not to last for long.

In 1806 Napoleon created his younger brother, **Louis Bonaparte**, King of the Netherlands. Louis converted Amsterdam's prized Stadhuis into a palace and demolished the ancient public weighhouse on the Dam because it spoiled his view. The outraged city was not consoled by the fact that it was now the new capital.

A Kingdom Again

On his first day in the new job Louis announced to his ministers, in heavily accented Dutch, '*Ik ben uw Konijn*' ('I am your rabbit') rather than '*Ik ben uw Koning*' ('I am your king'). But though he had started off on the wrong foot, Louis soon endeared himself to the people by visiting the stricken during smallpox epidemics, actively supporting the arts and sciences and rather foolishly standing up to his older brother. (He allowed Dutch smugglers to break Napoleon's blockade of British ports.) Napoleon hadn't expected his young sibling to be such an upstart, so in 1810 he deposed him and incorporated the Netherlands into the French Empire. But **Waterloo** was just around the corner. Even before that battle, in 1813 (after Napoleon's retreat from Moscow) the French garrison withdrew from Amsterdam and the Netherlands was proclaimed a constitutional monarchy under the House of Orange. The 1814 **Congress of Vienna** united all the Netherlands provinces (north and south) for the first time, under **King William I** (1772–1843), son of *stadhouder* William V (who had died in 1806), as a constitutional monarch. But the proud new kingdom lasted only until 1831, when the predominantly Catholic and anti-Orangist southern provinces rebelled and formed a new independent kingdom called **Belgium**, unrecognised by the north until eight years later, when the disputed southern province of Limburg was finally ceded to the north.

From Gloom to Boom

After months of bickering with The Hague, Amsterdam had become the capital of 'the Netherlands', and home to the Netherlands Bank. But the new nation was in something of a decline. The city's coffers were empty. Napoleon's blockade of English ports and the British occupation of Dutch colonies during the Napoleonic wars had strangled trade, the money market had slipped across the channel to London, and Dutch entrepreneurs had disdained the inventions of the Industrial Revolution. The trading companies' dainty sailboats were soon to be eclipsed by heavy steamships, too bulky to negotiate the Zuider Zee. In 1824 the North Holland Canal (between Amsterdam and Den Helder) was given a festive opening, but the bravado was misplaced. The numerous bends and locks compelled such creeping progress that it was hardly worth the merchants' while. From now on it was **Rotterdam**, rather than Amsterdam, that was destined to become the country's premier port.

As the disconsolate country limped through the early decades of the 19th century, a few valiant paladins of the new industries set their minds to revitalizing her. The king set up the **Nederlandse Handelsmaatschappij** (Netherlands Trading Company) to perk up the drooping trade in tropical products. In 1825 Paul van Vlissingen started running regular steamship services to London and Hamburg and built an engineering works on Oostenburg island in east Amsterdam. Peppy doctor and philanthropist Samuel Sarphati founded a commercial college, several banks, a construction company, the Amstel Hotel (still one of the best in the country) and an efficient and profitable refuse disposal service (Amsterdam's stinking waste was shipped out in sealed barges, composted and sold to farmers). He founded the **Vereniging voor Volksvlijt** (Industrial Society) to knock new life into flagging manufacturers and to inject new technology into factories. His sparkling glass Palace of Industry rose up dramatically on Frederiksplein in Amsterdam and was home to countless displays, exhibitions and concerts until it burnt down in 1929.

Towards the end of the century the Netherlands began to thrive once more. New industries—even a motor car factory—flourished. The opening of the Suez Canal in 1869 meant easier access to the Orient, and in 1876 the North Sea Canal was cut through the dunes to give Amsterdam proper access to bigger ships. The Netherlands became the main supplier to a newly unified Germany, and manufacturing and shipbuilding industries revived. The discovery of diamonds in South Africa led to a boom in the diamond-cutting trade, with workers becoming deliriously rich overnight. In 1839 the first railway in the Netherlands ran from Amsterdam to Haarlem; fifty years later there were nearly 200 trains running to destinations all over Europe, and grand new railway stations were springing up in cities along the way. During the 1880s the first trams and bicycles made their appearance. The arts blossomed: national institutions such as the Rijksmuseum and Concertgebouw have their origins in the last two decades of the century. By 1883 the Netherlands had regained enough of her former grace for Amsterdam to host the **World Exhibition**.

The 19th century also saw an increase in **parliamentary democracy** in the Netherlands. The 1848 revolts in the rest of Europe made King William II nervous. In 1848 the king set up a reform committee under the liberal Rudolph Thorbecke and changes were hurried through after a mob stormed around the Dam in Amsterdam in 1849, with the alarming proclamation that 'All men are brothers.' As the franchise was extended, support grew for the socialist movement. A Socialist Party was founded in the 1880s, without much success, but the Social-Democratic Workers' Party (SDAP) founded in 1894 was the forerunner of today's Partij van de Arbeid (PvdA—Labour Party).

Amsterdam entered the 20th century on the crest of a boom. The Netherlands remained neutral in the First World War. The Dutch happily traded in arms with both sides, and emerged comparatively unscathed—though the rest of the country's trade had taken a blow and food shortages in 1917 had provoked riots in Amsterdam. The population had been growing fast—from 3 million in 1846 to 6 million in 1913.

In 1920 two converted De Havillands, carrying two passengers apiece, began to fly regularly to London. The world's first air travel booking office opened at Schiphol in the following year. In 1928 Amsterdam hosted the Olympic Games, but the 1929 Wall Street Crash slid the country into an economic depression. The 1930s also saw the growth of a small but vociferous Dutch Nazi Party (NSB)—though the fascist movement didn't gather anywhere near the support it did in Germany.

The Second World War

The Netherlands hoped to remain neutral in the Second World War, as they had in the first. But on 10 May 1940 the Germans attacked Dutch airports and military barracks. Queen Wilhelmina and the Dutch government lost little time in skipping across the Channel to the relative safety of England. They left Supreme Commander Winkelman to deal with the advancing Germans. He held out for five days, during which Rotterdam was mercilessly bombed from the air. On 15 May the German army occupied the Netherlands and Hitler declared the cool Austrian Nazi Arthur Seyss-Inquart *Rijkscommissaris* (State Commissioner). Members of the NSB who had collaborated with the invaders were catapulted to positions of high office.

At first life carried on much the same as before, with the Dutch exercising their indefatigable capacity to turn a blind eye to anything that threatened to ruffle the smooth flow of daily business. However, when Seyss-Inquart's early softly-softly attempt to *nazificeren* ('nazify') Holland met with stolid Dutch inertia, he became more brutal. Young Dutchmen were sent off to work in Germany, soldiers who had been captured during the invasion and then released were re-arrested as prisoners-of-war. Jews, especially, were the butt of systematic oppressive decrees. The wearing of yellow stars was compulsory and Jews were banned from driving or from using trams. They had to hand in their bicycles, be indoors by 8 o'clock (not even out in their own gardens), were allowed to shop only in Jewish shops between 3 and 5 o'clock in the afternoon, and couldn't visit theatres, cinemas or sports grounds. Soon they were forbidden to visit Christians, had to go to separate schools and were fenced off in ghettos. On 22 February 1941 German trucks rumbled into the Jodenhoek (Jewish Quarter) in Amsterdam and the first round-up of Jews began. In the years that followed nearly all of Amsterdam's Jews (10 per cent of the city's population) were transported, along with gypsies and homosexuals, to concentration camps in Germany. Hardly any survived.

The February *razzia* (raid on Jews) sparked off a spontaneous Amsterdam-wide strike that was viciously put down. Right through the occupation heroic Resistance fighters sabotaged German munitions and supplies stores, attempted to assassinate Nazi leaders, spawned batches of false documents and reeled off secret newspapers to keep the public properly informed. Nazi retaliation was diabolical. If they couldn't dig out the ringleaders, whole groups of innocent people would be shot in reprisal for any Resistance activity. Opposition also went on in quieter, but no less courageous ways. Many non-Jews wore yellow stars in sympathy and thousands gave shelter to *onderduikers* ('divers')—members of the Resistance, or Jews (like the Frank family), who went into hiding around the city. On Prince Bernhard's birthday, thousands imitated his habit of wearing a white carnation, much to the confusion of the Nazis who didn't know quite what to legislate against. Queen Wilhelmina re-established herself in the good opinion of many Amsterdammers by broadcasting cheering messages to her people from the security of a BBC studio.

By the winter of 1944—'Hunger Winter'—the fabric of life had all but collapsed. Everybody was starving (especially those sharing ration books with *onderduikers*), as the Germans had restricted the flow of food in retaliation for a Dutch railwaymen's strike. Walking was the only means of transport and rubbish bins and sewers overflowed. Fuel was impossible to come by, so people stole any wood they could lay their hands on. Sleepers were torn from the tram tracks, parks thinned out mysteriously overnight and any empty houses were stripped of furniture, beams and floorboards.

On 5 May 1945 the Netherlands was liberated. On 7 May jubilant crowds crammed the streets of Amsterdam to greet the Canadian liberation force. In a final lash of malice, German soldiers opened fire on the crowd, killing 22 people.

Post-war Blues

The Netherlands was devastated by the war. Its transport system was paralyzed, industrial production had slumped by 30 per cent and the Germans had broken dykes, flooding much of the countryside. Despite chronic shortages of almost everything, the Dutch bounced back with a lively resilience, enthusiastic for a quick recovery. They even managed city-wide street parties in 1948 to celebrate Queen Juliana's coronation and Dutch victories in the Olympic Games. The granting of independence to former colonies knocked the edge off the tropical trade, but the Netherlands soon got down to the more mundane business of keeping the hungry new Ruhr industries fed. From the outset, the country participated in the economic recovery that swept continental Europe in the 1950s. After the widening of the North Sea Canal and construction of the new Amsterdam-Rhine Canal in 1952, regeneration was meteoric. Garden-city suburbs sprang up to house the swelling population.

Unity and Prosperity

The Netherlands, together with Belgium and Luxembourg, formed the **Benelux Customs Union** in 1948, and the **Benelux Economic Union** in 1958—organizations that played an important role in the establishment of NATO and of the **European Economic Community**.

The 1960s saw increasing prosperity, and the foundation of the Dutch welfare state. Old patterns began to emerge. The solid Calvinist burgers were still very much in control, but the traditional tolerance of minorities and deviants soon made space, not for the naked dancing Anabaptists of yore, but for a new phenomenon of dreamy hippies and tatty youth. In the 1960s Amsterdam became a mecca of the blossoming youth culture. Troupes of long-haired, denim-clad, gently stoned young people hung out and slept around Centraal Station, the National Monument on the Dam and in Vondelpark. In 1969 John Lennon and Yoko Ono staged their week-long 'Bed-in' for world peace in the Hilton Hotel. An old church near Leidseplein was converted into the Paradiso—a place where you could puff away on marijuana without fear of arrest, and have your ears blasted by the latest music. Homosexuals began to join the party, and soon Amsterdam was known as the gay capital of Europe.

The 1980s and 1990s have seen an era of extraordinary wealth and economic stability for the Netherlands—even during the rollercoaster rides other European economies were taking at the end of the 1980s boom years. Based on open and easy industrial relations and good Protestant moderation, the 'polder model' economy, as it has come to be known (after Dutch '*polders*'—reclaimed land) has been the envy of many an EU finance minister. At one point, the Netherlands was almost the only country that met all the criteria for entry into the single currency without having to resort to imaginative accounting.

The 21st century began early in the Netherlands. The first non-military **Internet** connection point in Europe was in Amsterdam, set up in 1988 at the Centre for Mathematics and Computer Science (CWI). And the city remains one of the six biggest Internet nodes in the world, transmitting over 100 million bytes per second. By the late 1990s, Amsterdam already had public Internet booths alongside telephone boxes on street corners. With a long history of formal and informal unions and alliances behind it, the Netherlands seems unruffled about entering a new millennium as part of a united Europe.

Art and Architecture

Dutch Painting

Sacheverell Sitwell, the English poet and essayist, wrote that painting is as endemic among the Dutch as poetry is among the English. During the 17th-century Golden Age (a high-water mark for painting, as well as an economic boom) an estimated 20 million paintings were executed. Even the humblest homes had the odd oil tacked up on the wall. A 17th-century English traveller observed that 'many times blacksmiths, cobblers, etc. will have some picture or other by their forge or in their stall. Such is the general notion, inclination and delight that these country natives have to painting.' These days there is still a feeling that art matters, is part of everyday life, and that even the zaniest of new painters belongs to a long continuum of artists working in Holland.

Before the Golden Age

It is important to draw a distinction between Dutch and Flemish art. In 1579 the Netherlands polarized into a Flemish, predominantly Roman Catholic south, and an alliance of seven Dutch, Protestant northern provinces. Eugène Fromentin, the 19th-century art critic, observed that 'Holland had never possessed many national painters. While she was blended with Flanders, it was Flanders that took upon herself to think, invent and paint for her.' Early Flemish art resounds with familiar names like Breughel, Bosch and van Eyck, while Holland musters Cornelis Ketel, a portrait painter who grew bored with his craft and, as a ruse to liven up his technique, started painting with his toes, with no noticeable loss in quality. However, in the 17th century migrations of prominent painters to the Protestant north, a blossoming national confidence and snowballing economic prosperity stimulated a new Dutch School. This exclusively Dutch painting was influenced by Flemish artists, but also by Italians and a small heritage of local painters less disgruntled with their lot than Cornelis Ketel.

In his *Book of Famous Men*, the 15th-century humanist Barolemmo Fayio lists only two Flemish artists: Jan van Eyck and Rogier van der Weyden—painters we still consider pivots of the period. Both had a strong influence on later Dutch painting. **Jan van Eyck** (1385–1441) and his shadowy brother, Hubert (some say they collaborated, some say that Hubert never existed) are credited with the discovery of oil paint. In reality, they merely perfected a technique that northern European painters had been using for some time. Oil paints, which can be applied in layers, give a rich, deep tone which was much favoured by artists who were fascinated by appearances—the glowing colours of objects as they were touched by light. Italian artists, on the other hand, tended to be more concerned with structure, bodies and movement: they worked in tempera (egg-based paint) which rendered sharper, brighter colours—but soon latched on to the practical and artistic merits of oils.

Early Netherlandish art was mainly devotional. Static groups of bodies crowded pictures crammed with detail and heavily symbolic bric-a-brac. **Rogier van der Weyden** (1399–1464) swept the canvas clean. He focused tightly on a few figures and injected a passionate, authentic emotional intensity into his work. This was extremely rare in religious art of the time, and had a powerful impact on later Dutch painters.

Albert Ouwater (active 1450–80) was the man who took these ideas north. He settled in Haarlem around the time that a book by the Florentine Leon Battista Alberti was being passed around painters' studios. Alberti argued that historia (narrative) was crucial to good art. Dutch painting became less static; small dramas and conflicts began to emerge from the canvas. **Geertgen tot Sint Jans** (c. 1460–95) was much influenced by Ouwater. He painted bright, beautiful pictures, still laden with symbolic references but with a much freer arrangement of figures. The figures themselves, however, were still rigid, with little real eloquence of human movement. **Lucas van Leyden** (1489–1553), a child prodigy who was already engraving in his native Leiden at the age of nine, burst on to the scene with sparkling, dynamic, densely peopled paintings that revolutionized Dutch art. As these various strands combine we can see, in the work of painters like Van Leyden and **Jan Mostaert** (1475–1555), the first signs of a separate Dutch school of painting.

In 1604 Karel van Mander, a painter and theorist working in Haarlem, published *Het Schilderboek*. This was a collection of biographies but also served as a theoretical handbook for artists. It was the first full-scale work of art theory to delineate Dutch and Flemish traditions. In his book, Van Mander exalted Haarlem as the cradle of Dutch art. The school of painters working there was developing its own style of Italian Mannerism. The Mannerists believed their work shouldn't slavishly imitate Nature, but instead improve upon it with imagination and Art. Paintings (even those with innocent titles like *John the Baptist Preaching*) swarm with lumpy nude musclemen and elongated female figures. They sport about in exotic settings in which piled-up fragments of Roman art, stylized plants and fabulous beasts abound.

The first Dutch painter to travel to Renaissance Italy (it later became de rigueur for any artist who wanted to be taken seriously) was **Jan van Scorel** (1495–1562). He passed through Germany and Venice on a pilgrimage to Jerusalem. On his way back he visited Rome, and was given the job of curator of the massive papal art collection by Hadrian VI, the only Dutch pope in history. This experience changed his painting style completely, and he returned to Haarlem (as Van Mander puts it) as 'the lantern-bearer and road-paver of the Arts in the Netherlands'. Others would claim that honour for Lucas van Leyden, but Van Mander thought that Van Leyden was a show-off—and, besides, he didn't come from Haarlem. Van Scorel's pupil **Martin van Heemskerck** (1498–1574) also travelled to Italy and was one of the main propagators of Mannerist ideas in Holland.

Mannerism made Dutch painting far more lively and flexible, but painters began to tire of its ornament. A move to greater realism and narrative clarity—more Nature, less Art—can be seen in the works of **Hendrik Goltzius** (1558–1616), another member of Van Mander's Haarlem mafia.

By the 1620s another school of painters had sprouted in Utrecht. Artists such as **Hendrick Terbrugghen** (c. 1588–1629) and **Gerrit van Honthorst** (c. 1590–1624) were ardent followers of the Italian painter Caravaggio, whose chiaroscuro technique (strong contrasts of light and shadow) influenced successive waves of Dutch painters all the way through to Rembrandt and Vermeer. Terbrugghen was the first Dutch Caravaggist to return to Holland (after a ten-year stay in Italy), but he was self-effacing and a bit of a misfit—he wasn't even elected to office in the Utrecht guild. The flattering and flamboyant Van Honthorst, on the other hand, ran up impressive lists of patrons wherever he went and became the best known of the Dutch Caravaggists. His beautiful nocturnal scenes—candlelight and shadow playing over huddles of faces—earned him the nickname 'Gherardo delle Notti'.

The Golden Age

France has shown a great deal of inventive genius, but little real faculty for painting. Holland has not imagined anything, but it has painted miraculously well.

Eugène Fromentin, art critic, writing in 1875

In 1565 mobs stormed through the Netherlands breaking church windows and destroying religious paintings and statues. In their enthusiasm to eliminate idolatry, these iconoclasts wiped out much of the country's artistic heritage. There seemed little call to replace it. The austere Calvinists who took control of the northern provinces after 1579 whitewashed the insides of churches and had no time for papish decoration. Italy and its art went out of fashion. The rising merchant classes seemed suspicious of unprofitable aristocratic foibles like patronage of the arts. Artists were in a dilemma: what were they to paint, and who would pay them for it? Eugène Fromentin comes right to the point.

The problem was this: given a bourgeois people, practical, not inclined to dreams, very busy withal, by no means mystic, of anti-Latin tendency, with broken traditions, a worship without images, parsimonious habits—to find an art to please [them]…there remained nothing for such a people to propose to themselves but a very simple and daring thing…to paint its own portrait.

And so the Dutch set about painting 'the portrait of Holland, its external image, faithful, exact, complete, life-like, without any adornment'. In the Golden Age that followed, you find few flamboyant devotional paintings or pompous, heroic battle scenes. Instead, you are given portraits of merchants, town squares, street scenes, glimpses of daily life, breakfast tables, brothels, taverns, the countryside, or moments in history. No other nation has managed a more intimate and beautifully executed chronicle of its life and times.

Genre Painting

Early English critics called the pictures of scenes from everyday life 'drolleries'—nowadays we refer to them as genre paintings. By the mid-17th century, genre was one of the most popular art forms in Holland as well as being the cheapest to buy. These were straightforward, unembellished paintings of taverns, brothels and family life, but they often contained a covert moral message. Sometimes the signal was crude—wildly copulating dogs in a doorway behind a flirting couple refer to the saying 'As with the woman, so with her dog.' Sometimes complex allegorical references and obscure symbols were knitted into the apparently simple pictures. Unravelling these was, for an educated 17th-century viewer, half the fun of genre paintings.

There are examples of genre work in the paintings of the Caravaggists Hendrick Terbrugghen and Gerrit van Honthorst, and in the work of some Mannerists, but it was the writing and painting of **Willem Buytewech** (1591–1624) in Haarlem, and the short visit to the town of Flemish painter **Adriaen Brouwer** (1605–38), that really established the style in Holland. Brouwer was a disorderly bohemian and a popular painter. Both Rubens and Rembrandt went to great lengths to add his work to their collections, though Haarlem society took some time to recover from his high spirits. He was strongly influenced by his compatriots Breughel and Bosch, and would sit about in pothouses knocking off cruelly realistic sketches of the clientele. The grotesque portrayal of peasants appealed to his Haarlem pupil **Adriaen van Ostade** (1610–85), and became a feature of one strain of Dutch genre painting. (As Van Ostade grew older and richer, however, his work became calm, cosy and far more respectable.)

Another style of genre grew up in Leiden around the painter **Gerard Dou** (1613–75). His meticulous, highly finished, almost slick work was widely imitated and gave rise to the school of Leiden *fijnschilders* ('fine painters'). The paintings, often of genteel middle-class interiors, have subtle chiaroscuro lighting effects and some very abstruse symbolic references. Leiden seemed to enjoy especially difficult allusions, maybe because it was a university town. Dou's pupils **Gabriel Metsu** (1629–67) and **Frans van Mieris** (1635–81) excelled in elegant genre work.

In far-away Deventer **Gerard ter Borch** (1619–81) was developing his own style—highly attentive to detail and with an especially fine touch in painting fabrics. In Delft **Jan Vermeer** (1632–75) was painting the hushed, softly lit interiors that have earned him the reputation (with Rembrandt and Frans Hals) of being one of the three great painters of the age. Vermeer produced 11 children, and only three times that many paintings in his life. In the midst of his tumultuous household, he would lock himself away and work painstakingly on tranquil portraits of Dutch homes and quiet, still moments from everyday life without a single child in sight. The reticent, and poor, painter would even hide from influential art dealers when they came to call.

The best recorder of riotous domestic uproar was tavern-keeper **Jan Steen** (1625–79). He paints the lewd, sozzled and wanton inhabitants of his sitting rooms, taverns and brothels with such verve and good humour that it's difficult to judge just what his moral attitude really is. The paintings of **Pieter de Hooch** (1629–after 1688) and **Nicholaes Maes** (1629–93), on the other hand, are closer to the subdued interiors of Vermeer. De Hooch is especially known for his sensitive portrayals of mothers and children. His paintings of the dark interiors of burgher homes with, somewhere in the picture, a door opening on to the bright outdoors, set a pattern for many other genre painters.

Historical and Biblical Painting

In the 16th-century the Mannerists had used Biblical and historical subjects as a pretext for fanciful flights of imagination, an excuse to adorn paintings with naked bodies and elaborate ornamentation. As we have seen, there was no place for this in respectable 17th-century merchants' sitting rooms, and the austere Calvinists proscribed art in churches. Most artists were launched into an open market of more acceptable styles—portraits, landscapes and genre scenes—but a few soldiered on in the grand old style. Many of these painters were simply out of touch with the spirit of the new age, but others came up with an innovative, more realistic style of historical painting.

The Dutch Caravaggists (*see* above) were prime movers in the new direction. Their bold realism appealed to painters in this Age of Reason. The new style of historical painting leant on experience, rather than invention, and had a much clearer narrative. Unlike the Mannerists, who had indulged themselves in flashy virtuoso performances without any deference to period, 17th-century painters painted scenes from the Bible or from history (especially banquet scenes or intimate group studies of Christ with the apostles), attempting to portray clothing, buildings and utensils with some sort of historical accuracy. (They were, however, usually quite spectacularly off the mark.)

The Amsterdam painter **Pieter Lastman** (1583–1633) was the spearhead of the new generation of history painters. It was to study as his pupil that **Rembrandt van Rijn** (1606–69, *see* pp.92–3) went to Amsterdam in 1624. Rembrandt clearly wanted to be part of the modern movement of realism. Kenneth Clark calls him 'the great poet of that need for truth and that appeal to experience which had begun with the Reformation'. His quest was for naturalness and authenticity. He used his neighbours in the Jewish Quarter for Biblical paintings, and infused his pictures with a powerful psychological realism. By the 1640s he was undoubtedly the best history painter in Holland, but it was a lonely mission, as the style remained unpopular during his lifetime. Only one of his pupils, the last, **Aert de Gelder** (1645–27) concentrated exclusively on history painting. He worked in a lighter, more sentimental style than Rembrandt would ever have allowed himself to fall into.

Portraiture

Portraiture is the most conservative of all the categories of visual art. Painters commissioned to record the wealthy, pompous and important for posterity usually opt for well-tried, acceptable forms. The Golden Age brought some exciting innovators—especially with double and group portraits—but the changes were subtle and the style soon hardened once more into an emptier, more formalized genre.

Anthonie Mor (1519–74), who Italianized his name to Antonio Moro, spent some time in the court of Emperor Charles V, and introduced the fashionable classical style of Italian portraiture to the Netherlands. It was taken up by **Michiel Miereveld** (1567–1641). He had a comfortable job in the court of Frederick Henry in The Hague, churned out competent, formal pictures and became the leading portraitist of the early Dutch Republic.

It was **Frans Hals** (1585–1666) who brought verve to portrait-painting. His acute psychological perception, comic wickedness and lightness of touch give his portraits an unprecedented vibrancy. For the first time the sitters seem unconstricted, even friendly. Though his work became very dark towards the end of his life, his early group portraits are exuberantly stage-managed and really capture the high spirits and optimism of Holland's new-found freedom.

Rembrandt's portraits are more introspective than Hals, with subtle nuances of light and mood, but portraiture was, for him, primarily a source of income. The earlier 'jugs on a shelf' approach to sitters had been corrected by Hals, but it was Rembrandt who gave canvasses real vitality, particularly in his larger works. His dynamic arrangement of the guardsmen in the *Night Watch* (1642; *see* p.93) turned group portraiture on its head. Although he brings his full artistic weight to the task, he reserves any radical experimentation for pictures of himself and his family. In these you find a sensitivity and flair quite beyond the formal traditions of the art.

Govert Flinck (1615–60) and **Ferdinand Bol** (1616–80), both students of Rembrandt, are admired as portraitists. Bol followed Rembrandt so slavishly that even art historians can't always tell them apart. Flinck had the awkward honour of being commissioned to paint for Amsterdam's new town hall after his teacher's sketches had been rejected. He died before completing his drawings, and Rembrandt was one of the painters employed to finish the job.

Frans Hals and Rembrandt gave portraiture a fresh burst of life, but by the middle of the century other artists were cementing their innovations into a new repertory of poses and gestures. Dutch society was becoming grander and more pompous, and the artists it commissioned to paint its picture—like **Bartholomeus van der Helst** (1613–70)—thought Hals' and Rembrandt's work too plain. Once again the portraits lost spontaneity and energy and, though often stylish, became formalized and rhetorical.

Landscape, Still Life and Specialist Paintings

In his *Natural History*, Pliny marvels at the exactness with which some ancient painters could imitate Nature: birds would crash into a wall on which Zeuxis or Apelles had painted a still life. Early Netherlandish painters were impressed by this idea and paid loving attention to background rocks, trees and landscapes—so much so that Sir Henry Wotton, a 17th-century English Ambassador to the Low Countries, could marvel at their 'Artificiall Miracles'. (Michelangelo, however, is reputed to have scoffed at the mundaneness and literalness of this Netherlandish style, saying it was fit only for young or very old women, monks, nuns and certain tone-deaf members of the aristocracy.) Although no painters actually took an easel out of doors until the 19th century, this interest in realism did mean that landscape established a sturdy niche for itself in Dutch art during the Golden Age.

The 16th-century Mannerists used natural scenery, laced with fantastical creatures, as an exotic backdrop to biblical and classical scenes. The well-travelled **Gillis van Coninxloo** (1544–1607) painted very much in the Mannerist style, but is generally regarded as the first Dutch landscapist. Mannerist pictures were usually painted from a high viewpoint. It was **Esaias van de Velde** (1591–1632) who, quite literally, brought things down to earth. He painted dry, rather matter-of-fact country scenes from a low, more naturalistic, point of view—a style adopted by practitioners of what became known as the **tonal phase** of Dutch landscape painting.

Paintings of the tonal phase, which lasted until the 1640s, are delicate, almost monochromatic and are animated by the atmosphere they create. The 17th-century poet and critic Constantijn Huygens praised the school for its ability to evoke 'the warmth of the sun and the movement caused by a cool breeze'.

The first tonal painter was van de Velde's pupil **Jan van Goyen** (1596–1656). Although he began painting in the bolder colours of his master, he was soon producing translucent worlds of hazy greens, browns and greys. **Salomon van Ruysdael** (1600–70) painted refined, spacious landscapes and is generally considered the second major tonal painter. **Hercules Seghers** (b.1590) painted some inspired and original scenes of waterfalls, desolate valleys and stormy mountains. Although he worked at the same time as the tonal painters, his unique style evoked the power of a much grander Nature. He had a reputation for being drunk and depressed, and disappeared in 1633. Nowadays the whereabouts of only 15 of his works are known, though there are records of another 30.

Rembrandt was a great admirer of Seghers, and owned eight of his paintings. His small oeuvre of landscapes strongly reflects Seghers' influence. From the 1650s a new generation of landscape painters started producing rugged, grandiose works with more solid forms and stronger contrasts of light and colour than the rather pale pictures of the tonal phase artists. Leaders of this new **classical phase** were **Jacob van Ruisdael** (1628–82; Salomon's nephew, though they spelled their names differently) and **Albert Cuyp** (1620–91). Ruisdael is acknowledged as the greatest Dutch landscapist and is especially admired for his stormy skies. Cuyp combined clarity and a firm classical structure with (especially in his late work) Italianate lighting that suffuses his pictures with a soft glow. Ruisdael's pupil **Meindert Hobbema** (1638–1709) produced paintings very much derivative of his master's work before marrying the burgemeester's kitchen maid and becoming a wine gauger in the Amsterdam customs house, abandoning painting almost entirely.

Cuyp, like many other Dutch landscapists, fell under the spell of Italy. Many Hollanders were drawn south by the warmth and shimmering light. Right from the beginning of the century Italianate landscapes existed alongside the more typically Dutch pictures. (The term, however, refers more to the subject matter than to the influence of Italian art.) The escapist, rather nostalgic paintings by artists like **Jan Both** (*c.* 1618–52) and **Nicolaes Berchem** (1620–83) were very popular with the Dutch public. The landscapes are imaginary (some of these painters didn't even visit Italy) and are populated by the beautiful shepherdesses and antique ruins also found in the pastoral literature of the time.

By the 19th century the style was beginning to lose favour. The English painter John Constable, in a lecture in 1836, berated Both and Berchem as specious painters whose reputation was propped up by dealers demanding high prices. When, reeling from the vehemence of the attack, an avid collector remarked that he had better sell his Berchems, Constable replied: 'No sir, that will only continue the mischief, *burn them.*'

The English term '**still life**' comes from the Dutch '*stilleven*', the word that began to be used around the 1650s to describe a theme in Dutch painting that was very typical of the 17th-century taste for the domestic and realistic. The stylistic development of still life painting parallels that of landscapes. Early works are 'tonal'—suspended against a plain background, suffused by a transparent, dull light. The objects painted are simple everyday things. The *ontbijtje* (breakfast piece) with bread, cheese and pewter mug is a favourite subject. Later *Vanitas* still lifes, reminding us of the ephemerality of life and earthly pleasures, became popular. Fruit is seen at its *toppunt,* the point of ripeness just before it goes bad, and darker symbols like skulls and snuffed out candles make an appearance. As the Golden Age society prospered, the simple *ontbijtjes* were replaced by *pronkstilleven* (*pronk* means ostentation). The style of these luxurious pieces is similar to that of the classical phase of landscape painters. Colours are brighter and each object seems sharply picked out, as if by spotlight. Gold, silver, china, expensive seafood and exotic fruit replace the simpler fare of earlier work.

Paintings of flowers were a specialized branch of still life. Real blooms were often cripplingly expensive, and short-lived and the 17th-century Dutch preferred pictures of flowers. The paintings were often complete fantasies—exotic blooms from all over the world, that flowered at different times of the year, would all be arranged in one vase, painted with an extravagant realism. Samuel Pepys enthuses in his diary over a 'little flower pott' done by **Simon Verelst** (1644–1721), marvelling that it was 'the finest thing that ever I saw in my life—the drops of Dew hanging on the leaves, so as I was forced again and again to put my finger to it to feel whether my eyes were deceived or no'. (Verelst was asking £70 for the painting. The notoriously mean Pepys 'had the vanity' to offer £20, which wasn't accepted.) **Ambrosius Bosschaert the Elder** (1573–1621) and his three sons were the most prolific flower painters of the period. By the time he died, Bosschaert could command 1,000 guilders a painting.

Sea, Buildings and Animals

Despite Holland's reliance on the sea, **marine painting** doesn't occupy an important position in its art. Early painters like **Jan Porcellis** (1584–1632) seem primarily concerned with atmosphere of the sea and sky, while later artists like **Willem van de Velde the Younger** (1633–1707) begin to reflect the nation's pride in the ships themselves. Of the **architectural paintings, Pieter Saenredam's** (1597–1695) exquisitely executed church interiors are the most pleasing—and so accurate that they are still used as blueprints for restoration work. The most interesting **animal painter** is **Paulus Potter** (1625–54), whose bulls and cows have an intense reality that is almost nightmarish.

The 18th and 19th Centuries

After decades of entrepreneurial adventure, Amsterdam settled back to enjoy its wealth, and seemed to lose the drive that had propelled it through the Golden Age. Society began to look to France as a model of graceful living, and associations for the promotion of French ideas and culture sprang up.

With the deaths of Frans Hals (1666), Rembrandt (1669) and Vermeer (1675), the Golden Age of Dutch painting also came to an end. The achievements of the 17th century were so great that they seemed to haunt 18th-century painters, who didn't dare do anything new. Paintings became over-refined and uniform in their imitation of French styles and reworking of old ideas. Much 17th-century painting had reflected the stern ethics of Calvinism, but the 18th century began to shed the moral sobriety that had been the dominant humour of the previous age. The freshest painting of the period comes from the few artists who reflected this change in mood and worked playfully with the established Dutch styles. The most impressive of these lighter-hearted painters was **Cornelis Troost** (1697–1750), whose delicately composed satires have earned him the title of the 'Dutch Hogarth'.

Much work was to be had painting the ceilings of grand mansions and decorating the interiors of new public buildings. **Gerard de Lairesse** (1640–1711) was the market leader in this field. His somewhat over-enthusiastic admirers dubbed him the 'Dutch Raphael'. His successor, **Jacob de Wit** (1695–1754), excelled as a trompe l'œil artist and a decorator of churches. Protestant churches were still bare, but Catholicism was tolerated provided that (a 1730 decree cautioned) care was taken 'that the meeting places of the Catholics do not have the appearance of churches or public buildings, nor should they strike the public eye'. There were no such restrictions, however, on interiors, and De Wit made his fortune on commissions from wealthy parishes.

During the 19th century, painting became more documentary—any allegorical meaning or high moral purpose disappeared entirely. Romantic painters such as **Jozef Israëls** (1824–1911) and **A. H. Bakker Korff** (1824–82) did imbue their work with emotion, but it was of the sober, cosy Dutch variety rather than anything explosive or passionate. Landscapists ploughed on in a neoclassical or grand Romantic manner, though in the world of **A. G. Bilders** (1838–65) you can see the beginnings of a simpler naturalism. In place of the distant, artificially constructed views found in previous paintings, the landscape is seen from close to. This radical change, which gave paintings the sort of perspectives seen in photographs, characterized much work later in the century. (This is particularly evident in the city scenes of the Amsterdam Impressionist **G. H. Breitner** (1857–1923). The landscapes and seascapes of

Johann Barthold Jongkind (1819–91), drawn from the 17th-century tonal tradition, influenced later French Impressionists and Dutch artists of the Hague School.

The Hague School was active between 1870 and 1890, an Art for Art's Sake movement made up of an enthusiastic group of Impressionistic painters. They became famous for their grey skies, and paintings of the long flat beaches and rainswept polders around The Hague. Subject matter was less important than personal feelings and style. **Anton Mauve**'s (1838–88) gently coloured landscapes are the best known. **Hendrik Mesdag** (1831–1915) was a skilled seascapist, and painted the impressive *Panorama* in The Hague (*see* p.192). The brothers **Maris-Jacob** (1837–99), **Matthijs** (1839–1917) and **Willem** (1844–1910)—contributed landscapes and nature studies to the movement.

Undoubtedly the greatest painter of the century was the man that a director of the Stedelijk Museum called 'the lowliest, most human', **Vincent Van Gogh** (1853–90). During his short, troubled painting career, Van Gogh produced work quite unlike any other Dutch artist; his work also takes its own quite individual course in the stream of postimpressionist painting in general (*see* pp.97–100).

Jan Toorop (1858–1928) trailed along with the stylistic changes of the century—from Pointillism to Expressionism. His best work, like that of his contemporary **Johan Thorn Prikker** (1868–1932), was in a delicate, almost fairytale Symbolist style that begins to point towards Art Nouveau.

The 20th Century

The individualism of the late 19th century undermined the supportive strength of the great painting traditions of the past. Twentieth-century Dutch artists were left not only with the question that had dogged their 17th-century forebears (what to paint), but also by a new problem: *how* to paint. There was no longer a framework of assumptions within which they could make their decisions. Twentieth-century art fragments into splinter groups trying to find their way through the dilemma.

The artists of *De Stijl* ('Style', or 'The Way') came up with a new set of assumptions, a theory they believed would take the place of the old traditions. This theory was propounded in a series of polemical articles in the periodical from which they got their name (published from June 1917 to January 1932). They claimed that they were getting rid of all the inaccuracies, obscurity and casual accidents of individualism, and had discovered the essence of art—a Platonic ideal that the world could understand. The best known visual expression of this great universal principle is the straight black lines and blocks of primary colours in the work of **Piet Mondriaan** (1872–1944). (He dropped the second 'a' in his name in order to appear more French—a pretension that most Dutch museums ignore.) Mondriaan gives us a one-man lesson in the development of abstract art. Even in early, recognizable landscapes you can see the germs of his fascination with horizontal and vertical lines. Gradually the figurative images dissolve and you're left with the dashes and criss-cross lines of what is aptly known as his 'plus-minus' period. Then the lines get straighter and bolder, and the colours resolve into bright, flat reds, yellows and blues. Mondriaan claimed he was aiming for the 'lucid tidiness' that the new age demanded. In this he is, paradoxically, very much part of a Dutch tradition of stillness and quiet, careful composition. As Kenneth Clark suggests: Mondriaan is Vermeer without the light.

The prime motivator of *De Stijl*, and editor of the periodical, was **Theo van Doesburg** (1883–1931). His paintings were more dynamic than Mondriaan's, and caused the final rift between the two artists. The work of a third member of the group, **Bart van der Leck** (1876–1958), is instantly recognizable—coloured triangles scattered on a white canvas. Van Doesburg was the real energy behind the movement. When he died, the magazine ceased publication and formal contacts between members dissolved. Though *De Stijl* lasted only 15 years, its impact was felt all over the world, not only in painting, but also in architecture, interior design, typography and even literature and music. The images are still plagiarized by trendy designers for company logos, coffee mugs and T-shirts.

Most of the major art movements of the early 20th century seemed to pass Holland by altogether. There were, however, two Dutch schools of Expressionists active before the Second World War worthy of note. The **Bergen School** centred on the recalcitrant work of **Charley Toorop** (1891–1955; daughter of the 19th-century painter Jan Toorop). **De Ploeg** ('The Plough') was led by **Jan Wiegers** (1893–1959) and influenced by Van Gogh and the German Expressionists. They painted angular and explosively coloured pictures, often of the countryside around Groningen.

The hard, nightmarish quality of the Dutch **Magic Realists** is reminiscent of Salvador Dali's Surrealism, but their scenes are not as hallucinatory. **Pyke Koch** (b. 1901) paints alluring, pithy works with awe-inspiring prowess. He is shamefully little known outside Holland. **Carel Willink** (1900–83) and **Raoul Hynckes** (b.1893) are two other prominent Magic Realist painters, if not quite as inspired.

Perhaps the most exciting movement to emerge after the war was **COBRA** (made up of artists from **CO**penhagen, **BR**ussels and **A**msterdam). These painters were inspired by primitive art and children's paintings to develop a *volwassen kinderstijl* (grown-up child style). Their keywords were vitality and spontaneity. **Karel Appel** (b. 1921) remarked 'I just mess about' and 'I paint like a barbarian in a barbarous age.' The gaudy, vibrant and topsy-turvy paintings of COBRA appear to represent a purposeful effort to wipe out any vestige of classical tradition.

During the 1960s minimalistic monochrome canvasses and white reliefs made an appearance. Work by **Jan Schoonhoven** (b. 1914) was influenced by the German **Zero/Nul** movement, which was trying to create a new beginning for art by reducing individual influence to nothing. **Ad Dekkers** (1938–74) and **Edgar Fernhout** (1912–74; Charley Toorop's son) produced similar work, but were more in the abstract geometrical tradition of Mondriaan.

The technological revolution has had its impact on Dutch art. **Peter Struycken** (b. 1939) began very much in the vein of Dekkers, but since 1968 has been using a computer to generate the colour and patterns of his work. **Jan Dibbets** (b. 1941) uses montages of photographs geometrically arranged on clean white canvasses, in a way that seems to link him to Mondriaan and Saenredam (the 17th-century painter of church interiors). Nowadays, the club scene and the computer revolution is spawning exciting multimedia art. Colourful pieces by **Dadara**, rather in the manner of Keith Haring, are proving commercially very popular, and finding their way on to T-shirts and mouse pads. Among contemporary artists, keep an eye open for witty sculptures by **Servaas**, innovative painting by **Aldert Mantje** and **Ger van Elk**, **Gijs Bakker**'s poised mixed-media pieces, **Arjan Lancel**'s inspired installations and sculpture, and beautifully shaped ceramics by **Wouter Dam**.

The delights of Dutch architecture are generally small-scale, domestic ones. Wealthy merchants over the centuries have built some grand mansions, but they're not gargantuan. Though you're unlikely to be bowled over by the sheer magnificence of some glittering edifice, you're sure to be stopped in your tracks, suddenly captivated by an ornamented gable, a witty façade decoration or a neat, perfectly poised little house.

In the Beginning...

The first houses made of wood, but soon people began building in brick, which was more resistant to the fires that could sweep through crowded cities. At first this only applied to the lower walls; the gables (which formed the outer walls of attics and were often shaped to give interesting definition to steep triangular roofs) were still wooden.

The shapes of early brick gables, called **spout gables**, are a direct reflection of their wooden ancestry. Wooden constructions were built with each successive storey sticking out a little further than the previous one, so that rainwater would drip on to the street and not seep back into the body of the building. Early **brick gables** leant over for the same reason, which is another contributing factor to the many tilting façades you see in Dutch streets. Most of the pre-17th-century buildings still standing around the country belonged to the city fortifications, built in stone after the 15th century to deflect the impact of newly invented gunpowder.

New Ideas

Towards the end of the 16th century, architectural pattern books from Italy made an appearance in Holland. The Dutch architects who pored over translations of these books were inspired both by the classical system of proportion, and by the ornamental designs. In the buildings these architects subsequently produced, the simple spout gable gave way to the more decorative **step gable**, and red-brick façades were lavishly decorated with plaster scrolls, escutcheons, vases and masks. The ornamentation reached a high point in the playful work of the Amsterdam architect **Hendrick de Keyser** (1565–1621). It took until the end of the 17th century for people to stop building in the Renaissance style, but the adventurous were already experimenting with a purer form of classicism in the 1620s. This new wave reacted against lavish ornament, and was far more intrigued by the strict lines and proportions of classical design. Fruit, flowers, animals and human figures do join the line-up of gable adornments, but not in such profusion. The larger houses begin to resemble temple-fronts, with garlands and festoons under windows. Smaller buildings sport **neck gables**. Simpler and more suitably classicist than the cascading step gables, neck gables are often topped off with a purely classical fronton and are a compromise between a vision of architecture that imitates the buildings of Greek and Roman antiquity, and the practicalities of building for a rainy climate. (The tall 'necks' mask steep roofs, something a conventionally classical straight cornice could not do. It was only in the 19th century that reliably leak-proof flat roofs could be built, and straight cornices became more widespread.) Notable architects of the period are **Jacob van Campen** (1595–1657), who built the city hall on the Dam in Amsterdam (*see* p.70) and **Philips Vingboons** (1607–78) and his brother **Justus** (1620–98), famed for their domestic architecture.

Decoration and Decline

Towards the end of the 17th century austerity set in, and architects began to emphasize simplicity and harmony. **Adriaan Dortsman** (1625–82) is the master of the school of 'Restrained Dutch Classicism'. Windows were made larger and façades became simpler and more rhythmical in design. In the 18th century, as the economy picked up, many merchant families gave their homes a facelift during which brick façades were plastered over or replaced by sandstone. But more money to spend also meant more decoration. The century is marked by a fascination with things French. Gables became draped with acanthus leaves (Louis XIV), encrusted with asymmetrical fripperies (Louis XV) or strung with modest garlands (Louis XVI). Sometimes buildings were crowned with excessively ornate balustrades—a nifty way of hiding a steep roof with what appeared to be a classical straight cornice. The 18th century also saw the advent of the standardized, **pre-fabricated gable**—a sort of architectural mix-and-match.

Public Pomp

The Netherlands suffered an economic slump for most of the 1800s. Little building went on until money began to dribble back into the coffers in the last decades of the century. The driving force behind 19th-century Dutch architectural innovation was **P. J. H. Cuypers** (1827–1921), the designer of the Centraal Station and Rijksmuseum in Amsterdam (*see* p.67 and pp.90–2). He based his work on indigenous brick and wood architecture, but was easily lured towards neo-Gothic extravagance. His belief that the entire building, from basic structure to the smallest detail of decoration, should be governed by a single coherent principle became the basis for modern Dutch architecture. Two other styles dominated 19th-century building: the upstarts of the **Architectura et Amicitia** society went in for idiosyncratic fantasies that outdid even Cuypers' ornamentation, while the more conservative members of the **Maatschappij ter Bevordering der Bouwkunst** (Society of Architects) favoured an eclectic approach, resulting in a mixture of diluted styles. Most of the interesting 19th-century buildings in the Netherlands today come from the boom period of the latter part of the century, and reflect this divergence of taste.

Modern Times

H. P. Berlage (1856–1934), the designer of the Beurs (Stock Exchange, *see* p.67), is known as the father of modern Dutch architecture. Like Cuypers, he used traditional Dutch materials. He relished displaying a building's structure with graceful brickwork, but was never tempted into frivolous ornamentation. The most exciting 20th-century school of Dutch architecture arose as a reaction to Berlage's homespun, rational buildings. Younger architects, many of them in the employ of Amsterdam's housing department, began experimenting with decorative folds and turrets of brickwork shaped around a more solid inner skeleton of concrete. These modern, quirky brick fantasies of the **Amsterdam School** (active from around 1912 to 1924, *see* p.112) have, until recently, been neglected, but an exhibition of photographs and architects' drawings at the Stedelijk Museum in the 1980s shot them back into fashion.

But the work of the Amsterdam School stands beside the mainstream Dutch architecture, and prime examples are confined to the capital. A second modern movement, which emerged as an extension of rather than a reaction to Berlage's work, was to prove more influential. Under the influence of *De Stijl* (*see* pp.48–9), Bauhaus in Germany, Frank Lloyd Wright in the USA and Le Corbusier in France, a new style of building emerged—all sharp edges, concrete, steel and glass. Like Berlage, the architects of what became known in the Netherlands as **Nieuwe Zakelijkheid** (New Functionalism), believed that they should use their materials to emphasize, not disguise, the basic structure of their buildings. Nieuwe Zakelijkheid dominated the middle decades of the century. Though it produced some neat and attractive buildings, and some fine domestic architecture by **Gerrit Rietveld**, it must also take the blame for the thinking behind high-rise 1960s horrors.

The Netherlands has suffered more than its fair share of architectural atrocities in recent years—tacky façades of insensitively used modern materials and buildings hugely out of scale. Notable exceptions are work by architects such as **A. Alberts**, who offers quirky exceptions to the norm with his gas-company headquarters building in Groningen, and the ING Bank headquarters on the outskirts of Amsterdam. This extraordinary brick building has hardly a right angle in sight, mineral water fountains instead of air-conditioning, a system that warms the building by recycling the heat generated by computers, and installations of mirrors and stone that play light tricks at the solstices.

The country's most impressive contemporary architecture is to be seen in Rotterdam, which embarked on a brave and adventurous programme of rebuilding after being flattened during the Second World War (*see* p.164). Elsewhere, the economic boom of the past two decades has resulted in competitive construction of showpiece office blocks. Dutch architects are encouraged to take chances, and business parks sprouting around Amsterdam and The Hague especially sparkle with glittering towers that show bravura and flair. Foreign architects invited to work on projects in the Netherlands have also made their mark in recent years: **Alessandro Mendini**'s zany and colourful Groningen Museum in Groningen, fellow Italian **Renzo Piano**'s New Metropolis Science & Technology Centre in Amsterdam, and Japanese architect **Kisho Kurokawa**'s new wing to the Van Gogh Museum, to name but a few.`

Amsterdam

Amsterdam is a practised but subtle temptress. Her gentle charms begin to work the moment you arrive, as they have for generations of travellers before you. You'll find yourself drawn along to nooks of curious architecture, and enticed into far more tantalizing cafés than could possibly be good for your health. You'll be lured down alleyways to glimpse the rough underside of town, then whisked back to the trim respectability of leafy canals. You'll be invited to admire wondrous treasures, and have secrets revealed to you that no other city would dare. Daily, you'll be launched into a farrago of sleek business people, droves of tourists, scruffs, bohemians and persons of decidedly ill repute. Yet everyone seems to get on remarkably well together, and the chance encounters with people here will be one of the lasting pleasures of your visit.

Amsterdam has an edge and verve that will keep you on your toes. As Henry James wrote after a visit to the Netherlands in the 1870s, it will 'at least give one's regular habits of thought the stimulus of a little confusion'. Three strands of life continually interweave: reminders of the wealthy Golden Age trading city dominated by a few Calvinist families, the sleazy port, and the radical hippie mecca of the 1960s grown comfortably liberal.

Over the past decade Amsterdam has notched up a high status in the business world, and seems anxious to become a little more respectable. Politics are becoming more conservative, police are clearing out junkies and dealers from the more squalid areas of the red-light district, and restaurants and galleries are appearing in their wake. But Amsterdam will never lose its alternative tang. It has a long tradition of liberal tolerance and is, after all, a port, with a port's hard edge. For centuries its heretics, whores and disruptive politicians have tugged, nudged and needled other Amsterdammers away from any tendency to complacency. Today you will still find a relaxed and tolerant city. Same-sex couples kiss in the street, whiffs of marijuana waft from psychedelic coffeeshops, clinics and crisis centres exist to help addicts with more severe drug habits.

Amsterdam offers all the advantages of a great metropolis, with few of the drawbacks. You can admire some of the greatest art in the world, listen to top-notch orchestras, and enjoy the summits of gourmet cuisine. Yet Amsterdammers are down-to-earth people, and in their compact city are more often to be seen cycling and walking than whizzing about in cars. The town's greatest attractions are still its simplest pleasures: strolls along the canals, time spent in front of a painting that takes your breath away and long conversations in quiet cafés where centuries of tobacco smoke have turned the walls quite brown.

See inside back cover for an overview map of Amsterdam.

Amsterdam's first inhabitants were probably fishermen and farmers who built a dam near where the River Amstel petered out into the tidal flats of the IJ. Little is known about this early period, until the 12th century, when a local bigwig, **Gijsbrecht**, built himself a castle at the spot where the River Amstel was dammed (on the site of the present day Dam Square). He called himself the first Lord of Amstel and laid claim to the countryside emerging from the water around him. The **Lords of Amstel** were answerable to the **Bishops of Utrecht**, and rather resented it. In the late 13th century Gijsbrecht IV felt he was powerful enough to rebel, but he didn't reckon on his neighbour, **Floris V**, the **Count of Holland**, joining in the fray. Floris had wooed popular support in 1275 by granting special **toll privileges** to the people who lived beside 'the Aemstelle Dam'. Floris defeated Gijsbrecht, but later Gijsbrecht crept up on Floris and murdered him. The Bishop of Utrecht took advantage of the confusion and confiscated Gijsbrecht's land. In 1300 he granted the town of 'Aemstelledamme' its **first charter**. When he died in 1317 he ceded Amsterdam and the surrounding countryside to his nephew, William III, the new Count of Holland. The people of Amsterdam took full advantage of their toll privileges and of William's wide influence and settled down to serious trading and money-making. In 1323 the Count of Holland granted Amsterdam the sole right to import beer from Hamburg—at that time northern Europe's largest brewing town and a prominent member of the powerful alliance of Baltic trading ports, the **Hanseatic League**. That, together with the growing grain trade, laid the foundation for Amsterdam's future prosperity.

During medieval times the town remained small. In 1300 Amsterdam had one church (the Oude Kerk) and two streets—the present day Warmoesstraat and Nieuwendijk. The town was razed by **great fires** in 1421 and 1452. Wooden buildings were forbidden after the second blaze, and only two remain today (*see* pp.74 and 76). By the 15th century the boundaries extended as far as Oudezijds Voorburgwal, Nieuwezijds Voorburgwal and Spui. There was a new church as well as a clump of monasteries, chapels and inns built to cope with pilgrims flocking to the scene of the **Amsterdam Miracle**. In 1345 a dying man had vomited up the host after his last communion. It was thrown on a fire but didn't burn. Later it developed healing powers, and would transport itself overnight between churches. A chapel of its own seemed to make it stay in one place and, though this burnt down, the host survived. It became an object of worship, and is still honoured today in the **Stille Omgang** (Silent Procession, *see* pp.81 and 84). One of those healed by the magic wafer was **Maximilian I**, Emperor of Austria (later Holy Roman Emperor). Amsterdam had further earned his gratitude by supporting his faction, the Kabeljauwen (Codfish), against the conservative Hoeken (Hooks) in the struggle for domination of the Low Countries. In 1489 he upped Amsterdam's prestige by granting the city the right to use his royal insignia in its coat of arms. Trade flourished, and by 1500 Amsterdam bustled with 9,000 inhabitants contained within its first city wall (following the line of the present day Gelderskade, Kloveniersburgwal and Singel canals).

During the **Reformation**, Amsterdam held out longer than most cities against the Protestant forces of **William of Orange**, but swapped sides when it was clear that he was winning. On 26 May 1578, as the city made peace with William, all the Catholic officials and most of the clergy were bundled into a boat, escorted to the outskirts of the city, and cast off. A Protestant city government was set up by members of the leading Calvinist families. With characteristic Amsterdam grace, the events of 26 May were referred to as the '**Alteration**'.

Having weathered both seige and iconoclasts during the Reformation, the city became even more prosperous. By the time of the **Union of Utrecht** in 1579 (*see* **History**, p.30), Amsterdam was by far the most economically powerful city in the Dutch federation. The siege of Antwerp had not only wiped out a major trade rival, but had despatched droves of refugees who made straight for the haven in the north. Amsterdam's famous tolerance paid off as the newcomers brought skills, such as diamond-cutting, that fired up the city's crafts and industries into a prosperous new life. Though the war with Spain had closed off normal trade routes, local merchants had managed to keep rich by supplying both sides in the conflict. Through much of its history Amsterdam seemed to operate on the principle that 'if we didn't supply the enemy, we couldn't afford to fight them'. Arms dealers would support entire wars all over Europe, and brokers of marine insurance (introduced in the late 15th century) had no qualms about insuring both sides in a battle. Amsterdammers excelled at making money and at the end of the 16th century they were on the brink of the most resplendent era of their history.

The **Dutch Golden Age** in the 17th century (*see* **History**, pp.32–3) was centred primarily on Amsterdam, which was home to both the Dutch East India Company (VOC) and the West India Company. People flooded into the city and by 1650 the population had shot past the 200,000 mark. As early as 1613, far-sighted town planners had begun an extension of three new **canals** around the perimeter of the city. Initially the Herengracht (Gentlemen's Canal), Keizersgracht (Emperor's Canal) and Prinsengracht (Princes' Canal) went only as far as the present day Leidsegracht, but further construction in 1662 gave Amsterdam its familiar half-moon shape. Malodorous industries and the poor were banished to the fields beyond, to the area now known as the **Jordaan** (*see* pp.89–90). The wealthiest merchants built themselves mansions along the new canals and the city built a Stadhuis that was proclaimed the eighth wonder of the world.

Power in the city itself was grasped by a handful of patrician families. The Catholic clique ousted during the Alteration was replaced by a Protestant oligarchy that became known as the **Magnificat**. Family names like Hooft, Pauw, Bicker, van Beuningen and Six can still raise an Amsterdammer's eyebrow. Wives and daughters sat on the boards of charities and almshouses (housed in confiscated monasteries) and sons would serve in the civil guard on their way up to becoming *burgemeesters* or magistrates.

But as the glory days of the Dutch Golden Age slumped into the **depression years** of the early 1800s, Amsterdam's fortunes sank too. The sagging city almost collapsed under the burden of a population that doubled in the latter part of the 19th century. Living conditions were horrific. Whole families were crammed into dark cellars. Areas like the Jordaan and De Pijp became squalid, overcrowded slums, ravaged by **cholera**. (There were 2,273 victims of the 1848–9 epidemic alone.) Amsterdam had fallen far from the glory days of the Golden Age. In 1838, with deft symbolism, the piles under the Stock Exchange gave way and the building collapsed.

Amsterdam figures such as **Paul van Vlissingen** and **Samuel Sarphati** (*see* **History**, pp.35–6) were in the forefront of the country's revival at the end of the century, and though Amsterdam did suffer in the early **1930s Depression**—when gangs of unemployed were set to work creating the Amsterdamse Bos (Amsterdam Forest) outside the city—the city approached the **Second World War** with renewed prosperity.

The city was ravaged by Nazi occupation (*see* **History** pp.36–7), but made a quick recovery during the 1950s, and by the 1960s was entering one of its all-time halcyon periods, when it was a prime focus of the Youth Revolution that swept Europe. At the centre of the Amsterdam counter-culture was a group of flamboyant jesters, the **Provos** (from '*provocatie*'—'provocation'). Philosophy student Roel van Duyn, and magician and one-time window cleaner Robert Jasper Grootveld, with a motley gang of accomplices staged 'happenings' on the Dam and around the statue of the Lieverdje ('Little Darling') on the Spui. The Provos were against capitalism, traffic and tobacco, and for free bicycles and free sex. The demonstrations were light-hearted, theatrical and endearing. Whenever the police were needled into retaliation, onlookers in the elegant cafés around the square branded them bullies. However, when Crown Princess Beatrix married a German, Claus von Amsberg, in the Westerkerk in March 1966, the mood soured. The royal family was, to the Provos, the distillation of the Establishment. Not only the Provos were angry. There was a traditional coolness between Amsterdam and the House of Orange, and ratepayers resented having to foot the bill for the celebrations. The older generation—still raw from the Occupation—was appalled that their princess could marry a German. Demonstrators lined the route of the wedding procession waving banners demanding 'Republic' and 'Give me my bike back' (the Nazis had confiscated bicycles during the war). Smoke bombs were thrown and, though the day passed without serious incident, discontent bubbled on right through the spring. One hot June day a minor industrial dispute over construction workers' holiday pay erupted into violence. During a scuffle with the police in the Jordaan, one worker, Jan Weggelar, died of a heart attack. Rumour spread that the police had killed him, and a full-scale riot spread right across the city, sucking in Provos, Nozems (youth gangs) and anyone who enjoyed a good fight. Shops were looted, cars burned and parking meters ripped out of the ground. By nightfall the *burgemeester* was about to call in the army, but Chief Commissioner van der Molen of the Amsterdam Police took the matter in hand. He donned full dress uniform, called for his sword and strode out bravely into the midst of a bemused crowd. At midnight he met union leaders and, though he didn't entirely defuse the situation, the disruption fizzled out two days later after the mob had stormed the Port van Cleve Restaurant and the offices of the right-wing newspaper, *De Telegraaf.*

Later that year, violence broke out again over proposals to build a huge bank on Frederiksplein. Amsterdammers felt that big money was destroying the heart of the city by denuding it of anything but banks and offices. But despite concerted opposition, the city regents voted in favour of the bank by 30 to 14.

Meanwhile, the crowds camping out, especially those around the new National Monument (a war memorial), had begun to test the patience of upright, patriotic citizens. In 1967 off-duty Marines had descended on the hippies outside the Centraal Station and cut off their hair. The mess left by the impromptu campsites was an affront to the neat Amsterdammers and a by-law passed in the summer of 1969 banned sleeping around national monuments. Initially it wasn't enforced—though the police would occasionally hose everyone down. In 1970, after violent clashes with the police had failed to oust the Dam dropouts, the Marines once again decided on unofficial unilateral action. Bands of strapping lads singing barrack-room songs belted arm-in-arm down the Damrak, and frightened the hippies away forever. Good burghers looked on from the surrounding balconies and cheered. Though the next morning the establishment press felt compelled to condemn, ever so lightly, the Marines' behaviour. Amsterdam's youth culture survived the attack, but was more formally accommodated in hostels and Sleep-Ins.

The Provos had broken up in 1967 'in order to avoid bloodshed', but Roel van Duyn went on to establish the **Kabouters** ('helpful gnomes')—a whimsical party of idealists with occasional flashes of common sense—they wanted more trees, fewer banks and polluting industries, a ban on traffic in central Amsterdam, and free white bikes for all. In the 1970 municipal elections they polled 11 per cent of the vote and won five seats on the city council. As the decade wore on, they lost their appeal and were finally disbanded in 1981.

Though the Provos were no more, and the Kabouters were on the wane, the late 1970s and early 1980s saw some spectacular battles. The council's plan to build a **Metro**—largely to serve the outer suburbs—met with outrage. It was expensive, and meant pulling down more houses in the inner city. Many people refused to move and on 25 March 1975—'**Blue Monday**'—there were violent demonstrations when officials tried to clear the first houses for demolition. Police fired tear gas through the windows and drove armoured cars into the doors. The ferocity of the opposition increased until 1978, when the council agreed to build new homes and renovate areas of the inner city. Skirmishes went on right up until the opening of the Metro in 1980.

In 1980 13 per cent of the city's population was on the housing list. Squatting had become a popular solution to the chronic shortages. Properties that had been vacated for the Metro, factories left empty when companies moved outside the city and houses bought by speculative investors (and then left to rot and fall down so that the land could be developed more profitably) were occupied by the paint-pot and hammer-wielding homeless. A lot of work went into the renovation of squatter homes, and the building of accompanying studios and cafés. The network became highly organized, and, with 10,000 members by 1982, was a force to be reckoned with. Police attempts to evict squatters were heavy-handed (they used tanks on a squat in the Vondelstraat) and not always successful. Battles would rage for days, and at one point the *burgemeester* had to declare a state of emergency. By 1984 the last of the big squats had fallen. On others a compromise had been reached—the council bought up the property, renovated it and let it back cheaply to the inhabitants. Squatting, and evictions, still go on, but in a calmer atmosphere.

Ed van Thijn, Amsterdam's (socialist) *burgemeester* for most of the 1980s and the early 1990s, was tough on squatters when he first came to office, but then initiated a strong programme of *stadsvernieuwing* (urban renewal) to help ease the severe housing crisis and to transform the city's image. Every few decades, the city fathers get it into their heads that Amsterdam is backward and old-fashioned and needs to be promoted as a modern metropolis. This usually leads to big new buildings in the centre of town. In the 1890s the Centraal Station, a temple to the new railways, blocked off Amsterdam's view of its harbour forever; in the 1920s the enormous Nederlandse Handels-maatschappij (Chamber of Commerce) building pushed aside rows of historic gabled houses near Rembrandtplein; during the 1960s concrete and glass monstrosities appeared all over town, the most controversial being the Nederlandse Bank on Frederiksplein. The 1970s and early 1980s saw the arrival, amidst violent protest, of the Metro and the 'Stopera', a combined city hall and opera house on Waterlooplein (*see* pp.78–9). In the 1990s Burgemeester Van Thijn began to emphasize Amsterdam's role as a tourist, banking and congress metropolis. (It is now Europe's fourth tourist city after London, Paris and Rome, and in the world's top ten as a congress venue.) Vast new development went on in the area around Centraal Station, a glittering casino complex was built alongside Leidseplein, and business parks bristling with skyscrapers appeared—though this time on the outskirts of town.

Van Thijn's successor, **Schelto Patijn**, assumed office in 1994. Amsterdam's mayors are not elected by the citizenry, but appointed (ostensibly by the Queen). Even so, they wield extraordinary civic power. Unlike Van Thijn, Patijn is not a born-and-bred Amsterdammer. What makes matters worse is that he hails from The Hague, which is seen as Amsterdam's arch-rival. It did not help his image at all when the news leaked out that he didn't even intend to live in Amsterdam—though this decision was hastily revoked. At first, mutterings in Amsterdam cafés had it that this outsider did not understand the city one bit, and that he was trying to change Amsterdam into The Hague (which has a reputation for staid prissiness). His efforts at giving Amsterdam a more upmarket, businesslike image resulted in such moves as the towing away some of the old houseboats on the canals (seen as illegal and messy), and an attempt at closing down a number of café terraces (which was thwarted by rousing local opposition).

Whatever one thinks of Patijn the city's notorious drugs problem does seem more under control. Heroin dealers have been cleared out of the tourist areas around Zeedijk and Nieuwmarkt and now hole out in the south of the city. The *stadswacht* (modern-day equivalents of the Civil Guards in the Old Masters' portraits) wander about, unarmed, in smart uniforms with red trimmings, keeping an eye on public behaviour and making sure that buskers don't play their music too loudly. Tourist figures over the past few years have risen steadily. Amsterdam is enjoying a quiet, rather comfortable moment in its history, but its age-old tolerance of mischief remains the finest antidote to complacency. Amsterdam's flourishing gay community, the bustling red-light district, the newest wave of immigrants (from Turkey and Surinam), the Kabouters' heritage of environmental awareness and the Amsterdammers' nose for disruptive politics keep the cafés alive and the old port rough beneath its smooth veneer.

Orientation

For an overview map of Amsterdam, see inside back cover.

Amsterdam is small. If you were single-minded about it, it would take you only 40 minutes to traverse its spider's web of canals all the way from Centraal Station to the Rijksmuseum on the other side of town. But you would need to know where you were going. The cobweb shape is confusing and disorientating. Arm yourself with a good map (those published by Falk are recommended). Along the way you'll be constantly surprised by the changes in pace and atmosphere of the *kwartiers* you passed through, some no bigger than a courtyard and a few gabled houses, yet every one of them has a distinctive, quite particular character of its own. Visit the '**Negen Straatjes**' (*see* pp.87–8) for quirky shopping, the **Jordaan** (*see* pp.89–90) for quiet charm; wander along the **Grachtengordel** ('Canal Belt' *see* pp.82ff) for elegance and grandeur, or sink into the tat surrounding the **Damrak** and **red-light district** (*see* pp.67 and 71–2).

Amsterdam is a sedate city. Pedestrians and cyclists set the pace, and you'll find most places you want to visit within comfortable walking distance. If your legs are tired, or you're in a hurry, yellow trams will whisk you to almost anywhere you want to go. A car is a liability. Parking is expensive (when it's possible), and driving in the narrow streets, which throng with bicycles and jaywalking tourists, is a nightmare. Public transport on the other hand is efficient, safe and cheap, and to be recommended.

Taxis into Amsterdam will cost you at least ƒ60, and hardly seem worth it given the ease, frequency and price of public transport. Trains leave for Centraal Station every 15 minutes (until 1am, then hourly until 5am). The journey takes about 20 minutes and tickets cost ƒ6.50.

Alternatively, you can swan into town on the plush KLM Hotel Bus. The service is available to anyone, even if you sneaked over on a bucket flight and intend sleeping in the Vondelpark. Buses leave at 15min intervals from 6.30am to 9.15pm and tickets cost ƒ17.50. Route A stops include the Pulitzer, Krasnapolsky, Jolly Carlton and Okura (i.e. mainly central Amsterdam). Route B focuses more on southern Amsterdam, stopping at such hotels as the Hilton, Beethoven and Apollo.

Amsterdam © (020–)   ### *Getting Around*

Maps, information and tickets are available from the **GVB** (Amsterdam Municipal Transport Authority), Stationsplein 15, opposite Centraal Station (open Mon–Fri 7am–7pm, Sat and Sun 8am–7pm, © (0900) 92 92). In the summer there's often a mobile branch on Leidseplein.

Once you've grasped the quirky logic behind it, the ticketing system used on public transport seems quite sensible. Although you can buy single tickets on boarding, it's cheaper and easier to buy a **strip ticket** (*strippenkaart*, ƒ11.75). Most tourist sights are within the central zone, but there are maps at all stations and stops, should you be in any doubt.

If you intend to use a lot of public transport, the most economical ticket will be a **day ticket** (*dagkaart*). This allows unlimited travel in Amsterdam and costs ƒ12 for 1 day, ƒ15 for 2 days, ƒ19 for 3 days, ƒ23 for 4 days, and ƒ27 for 5 days. You can buy *dagkaarten* from drivers or the GVB. Weekly, monthly or annual season tickets (*abonnement*) are also available from the GVB, starting from ƒ17.75.

Bus and tram drivers can also sell you an **hourly ticket** (*uurnetkaart*, pronounced 'oornetkart') for ƒ4.50 which allows you to travel anywhere in Amsterdam within an hour of its validation.

by tram

Trams run from 6am Mon–Fri and 7.30am Sun. Last trams are around midnight. On most trams you can get on or off through any one of the three doors (which open after you press the adjacent metal button). Some lines have conductors, who sit at the back. On these trams you can only alight through the rear door. Tram stops have yellow boards showing the numbers of the trams they serve and listing further destinations along the route. Of special benefit to visitors is the **Circle Tram**, running from Centraal Station to all the major sights and back.

by bus

Buses work on the same system as trams, though you must board at the front door. You're much less likely to use them, unless you need a **night bus**. A black square with the bus number printed on it is shown on the board of night bus stops. By some inscrutable logic the night buses decrease in frequency at about the time the bars close (2am). After this time there is only one bus an hour on some routes, and none at all until 4am on others. So your alternatives are a late night out, a very late night out, or walking home. You can, of course, always get a taxi.

by metro

The metro is used mainly by commuters from the eastern and southeastern suburbs. There are only two lines, both terminating at Centraal Station. Running times and ticketing are the same as for trams.

by taxi

Theoretically, you can hail an Amsterdam cab in the street, but you're unlikely to have any luck at all. Best bet is to pick one up at a rank, or telephone the 24-hour central control, ✆ 677 7777 or ✆ (0900) 0724. The main **ranks** are at Centraal Station, Rembrandtplein and Leidseplein. Cafés, restaurants or nightclubs will usually phone a cab for you and one will arrive in ten minutes or so. When you set off, the meter should be blank, except for the minimum charge. Even short journeys are expensive, with a flat rate of ƒ5.80 for starters, then ƒ2.85 a kilometre (ƒ4.50 a mile) and increasing after midnight.

by bicycle

Cycling is the perfect means of transport in Amsterdam. It's convenient and gets you about at just the right speed to enjoy the city to the full. It's also a very Dutch way to travel. There are 700,000 people living in Amsterdam, and 550,000 bicycles. The city has an excellent network of cycle lanes, and bicycles are cheap to hire, though it can be more economical to pick up a second-hand one. This you can do from markets or cycle shops for around ƒ150.

For bike hire try Rent-A-Bike (Pieter Jacobsdwarsstraat 11, ✆ 625 5029) or Macbike (Mr. Visserplein 2, ✆ 620 0985) and Take-A-Bike (Stationsplein 6, near Centraal Station, ✆ 624 8391), which are a little cheaper.

by water

If you have the time for the leisurely journeys, canal trips can give you an eye-opening perspective on the city. The moment you step on a boat you seem to cross a mysterious boundary. People on shore carry on with their lives—nicking bicycles, arguing, making love—apparently oblivious of you sailing past only a few feet away. The **Canal Bus** takes you on a gentle dawdle along some fine stretches of canal between the Rijksmuseum and Centraal Station, stopping at Leidseplein, Leidsestraat/Keizersgracht and the Anne Frank Huis. Buses leave at 45min intervals between 10am and 6pm. A day ticket costs ƒ22. The new **All Amsterdam Transport Pass** is a day pass that for ƒ27.50 includes all public transport as well as unlimited use of the canal bus.

Water Taxis can be great fun if you are feeling in the mood to live it up a little—the company will even lay on a guide, food and drink for appropriate extra charges. If you're lucky you can hail an empty water taxi as it putters past (they can stop anywhere along the canalside). You can also order them from the **Water Taxi Centrale** (Stationsplein 8, ✆ 530 1090; open daily 9am–1am; major credit cards accepted). Fares are metered—an 8-seater boat works out at around ƒ125 for the first half an hour irrespective of the number of passengers, and ƒ75 for every subsequent half-hour.

If you're feeling energetic you can hire a **Canal Bike** (a pedalboat that seats two or four people; costs ƒ25 per hour for two people and ƒ40 for four; deposit ƒ50; no credit cards). Explore the canals for a while, then drop it off at any one of the hire company's four moorings—at Leidseplein (between the Marriott and American Hotels), at the Rijksmuseum, at the Anne Frank Huis, and on the Keizersgracht near Leidsestraat. Remember to keep to the right, and keep an ear open for warning hoots emitted by the long canal boats as they approach sharp corners or narrow tunnels. **Canal Motor Boats** (on Kloveniersburgwal, ✆ 422 7007) offer electric boats for hire at ƒ65 for the first hour, and a declining rate for subsequent hours.

by car

If you do find yourself lumbered with a car in Amsterdam, you can find covered **car parks** (indicated by a white P on blue background) at De Bijenkorf (on Beursplein), Byzantium (Stadhouderskade, opposite Leidseplein), Europarking (Marnixstraat 250), RAI (on the Europa Boulevard) and under the Muziektheater (Waterlooplein). Charges are around ƒ5 an hour. Parking beside the road works out at about ƒ4 an hour, and street parking works by the 'pay-and-display' method. You put your money into a machine (often cunningly concealed behind a tree halfway down the street), estimate your time of return, then leave the ticket it prints out on your dashboard. If you park illegally your car will be towed away before you've had a chance to buy an ice-cream. It will cost you at least ƒ400 to get it back from the pound (Dani, 1 Goedkoopstraat 7, ✆ 553 0333), and they won't take credit cards. If you overstay your time in a parking bay, your car will be clamped. A yellow sticker on the windscreen tells you where to pay the fine (which will be at least ƒ126). Some meters are free after 7pm and on Sundays, but in the city centre you have to pay up to 11pm, Sunday inclusive. It's always best to check before abandoning your car to the clampers.

If you are in Amsterdam with a car for any length of time, it is a good idea to buy a **parking card**. This costs ƒ30 (9am–7pm), ƒ33 (9am–11pm), or ƒ7 (7pm–11pm), and is available from the Dienst Stadstoezicht (Weesperstraat 105a, Beukenplein 50, Ceintuurbaan 159, Kinkerstraat 17, ✆ 553 0333). A **park-and-ride system** (known to the Dutch as a Transferium) operates from the Amsterdam ArenA, in Amsterdam southeast. Amsterdam city council hopes to open more park-and-ride lots around the outskirts of town.

The most convenient 24-hour petrol stations are at Marnixstraat 250 and Sarphatistraat 225.

If you'd like to **hire a car**, you'll find the international companies well represented: Avis (Nassaukade 380, ✆ 683 6061); Budget (Overtoom 333, ✆ 612 6066) and Hertz (Overtoom 85, ✆ 612 2441). Local companies provide a good service, sometimes at less than half the price. Try Diks (Van Ostadestraat 278–80, ✆ 662 3366); Drive Yourself (Cruquiuskade 5, ✆ 627 4001) or Kuperus (Middenweg 175, ✆ 693 8790).

On the jetties around Centraal Station you'll find companies offering canal tours, and cruises. Prices and standards are almost uniform, but **Lovers Rondvaarten** (Prins Hendrikkade 25–27, ✆ 530 1090) has the best reputation.

The **Amsterdam Tourist Board** (*see* below) not only takes bookings for canal cruises, but constantly comes up with new ideas for touring the city—its staff can suggest all sorts of walking and cycling routes in and about Amsterdam. **Yellowbike** (NZ Kolk 29, ✆ 620 6940) also offers guided cycle tours around the city and surrounding waterlands. **Audiotourist** (Oude Spiegelstraat 9, ✆ 421 5580) will rent you a personal stereo plus guided tour on cassette for ƒ15 (plus deposit). There are three different walks that last two to three hours each.

More rewarding than the commercially organized tours are the informal walk-abouts with old Amsterdam residents offered by **Mee in Mokum** (✆ 625 1390; open Mon–Fri 1–4 pm). The guides aren't professional, but give a homely, resident's touch that you're unlikely to find elsewhere. The tours are usually done in Dutch, but since the groups are small (about eight people), it's often possible to arrange an English alternative. **Archivisie** (✆ 625 8908) offers specialist architectural tours.

Amsterdam ✆ (020–)   **Tourist Information**

The **Amsterdam Tourist Board** has English-speaking staff who can help with information about tourist sights, events and transport. They can change money and (for a ƒ3.50 fee) arrange hotel and theatre bookings. They sell a range of maps and brochures and can suggest tours and walks. The main Amsterdam branch is opposite Centraal Station at Stationsplein 10. There is another, less busy branch at Leidseplein 1, a small branch in Centraal Station and one in the south of town on the corner of Stadionplein and Van Tuyll van Serooskerkenweg. All these branches are open Mon–Sat 9–5. During the high season some offices may extend their hours, and open on Sunday. There is a central information telephone number: ✆ (0900) 400 4040, but it costs ƒ1 a minute and you are usually kept for ages in an electronic queue (paying for every second of the wait), often to be told at the end of it all that the office is too busy anyway and that you should phone back later.

Information about public transport is given by the **GVB** (Amsterdam Municipal Transport Authority), Stationsplein 15 (open Mon–Fri 7–7, Sat and Sun 8–7).

The **AUB Uitburo** (Leidseplein 26, ✆ 621 1211; open Mon–Sat 10–6) gives information and sells advance tickets (booking fee ƒ2) for the city's theatres and concert halls and for many other cultural events. It also distributes leaflets and listings magazines. Entertainment info is also at the end of a phone line: Uitlijn, ✆ (0900) 0191.

The information desk at Schiphol Airport can give you a free English copy of the *Visitors' Yellow Pages*, a slim book of useful telephone numbers. You can also pick it up at police stations or from the Amsterdam Tourist Board.

You can visit the city **website** on *www.amsterdam.nl*. For business-orientated information visit the website of the Amsterdam Promotion Foundation at *www.amsterdampromotion.nl*.

addresses

Houses on the main canals are numbered from west to east, even numbers on the outer circumference. Amsterdammers seem to have run out of imagination when naming their streets. If they think they've hit on a good name they'll use it again and again, so you get not only Eerste/1^e (1st) Helmersstraat but also Tweede/2^e (2nd) Helmersstraat and Derde/3^e (3rd) Helmersstraat. Transverse streets get the epithet 'dwars', and also appear in multiples, so Tweede Egelantiersdwarsstraat will be the second street off Egelantiersstraat. The Oudezijd (old side of the city, east of Damrak) and the Nieuwezijd (new side, west of Damrak) are abbreviated in addresses to OZ and NZ—Oudezijds Voorburgwal, for example, is usually written OZ Voorburgwal.

babysitters

You can get hold of vetted and reliable babysitters from **Oppascentrale Kriterion** (✆ 624 5848; open 24 hours). Prices start at about *f* 7 an hour and you're expected to provide drinks, food for long sessions and the cost of transport home after midnight. Over weekends there is a minimum charge of *f* 20.

discounts

The **Amsterdam Culture and Leisure Pass** entitles you to all sorts of discounts on museums and restaurants. It costs *f* 39.50—though it can pay for itself within a few days. It's available from the Amsterdam Tourist Board.

emergencies

The national emergency number is ✆ **112**.

Main police stations are at Elandsgracht 117 and Warmoesstraat 44. Report any theft immediately, and get a written statement for your insurance claim. The **Amsterdam Tourist Assistance Service** (ATAS, NZ Voorburgwal 114/8, ✆ 625 3246) is on hand to offer victim support, should you have been shaken up by your experience, or feel at a loss as to what to do.

If you are a victim of rape or sexual abuse contact **De Eerste Lijn** (The First Line) on ✆ 613 0245 (24 hours). You'll find main **police stations** at Elandsgracht 117 and Warmoesstraat 44. It's a good idea, for insurance purposes, to report lost or stolen property to the police as soon as possible. There are **lost property offices** at Centraal Station, GVB Head Office, Prins Hendrikkade 108–14 (open Mon–Fri 9–4, for items lost on public transport), and at Waterlooplein 11 (open Mon–Fri 11–3.30, for items lost in parks and on the streets). It's best to allow a day or two for your property to filter through the system before trying to reclaim it.

health

The most useful place to ring if you are ill or need a dentist is the **Central Medical Service** on ✆ (0900) 503 2042. This 24-hour service will refer you to a duty practitioner. The most central **hospital** with an outpatients department is Onze Lieve Vrouwe Gasthuis, Eerste Oosterparkstraat 179, ✆ 599 9111. **Chemists** (*drogisterij*) sell non-prescription drugs and toiletries. If you need a prescription made up you should go to an *apotheek*. The Central Medical Service can also advise you on this. If you've crushed your contact lenses or dropped your specs in a canal, try **York Optiek**, Heiligeweg 8; ✆ 623 3295 (open Mon–Fri 9.30–6, Sat 9.30–5, appointment advisable, major credit cards accepted). If your dentures take a crunch try **Accident**, Amstelveenseweg 51, ✆ 664 4380 (open 24 hours). There's a free and confidential VD clinic at Groenburgwal 44, ✆ 555 5822 (open Mon–Fri 8–10.30 and 1–3, but arrive before 10.30am for first consultation; appointment not necessary). The **Polikliniek Oosterpark**, Oosterpark 59, ✆ 693 2151 (open Mon–Fri 9–5) offers contraception, abortion and morning after pills, but its services are not free.

post

The main **post office** is at Singel 250 (open Mon–Fri 9–6, Sat 10–1.30; late opening Thurs until 8; ✆ 556 3311) and, as well as the usual facilities, has phones, photocopiers, a gift shop and a philately counter. Parcels can be sent only through this office, or the **sorting office** (Oosterdokskade 3, near Centraal Station; open Mon–Fri 8.30–9, Sat 9–12 noon; ✆ 622 8272).

religious services

Roman Catholic services in English are held at an old clandestine church: St John and St Ursula (Begijnhof 30, ✆ 622 1918; Sun 12.15 pm). There's a Latin High Mass at De Papegaai (St Peter and Paul, Nieuwezijds Voorburgwal 293; also entrance on Kalverstraat, Sun 11.15am).

Protestant services in English are held in the serene English Reform/Scottish Presbyterian Church (Begijnhof 48, ✆ 624 9665; Sun 10.30am) and at the Anglican Church (Groenburgwal 42, ✆ 624 8877; Sun 10.30am and 7.30pm).

Times of **Jewish** services vary. You can contact the Liberal Community at Jacob Soetendorpstraat 8 (✆ 642 3562) and the Orthodox Community at PO Box 7967, Van der Boechorstraat 26, 1008 ad (✆ 646 0046).

Festivals

Perhaps because of Amsterdam's Puritan heritage, you'll find little civic or royal pomp. Instead, the city lets its hair down at a number of fairs, arts festivals and street parties. *See* also **Practical A–Z**, pp.14–5 for nationwide festivals.

February: Commemoration of the February Strike—a solemn gathering on 25th at the Dokwerker statue on J. D. Meijerplein (*see* p.82).

March: The Stille Omgang (Silent Procession) takes place at night on the Sunday closest to the 15th. Roman Catholics from all over the world walk in silence along the Heiligeweg and up to Sint Nicolaaskerk to celebrate Amsterdam's 'Miracle' (*see* pp.55 and 67).

The Meervaart Theatre hosts a Blues Festival and there's a boat show featuring the latest pleasure craft at the RAI Congress Centre (on Europaplein).

April: 30 April is Koninginnedag (Queen's Day—a national holiday to celebrate the Queen's birthday). Amsterdam declares a 'free market'. Anyone can sell anything anywhere and all bar and restaurant takings are tax-free. Holland converges on the town to eat, drink, dance and be exceptionally merry, but with the usual charming Dutch relaxed tolerance. Up to three million people throng the streets (Amsterdam's population is only 700,000), yet you hardly *see* a policeman, there are no barricades, no rules and no problems—seldom upwards of ten arrests over the whole day, and those are usually for pickpocketing. The best time to join in is after midnight on the 29th, when everyone is setting up stalls and people are as fresh and excited as children on Christmas Eve.

An internationally respected World Press Photo Exhibition displays the pick of newspaper and magazine photography from the preceding year. (In the Nieuwe Kerk from mid-April to mid-May.) Watch out also for GRAP Day at De Melkweg (*see* p.136), when Amsterdam's best new bands blast away well into the night.

June: The Holland Festival runs for the whole month of June. This is Amsterdam's answer to the Edinburgh Festival, with an impressive constellation of international performers booked into opera, dance and theatre venues around the city. The festival forms part of the Amsterdam Arts Adventure.

Around the beginning of the month (or at the end of May) the RAI Congress Centre plays host to Kunst RAI, an international contemporary art fair. Later in the month, the World Roots Festival—nine days of music, dance and theatre from non-Western cultures—takes place at De Melkweg.

July: The July Summer Festival is a bonanza of the avant-garde that goes on all over town (sometimes in the strangest places).

August: For most of the month of August the Martin Luther King Park, beside the Amstel on the southern outskirts of town, is the scene of De Parade, a 'theatre funfair'. Various theatre groups and performers arrange bright show booths, some of them dating back to the first half of the century, in a vast circle, and offer everything from cabaret to performance art. The Masters (and Mistresses) of Ceremonies present the players on stages outside the booths, then everyone troops in for the show. There's lots to eat and drink too.

The Uitmarkt (Entertainment Market) takes place in the last week of August. Groups from all over the Netherlands offer tantalizing snippets of what the coming cultural season has to offer. It's free, and takes place in theatres, in the open air—in fact anywhere a company can find a suitable space.

More open-air music is played during the three-day-long Grachtenfestival (Canal Festival)—this time from boats opposite the Pulitzer Hotel (Prinsengracht 315–31; also in the last week of August).

September: Bloemen Corso (Flower Parade) is a parade of floats from Aalsmeer ('the flower capital') to Amsterdam on the first Saturday of the month. Check with the Amsterdam Tourist Board (*see* p.63) for details of the route and arrival times. Vijzelstraat and the Dam are the best places to watch from.

The Jordaan Festival is the liveliest of a series of neighbourhood street parties. All over the Jordaan, the residents come out into the streets to booze, barbecue and try their luck in the often unabashedly dire local talent contests.

November: In mid-November St Nicholas (Sinterklaas/Santa Claus) arrives by steamboat at Centraal Station (supposedly from his home in Spain). He parades through the city on a white horse with his slave Black Pete (an oddly persistent tradition in racially aware Amsterdam) and is given the keys of the city by the *burgemeester* on the Dam. Relax on Rembrandtsplein and watch the early part of the procession in relative comfort.

Stationsplein

The **Centraal Station**, built between 1884 and 1889 atop thousands of wooden piles on an artificial island, is such an elaborate and sustained exercise in 19th-century ornament that it can almost be forgiven for screening off Amsterdam's view of the old harbour. The architect P. J. H. Cuypers (also responsible for the Rijksmuseum) succumbed to every temptation to gild bits of his red-brick extravaganza, so that it sparkles in the sunlight like a Walt Disney palace. Its twin towers are adorned not only by a clock, but also by a wind-rose, a delightfully superfluous instrument that rotates languidly showing the frequency of winds blowing from the various leading points of the compass. The roof bristles with stone and iron spikes and the central section sports classically inspired reliefs showing allegories of sailing, trade and industry. There's a large section over the entrance depicting the peoples of the world paying homage to the maiden Amsterdam.

The building seems very much in the tradition of the triumphal arch or elaborate city gate and is indeed a grand place to arrive in Amsterdam. The city is laid out like a semi-circular spider's web with the Centraal Station in the middle. As you step out of the main entrance you get the full impression, across the shapeless open space of **Stationsplein**, of the spires, gables and cupolas of Amsterdam's delicate skyline. To the left across the square is **Sint Nicolaaskerk** (St Nicholas Church; *open April–Oct, Mon–Fri 11–4, Sat 2–4*), a sprucely restored 19th-century neo-Renaissance building with a murky interior. A small ship set above the door at the back is the only remainder that it was a seamen's church. Every March during the Stille Omgang (Silent Procession), Roman Catholics walk silently through the streets to the Sint Nicolaaskerk to commemorate Amsterdam's miracle (*see* p.55). Paintings in the left-hand transept depict the story.

Along the Damrak

From Stationsplein leads the **Damrak**, once a busy port built along the Amstel, but these days a street lined with the fast food joints, rip-off bureaux de change, tacky restaurants and tackier hotels that usually cluster around tourist inlets. The only remaining patch of water is a tiny dock filled with the glass-covered boats that bus you around on hour-long canal trips (for details, *see* pp.61–2).

Amsterdam grew up in the early 13th century along Kerkstraat (Church Street, later renamed Warmoesstraat) on the left (east) side of the river. Towards the end of the 1800s the village expanded along Windmolenstraat (Windmill Street) on the right (west) bank. The Church Side and the Windmill Side soon became known as Oude Zijd (Old Side) and Nieuwe Zijd (New Side) and the corresponding sides of Damrak are still called that today.

Halfway up Damrak, on the left-hand side, you come to the **Beurs van Berlage** (*museum open Tues–Sun 10–4; basic adm, includes visit to tower*). The first Beurs (Exchange) was built by the prolific 17th-century architect Hendrick de Keyser in 1608. The city council thought it necessary to confine all the outdoor wheeling and dealing that took place along Damrak and around the Oude Kerk to one (warmer and drier) venue. The result was deafening. As international trade expanded, such exotica as Turks, Indians and Hungarians joined the locals packed around the pillars and arcades of the small hall on the Rokin, bargaining madly for silks, shares, tobacco and tulips—or anything the boats brought in. De Keyser's Beurs held out for two hundred years. The building that replaced it (on the site of the present De Bijenkorf department store) was universally unpopular and in 1874 the city held a competition for a new design. When it was revealed that the winner had cribbed the façade from a French town hall, H. P. Berlage (who had come third) smartened up his original plans and landed the prize. Many revisions later (he was still at the drawing board while the builders were at work), he came up with a building that has become an Amsterdam landmark and earned him the reputation of being the father of modern Dutch architecture. The Beurs van Berlage (completed in 1903) is all clean lines and functional shapes. Berlage allows himself some gently patterned brickwork, but there's not one extraneous twirly bit nor a glimmer of 19th-century Gothic fantasy. The pillars and arcades inside are an echo of the original Beurs.

These days part of the Beurs is used for concerts, while the rest is a museum (comprising a modest display on the history and design of the building) and exhibition hall. A visit to the museum gives you access to the clock tower and a view over the oldest part of town. In the smaller of two concert halls you sit and listen to the music in an enormous glass box which has solved the problem of abysmal acoustics without defacing the original interior. You can get a glimpse inside without buying a ticket by popping into the café at the south end.

The café opens out on to **Beursplein**. To the right the traffic on Damrak hurtles past. The dainty neoclassical **Effectenbeurs** (Commodities Exchange) on the left is the place where the real trading now happens. Across the square, a row of silently chewing, blank faces stare out at you from behind a sheet of plate glass. These are exhausted shoppers propped up along a snackbar in the back window of De Bijenkorf, though they look as if they're for sale.

The Dam

Riots, garrottings, camping hippies—the Dam has seen it all. Reputedly the site of the original dam across the Amstel, it hit its zenith as city centre in the 17th century. Pragmatic Amsterdam merchants wouldn't stand for any decorative open space at the heart of the city and the Dam bustled with a fishmarket, a public weighing house, a communal crane and a dock that allowed ships to sail right up into the middle of town to offload. Popular tunes rang out from the Stadhuis carillon and, above all the racket, the town crier's horn would from time to time blast out (once for good news, twice for bad). When you needed to go home, you could ring a bell to summon a taxi. After a brief wait for the drivers to throw dice to decide who should take you, you'd set off at reckless speed in a slide carriage (wheels presented a problem on the hump-backed bridges), accompanied by packs of sprinting boys throwing water and greased rags under the runners to make the carriage go faster, or straw to make it stop. You'd have to drop out coins at intervals to ensure your rapid progress, and a few more at the humpy bridges to the stalwart lads who hung around to give a much-needed extra push.

Traffic on the Dam these days is just as frantic, but the square has lost all its verve. It's still the city centre and the carillon still peals out pop tunes, but the Dam is soulless, fumid and dull. The eastern end is dominated by the towering, phallic **National Monument**, erected in 1956 as a memorial to the people killed in the Second World War. In the 1960s it became a sort of hippie totem pole and hundreds of people would sleep around it in the summer. Police attempts to put a stop to this (such as washing it down with firehoses) led to protest riots, but in 1970 a marauding group of off-duty marines chased away the campers forever (*see* p.57).

Central Amsterdam (West)

Het IJ

PRINS HENDRIKKADE

Centraal Station

STATIONSPLEIN

Post Office

Herengracht

Singel

SPUISTRAAT

NIEUWEZIJDS VOORBURGWAL

HEKELVELD

NIEUWENDIJK

DAMRAK

Damrak

Schreierstoren

Amstelkring Museum

ZEEDIJK

Gelderschekade

Beurs van Berlage

BEURS-PLEIN

Oude Kerk

LANGE NIEZEL

WARMOESSTRAAT

OUDEKERKSPLEIN

Nieuwe Kerk

GRAVEENSTR.

De Bijenkorf

PAPEN-BURGSTG.

DAMRAK STG.

ST.ANNENSTR.

OUDEZIJDS VOORBURGWAL

Achterburgwal

Post office

Koninklijk Paleis (Stadhuis)

Grand Hotel Krasnapolsky

DAM

Madame Tussaud's

Nationaal Monument

DAMSTR.

NES

SPUISTRAAT

KALVERSTRAAT

ROKIN

Bank van Lening

OUDE DOELEN STR.

Oudezijds

Hash Museum

KOESTRAAT

Kloveniers-burgwal

NIEUW MARKT

Post Office

Oude Schans

Gate to Spinhuis

OUDE HOOGSTRAAT

RUSLAND

Amsterdam Historical Museum

Begijnhof

GED. BEG. STG.

NES

GRIMBURGWAL

Agnietenkapel

Gate to Oudemanhuis

Zwanenburgwal

WATERLOOPLEIN

SPUI

KALVERSTRAAT

VOETBOOGSTRAAT

HANDBOOGSTRAAT

Gate to Gasthuis

Rokin

Stopera

Gate to Rasphuis

Singel

AMSTEL

Binnenamstel

N

REMBRANDT-PLEIN

Herengracht

200 metres
200 yards

At its southern end the Dam leads into **Kalverstraat**, a pedestrianized shopping street where shoulder-to-shoulder consumers push in and out of Euro-high-street stores, scrabble about in the sales baskets and devour pungent fast food. While on the northwestern corner stands the **Nieuwe Kerk** (*open daily 11–5*). Of course the Nieuwe Kerk isn't all that new and construction on the building actually began nearly 600 years ago. It's a soaring Gothic heap without a steeple. (In the 17th century, Oude Kerk parishioners, who had always been jealous of the flash rival church, were delighted when the city council stopped construction of the tower because it was going to be higher than the town hall.) Until 1890 all the city's clocks were set weekly by the church's sundial. Like most of Amsterdam's large churches, the Nieuwe Kerk is now used mainly for exhibitions and concerts. Even if you can't catch a recital on the sumptuous Great Organ, the instrument itself, fluttering with angels and cherubs and surrounded by soft-painted shutters, is well worth a visit. Admiral de Ruyter, the Dutch naval hero, is buried in the choir. (His invasion of the River Medway in England caused Sir William Batten, Surveyor of the British Navy, to explode to Samuel Pepys: 'I think the devil shits Dutchmen.') There is also a memorial to the poet Vondel (*see* pp.104–5) near the west door. Before you leave, have a look also at the richly carved pulpit and ornate copper choir screen.

Next door to the Nieuwe Kerk, taking up the entire western end of the square is the **Koninklijk Paleis** (Royal Palace; *opening times vary, in summer generally daily 11am–5.30pm, sometimes closed for state functions; information on © (020) 620 4060*). The Koninklijk Paleis was the **Stadhuis** (City Hall) until Louis Bonaparte decided he wanted to live there in 1808. It has been a royal palace ever since, though Queen Beatrix prefers the leafier groves of Huis ten Bosch in The Hague and never spends the night here. The area in front of the Stadhuis was a favourite spot for theatrical public executions. On the right, above the entrance arches, you can still see the blocks where the scaffold slotted into the wall. The ornate street lamps along the front were commissioned by King Willem Frederik in 1840. They were the city's first gas lamps, but were so expensive to run that the council secretly turned them off whenever the king was out of town.

When the Stadhuis was built in the mid-17th century, only St Peter's, the Escorial and Venice's Palazzo Ducale rivalled it in grandeur. The poet Constantijn Huygens dubbed it 'the eighth wonder of the world', and a passing Englishman wrote of 'a most neat and splendid pile of a building'. But Sir William Temple, the British Ambassador to the Netherlands, harrumphed that it was '*una gran piccola cosa*' ('a big little thing'—he was quoting someone else's remark about the Louvre). The architect, Jacob van Campen (designer of the ill-fated Nieuwe Kerk tower), had produced a grandiose celebration of Amsterdam's mercantile supremacy and civic might—a classicist heap of windows, pilasters and relief carving. On the front pediment, collected water deities worship an allegorical Maid of Amsterdam; at the back of the building the trading nations of the world grovel to her. Peace stands high under the dumpy dome (a cornucopia overflowing at her feet) holding not only an olive branch, but also Mercury's staff (a symbol of commerce). Atlas buckles under a copper globe so heavy that it needs iron rods to prop it up. Despite all this confident symbolism, there's no grand entrance (the eight little arches along the front look more like tradesmen's gates or the way into the stables) and nowadays you are more likely to agree with Sir William Temple than Constantijn Huygens: the rather grimy palace in a busy city centre has as much architectural impact as a main post office or magistrates' court.

However, if you're passing during the rather restricted opening hours, don't miss the chance of popping inside to be dazzled by the **Burgerzaal** (Citizens' Hall). It's a vast space encrusted with marble carving that glints in the light pouring in from all sides. Rows of chandeliers drip from the distant ceiling, and brass inlaid maps on the floor show the heavenly and terrestrial worlds (with Amsterdam very much at the centre of things and the enthroned Maid of Amsterdam proudly surveying it all). The few chairs around the edges, even a grand piano for the inevitable recital, look like doll's house furniture. Scattered throughout the building are delicate and often witty marble reliefs (Icarus takes a tumble outside the Bankrupts' Court, caryatids look bored with holding up the cross-beams). Most of them are by Artus Quellinus, the noted Golden Age sculptor who also carved the pediments outside. The city fathers, however, blundered when it came to commissioning the wall paintings: they sent Rembrandt packing after he had presented his preliminary sketches.

The Empire furniture dispersed around the building was left behind by Louis Bonaparte. When he took over the Stadhuis he carpeted the marble floors, boarded up the galleries, turned the virtually empty upper storey into living accommodation and also had the weighing house on the Dam demolished because it spoiled his view. When the bored and wayward Queen Hortense granted a royal pension to a foundling abandoned at the palace door, he forestalled an inundation of hapless infants by surrounding the entrance with cobblestones and appointing guards to prevent anyone from stepping on them. His wooden-partitioned upstairs apartments lasted well into the last century and were such a fire risk that whenever Queen Wilhelmina used the palace everyone was instructed not to smoke and to sleep with the doors open. A fireman in gym shoes would creep about at night to catch offenders.

The Red-Light District

Amsterdam's much-hyped red-light district (known to locals as 'De Walletjes'—the little walls) lies east of the Damrak, and you can reach it from the Dam along Warmoesstraat or Damstraat. **Warmoesstraat** is Amsterdam's oldest street. Originally a cluster of wattle and daub cottages, it was by the 16th century a row of prosperous merchants' houses and powerful banks. The Duke of Alva lived here in 1574 during his reign of terror (the rest of the street was understandably empty at the time) and left without paying his rent. Vondel (the 'Dutch Shakespeare') had a small hosiery business at the Dam end before he became a famous poet; and Sir Thomas Nugent, a seasoned 17th-century traveller, recommended it as the only street where you'd find English inns and so avoid being cheated by wily Dutchmen. In 1766 Mozart senior held court in the tavern of De Goude Leeuw and sold tickets for his son's recitals at ƒ2 apiece; and a century later Karl Marx pondered and scribbled away in the inn next door. These days Warmoesstraat is the first layer of the red-light district, and a strange mixture of past respectability and the seediness which lies beyond. It's a grubby, dishevelled street, but no one seems to take it seriously enough for it to be sordid.

In the alleys off Warmoesstraat women sit, barely clad and deeply bored, perched on bar stools in the windows. Catch someone's eye and immediately there's a bright smile and a sparkle which disappears the moment you look away. If business is bad, or if you walk with eyes downcast, you'll hear the windows being rapped noisily. In the mornings the little alleys, some narrower than a doorway, are inhabited only by the desperate (on both sides of the glass) and the area has a feeling of secrecy and expectancy, rather like an empty theatre. Off-duty prostitutes join friends to go out shopping, or wander off in groups to the clinic for a check-up. In the afternoons it all seems too blatant and seedy, but later a wild festivity sets in as the lanes fill with the merry, the lecherous and the plain curious. Phalanxes of Japanese businessmen troop about aching to take photographs, drunken schoolboys gawp and try to pluck up courage, tight clutches of Dutch families from the provinces ooh and aah and snicker at all the wickedness.

In the heart of it all is Amsterdam's oldest building, the **Oude Kerk** (Old Church; *open summer Mon–Sat 11–5, Sun 1–5; adm*). Only the tower of the Oude Kerk actually dates from 1300. The original basilica disappeared behind an increasingly haphazard outgrowth of side chapels, transepts and clerestories. Most of what you see today is lofty early 16th-century Renaissance, but even that has a crust of warden's offices, choir rooms and houses, built over a period of three centuries. The interior has survived frequent bouts of heavy-handed restoration, an engulfing coat of Prussian blue paint in the 18th century and violent attacks by iconoclasts. In August 1566, roused by the sight of fragments of statuary from smashed-up churches in Antwerp, Protestant mobs stormed the church, breaking windows and destroying all graven images. A local girl, Lange Weyn, threw her shoe at a picture of the Virgin Mary in the excitement, and was later drowned in a barrel on the Dam for the outrage.

After what is discreetly called the 'Alteration' of 1578, when the Protestants finally took control of the city, the new Calvinist city fathers stripped the church of its dedication to St Nicholas (patron saint of sailors and so, aptly, of Amsterdam) and the popular title of Oude Kerk became official. They also set about turning it into a more sombre place of worship. It had become a hearty communal gathering place. Dossers and travellers slept in the corners, pedlars set up stalls in the aisles, merchants clinched deals on the square outside and dog-owners crowded the entrance. (Only certain classes of Amsterdam society were allowed big dogs, and if your mutt couldn't squeeze through the special iron hoop at the church door, its days were numbered.) These days the church plays host to travelling exhibitions and the occasional concert. Inside you can see the **tomb of Rembrandt's wife**, Saskia van Uylenburgh (near the Weitkoperskapel on the north side); some beautifully restored and remade stained glass (especially the windows depicting the Annunciation in the Mariakapel); and the secret door (once covered by plaster, 5m above the ground in St Sebastiaanskapel) to the **IJzeren Kapel** (Iron Chapel), a hiding place for important city documents until 1892.

Oudezijds Voorburgwal

Oudezijds Voorburgwal was the canal immediately inside (voor, 'in front of') the first city wall. Today it's a brash, brazen strip of porn shops, video booths and peep-shows, though some stylish gables and façades poke out above the lurid layer at street-level. Look out for: the diving dolphins opposite the Amstelkring; a mask- and bust-encrusted house by Hendrick de Keyser opposite the Oude Kerk; Africans and Indians relaxing on tobacco bales on the neck-gable at No.187; and an elegant neoclassical building by one of the three great 17th-century domestic architects, Philips Vingboons, at No.316.

At No.40 you'll find one of Amsterdam's most charming small museums, the **Amstelkring Museum** (*open Mon–Sat 10–5, Sun 1–5; adm*). Also known as Ons Lieve Heer op Solder (Our Lord in the Attic), the Amstelkring was a *'schuilkerk'*—a clandestine church. During the 17th and 18th centuries Roman Catholic services were illegal, but ever-tolerant Amsterdam turned a blind eye to what was going on behind domestic façades. The attic of the little spout-gabled house joins up with two others in the houses behind and was consecrated as a church in 1663. Inside the museum you can wander about an 18th-century reception room, into a classic 17th-century Dutch 'sael' (living-room) with symmetrical black and white marble flooring and a monumentally grand walnut fireplace, up through bedrooms with quaint box-shaped cupboard-beds, higher and higher to a small wooden staircase. Turn the corner at the top of the stairs and suddenly you're in what seems an enormous church with two galleries, light streaming in, an abundance of carving and painting and a voluptuous organ that must have been audible throughout the neighbourhood. The church is filled with treasures and mementoes of oppressed Catholicism (you can get an explanatory pamphlet downstairs). Try to get there early in the day, when you can appreciate the dream-like atmosphere in relative solitude.

Halfway down Oudezijds Voorburgwal the sleaze shops suddenly come to an end and you find yourself in a leafy nook of old Amsterdam. At No.300 is the Municipal Pawn Broker—the **Bank van Lening**, euphemized as 'Ome Jan' (Uncle John's). For the past three hundred years it has been a more sympathetic alternative to professional moneylenders—interest is fixed at a rate that corresponds to your ability to pay. Vondel, bankrupted by his playboy son, spent his septuagenarian years here as a clerk, going to work each day through a gateway that had one of his own poems inscribed in the arch. (It's still there, advising the rich to hurry past, as they have no business inside.)

Oudezijds Achterburgwal

Oudezijds Achterburgwal was the canal just outside (*achter*, 'behind') the first city boundary. Most of the buildings in this area are now part of the University of Amsterdam, but they were once (in the words of a 17th-century visitor) a collection of 'almshouses which look like princes' houses, hospitals for fools and houses where beggars, frequenters of taphouses, women who feign great bellies and men who pretend they have been taken by Turks' were confined and set to hard work.

These institutions, a product of prosperous and Calvinistic Amsterdam, were considered far-sighted and revolutionary by the rest of Europe. The gateway on the corner, copied from a Michelangelo design, led to the **Gasthuis** (hospital). A little further down you come to another elaborate arch, the entrance to the **Oudemanhuis**, an old men's almshouse. These days glass doors slide back as you approach and you find yourself in a dim arcade of second-hand bookstalls. Halfway along is a door that leads to the elegant almshouse courtyard. It's a private court belonging to the university, but nobody will stop you if you want to have a look.

The **Spinhuis** (on Spinhuissteeg) was a place where 'incorrigible and lewd women' were made to spin cloth for the poor. A rather alarming relief above the door shows women whipped with a cat-o'-nine-tails. Underneath is the not entirely convincing inscription:

> *Schrik niet, ik wreek geen quaat maar dwing tot goet.*
> *Straf is mijn hand, maar Lieflijk mijn gemoed.*
>
> *Cry not, for I exact no vengeance for wrong, but force you to be good.*
> *My hand is stern, but my heart is kind.*

The altruism of successive custodians seems to have been directed more towards passing gentlemen. For a small fee they were given access to the wicked inmates.

Modern attractions on Oudezijds Achternurgwal include the **Hash and Marijuana Museum**, at No.148 (*open daily 11am–10pm; adm*), devoted to a history of hemp and dope, and the **Tattoo Museum** at No.130 (*open Tues–Sun noon–6; adm*), which is not as tacky and sensationalist as one might expect, but a genuinely well-researched survey of the history of tattooing and body art in a variety of cultures.

Around the Nieuwmarkt

The Nieuwmarkt (New Market) is an open, brick-paved square that connects some of the more sinister alleys of the red-light district. Furtive men pop out of side streets, blink uncertainly in the bright light, then slip away. The police have cleared out the junkies and dealers who used to hang about the square, and it's been given a facelift. Now that the underworld is banished, Nieuwmarkt is moving upmarket. The once barren square is beginning to fill up with terraces and regain some of its old liveliness. On Sundays in the summer months there's a bustling antiques market and on feast days you can sometimes find a fairground or one of the old Dutch travelling dance halls.

A ring of modern street lamps, like giant mauve praying mantises, seem about to devour the solid medieval **St Antoniespoort** which huddles, flanked by dumpy towers, in the middle of the square. St Antoniespoort began life in 1488 as one of the main gates in the city wall. It was a popular spot for public executions. If you have a look on the south side you can see the rectangular holes (now bricked up) where the support beams of the scaffold slipped in. In one of the octagonal towers was a *galgekamertje* (little gallows room). From here the hapless prisoner got a foretaste of what was to happen to him: a small window looked out on the hangings, brandings and chopping off of bits going on a few feet below. In 1617 the gate was converted into a public weighing house. As all wholesale goods had to be weighed for taxes, 'De Waag' was the centre of trading activity. Liveried porters carried produce to and fro. Fierce armed guards were posted everywhere to keep an eye on the filling coffers and to arrest defaulters. (The sewer below the square was a highway for smugglers and bandits.) In 1691 St Antoniespoort housed the dissecting room of the Guild of Surgeons (cadavers being so conveniently at hand). You can just make out their inscription above the door in the south tower. On the other side bricklayers decorated the door to their guild room with elaborate wreaths of trowels. Today De Waag houses a trendy café.

Leading off Nieuwmarkt are Zeedijk and Geldersekade. In the 14th century **Zeedijk** marked the city limits. Modern Amsterdammers associate it with the *rode knipoog en witte kick* (the 'red wink' of prostitution and 'white kick' of heroin). A massive clean-up campaign by the council and police has turned most of Zeedijk into a respectable street of restaurants and galleries.

The timber house at No.1 is one of the oldest buildings in the city and one of the two remaining wooden buildings in central Amsterdam. It was built in 1550 as a seamen's hostel. The innkeeper allowed sailors who'd drunk or gambled away their wages to leave pet monkeys in payment. The hostel became infested with apes and fleas and became known as 'In 't Aepjen': you could always spot the poor scratching seamen who'd slept 'in the monkeys'. The Dutch still say of someone who is in difficulty that they have *in de aap gelogeerd* (literally, 'stayed in the monkey'). **In 't Aepjen** is now a café. The drinking-houses on the right-hand side of **Geldersekade** were notorious. A 17th-century British ambassador to the Netherlands was horrified: 'There are tolerated in the city of Amsterdam, amongst other abuses, at least 50 musick-houses where lewd persons of both sexes meet to practise their villainies.' His moral outrage didn't preclude him from having a detailed knowledge of the prices and opening times of the 'Long Seller', a public meeting house where 'rogues and whores make their filthy bargains'. The red-light district has moved fractionally eastward and Geldersekade is now the backbone of Amsterdam's small Chinatown.

At the northern end of Geldersekade is the **Schreierstoren** (built 1480), a dwarfish brick tower with a pixie-hat roof. It's one of the few remnants of Amsterdam's first city wall. Romantics maintain the tower gets its name because sailors' wives would gather on the battlements to see the men off the sea. Well might they weep and wave. Voyages could take up to four years and, on average, two-thirds of the men who set off never returned. More pedantic linguists point out that '*schreier*' comes from the old Dutch word for 'astride' or 'angle' and that the tower straddles two canals. The romantics win: a stone tablet on the wall depicts the wailing wives. Henry Hudson also has a plaque, as it was from here, in 1609, that he went off to discover a new route to the East Indies and found Manhattan instead, giving his name to the Hudson River. The Schreierstoren was originally a solid defence tower; the top storey, windows and doors were all added later. Nowadays it houses a café.

Amsterdam Historical Museum

Kalverstraat 92; open Mon–Fri 10–5, Sat and Sun 11–5; adm.

Situated in the old Burgerweeshuis, a home founded in 1520 for orphans, the Amsterdam Historical Museum offers an accessible introduction to the city's history. In the quiet loggia and courtyard of what was the boys' section, now a café, the boys' wooden lockers are still visible in the wall. Through the next arch is the girls' courtyard, a sober red brick court with sensible Ionic pilasters. The girls had their own gate, on the right side of the courtyard. The thrifty governors transferred it stone by stone from a building that was being demolished nearby and had a mason carefully alter the date stone from 1571 to 1634. Boys and girls were effectively kept separate by an open sewer that ran between their respective dormitories. The sewer has been covered and the resulting passageway converted into a promenade gallery for civic guard portraits which are too big to hang anywhere else (not particularly riveting viewing).

Inside the museum proper, the exhibition is arranged chronologically from Amsterdam's foundation right up to the 20th century and, armed with a file of English explanations of all the exhibits (free from the ticket desk), you can skim round quickly or stop to pick up details . A map on the ground floor lights up in sections showing different phases of Amsterdam's growth. There's a sudden expansion in the Golden Age and an even bigger one in the late 20th century, after which all the lights go out with an alarming thud. You can get a bird's eye view of early Amsterdam from a medieval painting (quite a feat of imagination for an artist who had never been higher than the top of the Oude Kerk tower); see a collection of the surprisingly basic navigational instruments that guided the Dutch East Indiamen all over the world; and push buttons that make period music come out from behind models and paintings. There's a whole room of paintings, banners and relics connected with Amsterdam's 'miracle' (*see* pp.55 and 67). Up a spiral staircase at the top of the building you can listen to recordings of the city's various carillons and even have a go at playing the one taken from the medieval Munttoren (*see* p.76)—though if you get too carried away an attendant clambers up to glower at you. The museum also stages excellent temporary exhibitions on aspects of Amsterdam's history.

The Begijnhof

The Begijnhof has the atmosphere of a quiet village square. You can hardly believe, in the leafy calm walled in by its neat gables, that the busiest parts of the city are only a few metres away. The Béguines were an order of lay nuns, founded in the 15th century, who, through self-effacement and powerful family connections, remained undisturbed by the religious upheavals of the following centuries. Sister Antonia, the last of the order, died in the house at No.26 in 1971. The small mound near the gate (covered by flowers in the spring) is the grave of another Béguine, Sister Cornelia Arens. When she died in 1654 she was buried, at her own request, in the gutter. Most of the houses were rebuilt in the 17th and 18th centuries, but at No.34 you can see the last remaining original façade, one of only two medieval wooden houses left in Amsterdam. Next door is an old clandestine church which still holds weekly mass. The church across the pathway was the original Begijnkerk, consecrated in 1419 and the only medieval church in the city with the tower in its original state. After a period of disuse during the Reformation, it was offered to Protestant dissenters fleeing England in 1607 and became known as the **English Church**. A plaque on the tower and stained glass in the chancel commemorate the fact that this group formed the core of the Pilgrim Fathers who sailed for America in 1620.

Some of Amsterdam's most enduringly popular cafés lie just outside the Begijnhof, around the Spui. At the southern end of this attractive square, the diminutive statue of *Het Lieverdje* ('The Little Darling', an impish Amsterdam rascal) was the focal point of provocative 'happenings' in the 1960s (*see* p.57). Down Voetboogstraat is the outrageous gate of the old **Rasphuis**, the male equivalent of the Spinhuis, where men had to saw wood into a fine powder used for dye. Carved figures are tied down by real chains. A castigating Amsterdam raises her hand high, but someone has pinched her flail. The Calvinist custodians of the Rasphuis thought up a most ingenious method of compelling the inmates to good soul-saving work. A 17th-century British consul in Amsterdam was much impressed: 'They are beaten with a bull's pissel [penis] and if yet they rebel and won't work, are set in a tub, where if they do not pump, the water will swell over their heads.'

Central Amsterdam (East)

The Flower Market and Rembrandtplein

After all the fuss that's made about it in the brochures, Amsterdam's **floating flower market** can be a bit of a disappointment. It's not very long, not all that cheap, you can't tell from the street that it's floating, and it's full of confused tourists clutching maps and asking each other: 'Is this it?' But the buckets of cut flowers and rows of potted plants are pretty to look at, and on hot days the mingling scents of the flowers fill the whole passage. If you're a keen gardener there's a tempting variety of seeds and bulbs that can be posted home (but *see* p.5).

At the eastern end of the market you come to **Muntplein** and the **Munttoren** (Mint Tower), a solitary clock tower with a polygonal base, that is yet another steeple by Hendrick de Keyser—a verticomaniac responsible for nearly every spike on Amsterdam's skyline. The base dates from 1490 and was part of Regulierspoort, one of the gates in the old city wall. The structure gets its name because the guard house was briefly used as a mint in 1672–3, when the French were occupying much of the rest of the Netherlands and the Amsterdam merchants couldn't get at their usual source of Rijksdollars and ductatoons.

Nieuwe Kerk

De Bijenkorf

DAM

DAMRAK STG

Koninklijk Paleis

Voorburgwal

NIEUW MARKT Ⓜ

Montelbaanstoren

KALVERSTRAAT

NES

Oudezijds

OUDE DOELEN STR.

Burgwal

Post Office

STANTONIESBREESTRAAT

ROKIN

NES

De Pinto House Ⓜ

Oude Schans

GRIMBURGWAL

Zuiderkerk

ST. ANT.

JODENBREESTRAAT

Klovenier-

SPUI

KALVERSTRAAT

HAUTBOOGSTRAAT

VOETBOOGSTRAAT

ROKIN

KLOVENIERSBURGWAL

GROENBURGWAL

Zwanenburgwal

Rembrandt huis Ⓜ

Fleamarket WATERLOOPLEIN

Moses en Aäronkerk MR VISSER PLEIN

Portuguese-Israelite Synago

NWE DOELENSTRAAT

STAALSTRAAT

Stopera

MUIDERSTRAAT

SINGEL

AMSTEL

Binnenamstel

TURFSTG Ⓜ

JONAS DANIEL MEIJER PLEIN

Munttoren

Flower Market

Tuschinski Cinema

VIJZELSTRAAT

REMBRANDT-PLEIN

Jewish Historical Museum Ⓜ

N

Herengracht HERENGRACHT

Amstel

WEESPERSTRAAT

Amstelhof

100 metres
100 yards

Halfway along Reguliersbreestraat—the road that conects Muntplein and Rembrandtplein—you'll find the **Tuschinski Cinema**. Abraham Tuschinski, a Jewish refugee from Poland, saw his first film in 1910 and immediately wanted to own a cinema. He got a friend to write to Pathé in French, requesting the machinery and rights to show films. His first 'bioscope' opened in 1911 in a disused seamen's church with a converted outside lavatory as the box office. But Tuschinski wanted a cinema where his 'guests' could lose themselves in another world. In 1921 he achieved his dream. You walk through a soaring Art Deco façade with flagpoles, camp statuary and curly iron lamps into an interior that lurches between heady luxury and high kitsch. It's a stylistic cocktail of five different colours of marble, Persian carpets, thousands of electric lights, wall decorations, stained glass and exotic *objets d'art*. You can go on a guided tour (*Sun and Mon during July and Aug, 10.30am; adm*), or come back later and see a film. Ask for a balcony ticket in the main cinema. On the first Sunday of each month during the winter, there's a special morning screening of a silent movie, with music from the original Wurlitzer organ.

The concrete and glass **Cineac** (opposite the Tuschinski) seems from another century. It's hard to believe it was built only 13 years later. The architect, J. Duiker, was a movie fanatic. The auditorium opened directly on to the street and the projectionist could be seen from outside through the glass wall on the first floor. Rebuilding in the 1960s and 1980s all but destroyed the original concept. In the late 1990s Cineac got yet another facelift, this time emerging as a restaurant in the Planet Hollywood chain owned, appropriately, by a group of movie stars.

Reguliersbreestraat opens on to **Rembrandtplein**, which was a butter market until the mid-19th century when a group of worthy burghers plonked a statue (Amsterdam's first) in the middle and grew some grass around it. Cafés sprang up. Variety artists from the halls along the Amstel would meet their agents at the posh Café Kroon, then retreat across the square to the darker recesses of the Hotel Schiller where they felt more at home among the artists, writers and other friends of proprietor Frits Schiller (whose paintings still decorate the walls). Nowadays the square is a favourite after-work stopover and a magnet to tourists, who come for the relaxed Amsterdam conviviality. You can lie about on the grass (among masses of tulips if it's spring) or sit and drink at one of the pavement cafés. Traffic is banished from most of the square but buskers keep the noise level high. When the sun sets, things get even livelier. The cafés change gear as the night staff come on duty. Music systems are turned on full, jazz from one corner, Dutch sing-along from another. Congas of drunken Dutchmen snake out of pubs and around bemused policemen. Spanish schoolgirls move about in wide-eyed groups. At one bar the three barmen break out at intervals into a well-rehearsed dance routine. Whether you're carousing with the revellers, or just sitting and watching it all, it's a cheerful place to stop for a drink.

Waterlooplein

Waterlooplein was originally the manmade island of Vlooyenburg, so named because the Amstel flooded it with monotonous regularity. (*Vlooyen* means 'flow', and also 'fleas', which seems rather more appropriate these days as Waterlooplein is the site of a fleamarket.) Vlooyenburg was built on a sandbank in the Amstel in 1593, and soon became a popular neighbourhood for Sephardic Jews arriving from Spain and Portugal. In the mid-17th century they were joined by the Ashkenazim (from eastern and central Europe), and Vlooyenburg became the heart of the Jewish quarter. Despite its sogginess, it was at first quite well-to-do. Prosperous Sephardim lived along the water's edge but, with the great influx of poorer Ashkenazim, buildings were constantly subdivided and more and more people were crammed into less and less space. The economic decline of the 18th and 19th centuries made conditions even worse. A contemporary traveller complained that everywhere there were 'horrible piles of excrement and offal, the walls around drenched with urine'. Later in the 19th century, however, the economy boomed and conditions improved. In 1882 the council reclaimed more land, and filled up two canals to create a large market square to replace the squalid, crowded network of alleys. In 1886 the clusters of market traders who had overrun the side streets were moved to the newly created Waterlooplein. There was much grizzling because it was so open and windy (an objection you're sure to sympathize with if the weather is bad) but soon the market had the reputation of being the busiest and most cheerful in Amsterdam.

The district was devastated during the Nazi occupation. Convoys of trucks would rumble into the market and cart away hundreds of people at a time. Of the 130,000 Jews living in Amsterdam in 1938 (10 per cent of the total population), 100,000 did not survive the war. The empty houses they left behind were stripped of anything burnable during the freezing winters. For a long time the old Jewish quarter lay empty and derelict, as if the buildings themselves were in a state of shock.

When the city council announced plans (in 1979) to build a combined city hall and opera house on the site, there was public outrage. The city hall was ugly, the opera house seemed unnecessary, and the few people still living in the neighbourhood would have to be evicted. The building was nicknamed the **Stopera**—from *stadhuis* (city hall) and opera. 'Stop the Stopera' campaigns were held all over Amsterdam but, as always, the council won.

The new **Muziektheater** (the opera house) opened in 1986, followed two years later by the Stadhuis. The city hall is indeed bland and ugly, but most Amsterdammers grudgingly admit to the beauty of the Muziektheater. Its glass walls, sweeping stairways, soft pink colour scheme and marble coliseum-like shell look their best in the early evening. As the light fades, the whole building seems to glow. The artists themselves are delighted with the state-of-the-art equipment and huge dressing rooms. There are even colour-coded stairways backstage (yellow for opera, pink for ballet and blue for technicians). But there were some massive architectural blunders backstage as well—the ballet rehearsal rooms have ceilings so low that dancers couldn't practise lifts, the orchestra didn't have a rehearsal room at all and the scenery lifts were at the opposite end of the building from the loading entrances. Both the Netherlands Ballet and Opera are resident, and the programme is varied, with many international visitors (*see* p.134, 'Entertainment and Nightlife').

In a passageway connecting the Stadhuis and Muziektheater three water columns show the tides at IJmuiden and Vlissingen (below knee-level) and the sobering sight of the level reached during the 1953 Zeeland flood (way above your head). You can walk down a flight of stairs, below sea level, and touch the bronze knob (its position was calculated in the 17th century) which represents the zero point from which heights in much of the rest of Europe are calculated.

Around the Stopera stretches Amsterdam's famous **fleamarket**. There's a wonderful lack of logic in its layout and a pervasive air of bargain-hunting and money-making. Antiquarian book-sellers rub shoulders with purveyors of used porn. Lines of Peruvians, Balinese and Indonesians sell bright national clothing and jewellery. There are heaps of mildewy second-hand overcoats and racks of precision-selected designer classics, tables of used kitchenware and haphazard conglomerations of expensive antiques. The rows of oddities and exotica are punctuated by more down-to-earth stalls selling bicycle parts, underwear or cleaning equip-ment. A fringe of derelicts gathers around the edge of the market, returning day after day with little spreads of unwanted (and sometimes unidentifiable) bric-a-brac. In one corner a muttering clump of old men surreptitiously flash watches and bits of gold at each other. A relentless stream of collectors, tourists, Amsterdammers looking for bargains and the openly curious flows up and down between the stalls.

Around Waterlooplein

The eastern corner of the fleamarket is dominated by the **Mozes en Aäron Kerk**. In 1649 it was a clandestine Roman Catholic church, named after the gable stones (one depicting Moses and the other Aaron) on the two house-fronts that hid it. The present rather heavy-looking neoclassical church (with wooden towers painted to look like sandstone) was built in the 19th century, but you can still see the original gable stones round the back. The church was famous for its choir and even the local Jews would come in for the music on Christmas night. The Jewish philosopher Spinoza lived in the house next door to the original church; the Sephardic community excommunicated him for his secular beliefs, but regretted their haste when he went on to become one of the most lauded intellectuals of his time.

Diagonally across from the church is the **Oudezijds Huiszittenhuis** (the rather Dickensian-sounding 'Old Side Home for the Domiciled Poor', built in 1654). The Alms Board Wardens would enter through a grand public staircase on the other side of the building. Paupers would huddle for hours in the courtyard waiting for handouts of bread, cheese and peat. The peat was stored next door in the Arsenaal (built 1610), and the road down the side of this warehouse is still called Turfsteeg (Peat Alley).

Off the northern end of the market, on Jodenbreestraat, is the **Rembrandthuis** (*open Mon–Sat 10–5, Sun and holidays 1–5; adm*). Rembrandt lived at Jodenbreestraat 4–6 for nearly twenty years (*see* pp.92–3) and his old house is now a museum. It has been carefully restored to its original state, using old plans and descriptions to ensure authenticity. In the adjoining modern wing you can see the pick of Rembrandt's etchings, including a series of tiny self-portraits of the painter pulling funny faces. Rembrandt used himself as a model more than any other 17th-century painter. He even slips into crowd scenes on some of his larger canvases. There's a slide-show on Rembrandt's life, in English, in the basement (hourly on the hour until 3pm).

Following St Antoniesbreestraat north from the Rembrandthuis, you come to the skull-and-crossbones adorned churchyard gate of the **Zuiderkerk** (*open Mon–Fri 12.30–4.30, Thurs 6–9; tower open June–Sept Wed–Sat 2pm–4pm, adm*), built between 1603 and 1614, which was the first Protestant church to be built after the Reformation, and is a triumph of Amsterdam's great steeple designer, Hendrick de Keyser. The soaring spire with its decorative Ionic columns and its clusters of slightly oriental pinnacles was much admired by Christopher Wren, and inspired the designs of his City of London churches. During the harsh winter of 1944–5 more people died in the neighbourhood than the authorities were able to bury, and the church had to be used as a temporary mortuary. Today it's a deeply uninteresting information centre for urban development.

Northeast of the church, on Oude Schans, is the **Montelbaanstoren**, a defence tower built in 1512 when the wharves were still outside the city walls. In 1606 (when the tower was no longer used for defence) the builder Hendrick de Keyser added a wonderfully gratuitous spire. This was an activity he apparently enjoyed: he's responsible for much of Amsterdam's spiky skyline. Five years after it was built, the Montelbaanstoren began to tilt over. Unlike their more flamboyant counterparts in Pisa, the good burghers of Amsterdam would have none of it: they attached ropes to the top and pulled it straight again. Rembrandt loved to draw it, and it's still a favourite subject for visiting artists. VOC sailors left from the Montelbaanstoren to join the large seafaring East Indiamen which were too bulky to navigate as far as Amsterdam and were moored far to the north. These days it houses the city water authority.

The Synagogues

Amsterdammers nickname their city 'Mokum', from the Yiddish '*Mokum aleph*', 'the best city of all', and they'll often leave you with a cheery '*de mazzel*'—'good luck'. As early as the 16th century, Amsterdam's religious tolerance was attracting Jews fleeing persecution in other European countries. This tolerance stemmed less from the milk of Christian kindness than from sound commercial reasoning. The Sephardic Jews brought good inside information on Portuguese colonies and trade routes. The Ashkenazim had skills that fuelled the Golden Age boom. The city's trade guilds, however, refused to admit Jews and so Jews could only find work in fields that did not present direct competition to locals. Many were physicians or apothecaries, or worked in high-risk finance and in the new trades associated with the cotton or diamond industries. But they could retain their religion and didn't have to live in ghettos or wear distinguishing badges. Amsterdam soon became known as the 'Jerusalem of the West'.

To the east of Waterlooplein, a complex of four old Ashkenazi synagogues now houses the **Jewish Historical Museum** (*open daily 11–5 except Yom Kippur; adm*).The Ashkenazim, fleeing pogroms in Poland and massacres in Germany, arrived in Amsterdam in the mid-17th century. They soon outnumbered the Sephardim (who had begun arriving half a century earlier) by ten to one, but were pitifully poorer. They really had to struggle to build themselves a synagogue. Just as they were about to begin, their attention was diverted by Sabbatai Zvi, a false Messiah who claimed he would lead them back to the Holy Land. They waited for four years before giving up on him and building the Grote Sjoel (Grand Synagogue) in 1671. As the congregation expanded, more temples were built on adjacent plots. The Obbene Sjoel (Upstairs Synagogue, 1686) was followed by the Dritt Sjoel (Third Synagogue, 1700). The Neie Sjoel (New Synagogue, 1752) opened with great ceremony. Tickets were sold at an outrageous ƒ10 (though crowds of poor were let in for free). Ashkenazi Congregation records revel in the pomp of the occasion and bristle with anti-Sephardic rivalry: 'An orchestra pit has been placed next to the bima (raised central platform), where the musicians took their places with their music. Below that there was an uncircumcised musician playing a contrabass and for the rest only Jews who played for free and even one Portuguese Jew.' The complex was gutted during the Second World War and remained empty until the 1980s, when the temples were restored and reopened as the historical museum.

The museum's displays do not dwell on gruesome images of the Holocaust and tales of woe, but are a combination of works of art, memorabilia and artefacts aimed at explaining Jewish life. Naturally it is moving to see one of the yellow stars Jews had to wear during the war, but the museum also diffuses a positive energy from the delicately embroidered prayer shawls, photographs of Bar Mitzvahs and overwhelmingly extravagant silverware also on show. The 'Jewish identity' displays in the New Synagogue explain aspects of tradition, Zionism and the reaction to persecution. Most of the Great Synagogue is given over to expositions of the religion itself—the rituals, festivals and rites of passage. You can see the original Mikveh (ritual bath) unearthed during the renovations, a rather cute circumcision set and some stylish modern temple silverware. In the galleries of the Great Synagogue paintings and old documents illustrate the history of Jews in Amsterdam. The connecting walkways house temporary exhibitions and work by Jewish artists (Jaap Kaas's fierce, funny bronze monkeys are worth looking for). The museum also has a library and media centre, a kosher café and a good bookshop.

Across the way from the museum is the **Portuguese-Israelite Synagogue** (*open April–Oct, Sun–Fri 10–4; Nov–March Mon–Thurs 10–4, Fri 10–3, Sun 10–12; adm*). There was little love lost between the Sephardim and Ashkenazim. Even today old Sephardic Jews can remember being warned off '*vrotte Tedesco*' (filthy Germans) with: '*Je kan nog beter met een Goya trouwen dan met een Tedesco.*' ('Rather marry a gentile than an Ashkenazi.') The Sephardim were a smaller but more powerful community with a class of wealthy professionals, and were happily welcomed into Dutch society. Their Portuguese-Israelite Synagogue (or 'Snoge' after the Spanish *esnoga*) was built between 1671 and 1675 as a showpiece. It was more than twice the size of the Ashkenazi temple completed the year before on the site next door. Only in Amsterdam could Jews make such an open display of their place of worship.

There was no established building style for synagogues, and the architect, Elias Bouman (who had also designed the Ashkenazi building), claimed he was creating an imitation of Solomon's temple following descriptions in the Old Testament. However, the building he produced, with its mahogany pews and brass chandeliers, bears a remarkable resemblance to the larger Christian churches of the period. It's an imposing brick block that dwarfs the buildings around it. The Hebrew letters of the name 'Aboab' are worked into the text above the door (which translates as 'And I—in Thy great love—shall enter Thy House') in acknowledgement of Rabbi Isaac Aboab de Fonseca's efforts to get the synagogue built.

Beside the synagogue is a peaceful square, the **Jonas Daniël Meijerplein**. Jonas Daniël Meijer (1780–1834) whizzed through his school years and was a Doctor of Law by the time he was 16. He was the first Jew admitted to the Bar and one of the first to fight for and get full Dutch citizenship. As a favourite of the potty but enlightened Louis Bonaparte and under William I, Meijer did a lot to improve the legal position of the Jews. In the middle of the square, standing stalwartly, his sleeves rolled up and chin cocked defiantly—ready for a fight—is Mari Andriessen's bronze statue **De Dokwerker** (The Dockworker, 1952). Every year on 25 February people lay flowers at its feet to commemorate the resistance to Nazi occupation. This is the anniversary of the general strike which swept through a shocked Amsterdam in a matter of hours as an expression of solidarity with the Jews after the first Nazi round-ups. During his brief spell as a theology student in Amsterdam, Van Gogh could be seen 'with his books clamped under his arm, holding snowdrops in his left hand in front of his chest, his head stooped forward slightly', making his way across this square to the third floor of the house at No.13, where he studied classics with Mendes da Costa for ƒ1.50 a lesson. (The original house has been demolished.)

The Canals

Amsterdam's population increased tenfold between 1550 and 1650. In the early 17th century the far-sighted city fathers were already planning to push the city boundaries outwards with three grand concentric canals. The Prinsengracht (Princes' Canal), Keizersgracht (Emperor's Canal) and Herengracht (Gentlemen's Canal, rather than Kings', a nice move by bourgeois Amsterdam) were intended for rentiers and rich merchants who wanted to live away from the smells and noise of the harbour. The shops and industries there were banished to poorer parts of town. The city hall parcelled out the land in 30ft, rather than the usual 20ft lots (though wily speculators would buy up two adjacent plots and split them into three and the really opulent merchants would combine two into a single house). Space was at a premium in Amsterdam and you were taxed on the width of your house, so height often became an expression of wealth and the boastful decoration was applied to the inside, or to the gables. Even the rear façades got special attention. ('Our Lord finished off a canary's behind as neatly as its front,' remarked one contemporary architect.) Narrow houses mean winding stairways, uncongenial to four-poster beds and heavy carved dressers, hence most Amsterdam buildings have a hoist beam poking out from the gable so you can winch your furniture up the outside. Many lean dangerously over the street, not necessarily because they're about to subside into the city's soggy soil, but because this shows off the gables to passing pedestrians and makes the building more imposing. It also stops rising furniture from crashing into the wall. Angles became so alarming that a bye-law was introduced in 1565 to put a stop to the more adventurous tilts.

The Herengracht

Fashion has claimed each canal, at one time or another, as Amsterdam's best address, but it was the Herengracht that was really built to impress. It's more grand than pretty, a little ravaged by centuries of ostentation. Subsequent occupiers have (until recently) thought nothing of pulling down old buildings to make way for bigger and better displays of wealth, but the survivors have an endearing panache. Some extraordinary gables poke up out of the trees that line the canal. Monumental sandstone frontages seem to push aside the traditional dainty gabled brick façades. Cornices curled with acanthus leaves, strung with garlands and surmounted by urns lord it over the modest step-gables, though the odd defiant bell or neck-gable might reply with an extravagant claw-piece.

At No.120 you can see one of the few smaller 17th-century houses to have kept its façade free of later additions and amendments. Farther along, at Nos.170–2 is the Bartolotti House, built in 1617 by Hendrick de Keyser (who designed most of Amsterdam's spiky towers) for West India Company director Van den Heuvel. (It was paid for by Van den Heuvel's mother-in-law who stipulated the house be called after her late husband.) Its enormous neck-gable is all but invisible under the encrustation of pilasters, pinnacles and decorative reliefs. These days part of it houses the **Nederlands Theater Instituut** (*open Tues–Fri 11–5, Sat and Sun 1–5; adm*) which always has good exhibitions, usually of the sort where you push buttons or pull levers and make things happen. If there are three of you, you can raise a storm with the wind, thunder and lightning machines on the ground floor.

The white sandstone house next door (known as the White House), built in 1668, was the first by the later famous 17th-century domestic architect, Philips Vingboons. The dignified row of four houses (Nos.364–70) farther down the canal, with clean lines, stately neck-gables and quiet decoration are also by Vingboons.

At No.366 is the **Bijbels Museum** (Bible Museum; *open Mon–Sat 10–5, Sun 1–5; adm; partially closed for renovation until late 2000*) worth a visit only if you are interested in models of Solomon's temple and the history of the Dutch Bible over the past millennium—though the interior does preserve ceiling paintings by the 18th-century design supremo Jacob de Wit.

No.380–2 is an outrageous confection—a late 19th-century imitation of a French Renaissance château scrunched down to city mansion size. Just up the canal is a pretty little 17th-century house with a simple festooned neck-gable (No.394), and across the way, No.401 manages to lean in three different directions at once.

The bit of the canal between Vijzelstraat and Leidsestraat is known as the **Golden Bend**, perhaps more for the wealth of the inhabitants than the refinement of the architecture. There are two clusters of more gorgeous and more graceful dwellings further up the canal that better deserve the epithet, though the elegant Louis XIV building with curved balustrades at No.475 does have the reputation of being Amsterdam's most beautiful house.

Amsterdam *burgemeesters* have been officially resident at No.502 since 1927, and next door (Nos.504–10) is a little stretch of wildly decorative claw-pieces. Tigers, dolphins and seagods curl about the gables and for once upstage the grander buildings.

At No.605, you'll come to the **Willet-Holthuysen Museum** (*open Mon–Fri 10–5, Sat and Sun 11–5; adm*), a 17th-century canal house. For two centuries it was occupied by a succession of Amsterdam glitterati. The last, Sandrina Holthuysen, had spent most of her life married to Abraham Willet, an avid collector of paintings, art books, glass, ceramics and silver. When she died in 1895, alone, riddled with cancer and surrounded by cats, she left the house and contents to Amsterdam as a museum. The city then filled it with pickings from a number of similar bequests. Most of the rooms are now reconstructed as 18th-century period pieces, with the different collections scattered about the house, mainly in rather stiff salons and boudoirs; there's also a crisp formal garden. Everything seems in its Sunday best—including the surreal headless mannequins that stand strategically about, sporting 18th-century costume. It's a good place to get an insider's view of one of the more stately canal houses.

The Keizersgracht

Less ostentatious than the Herengracht, the Keizersgracht nevertheless offers some architectural gems. At No.319 you can see the first house (built in 1639) in which architect Philips Vingboons combined classic elements (the Doric pilasters) with the traditional Dutch style. Nearby is the imposing classicist **Felix Meritis building** (No.324 on the left-hand side; *open daily 5pm–midnight*). It was built in 1778 to house an arts and scientific society founded in the spirit of Voltaire and Rousseau. With an observatory, library, laboratories and a small concert hall, the Felix Meritis Foundation became the cultural centre of the Dutch Enlightenment. When Napoleon made his triumphal entry to Amsterdam, he was punted up the canal and ushered with pride into the building. He got no further than the foyer, spat on the floor, said the place stank of tobacco smoke, and strutted back to the boat. Towards the end of the 19th century the society went into terminal decline. The building was later used as the Communist Party headquarters, but won back its cultural prominence in the 1970s when it housed the Shaffy Theatre, in the forefront of the European avant-garde. The theatre lost some of its significance and impact during the 1980s, but the Felix Meritis Society has been revived. As an arts complex and the home of Amsterdam's Summer University, the building is once again playing host to artists and intellectuals from around the world.

A wander farther along the canal reveals more architectural delights. The startlingly large windows of No.440 (built 1897) originally lit a clothing design studio and factory. It must have been the world's most gracious sweatshop. The bank at No.452 was once a private residence. Designed by Outshoorn in 1860, it is one of the last of a series of grand canal houses, influenced by French and Italian architecture, that were built by the three great domestic architects—Vingboons, van Campen and Outshoorn—over a period of 200 years. At No.546 nothing of the façade, except the windows, has changed since it was built in 1760. The bell-gable is a good example of the playful cake-icing Louis XV decoration. The ornately decorated building that cuts the corner with Leidsestraat is German-inspired—the Dutch were more into solid right angles at corners. A frieze of fat naked babies, lurking in shrubberies and grumpily pushing carts and canoes, runs around the wall. The bust commemorates the 17th-century poet Pieter Cornelisz. Hooft. The pompous building on the opposite corner was built on the site of Van Gogh's uncle's art shop for an insurance company in the late 19th century, but is now the refined **Metz** department store. Inside, you can mount stairs, passing racks of tasteful kitchenware and mounds of Liberty prints. As you climb, the atmosphere becomes increasingly rarefied and the floors emptier and emptier. By the time you're nearing the top, there's hardly anything for sale at all. The few pieces of designer furniture scattered about look more like museum pieces than anything you could put in the dining-room. At the top is a café designed by Gerrit Rietveld. Gazing through its glass cupola, you have a rare opportunity to view Amsterdam's spider's web from on high. Back down on ground level, try to get to the **Van Loon Museum** at Keizersgracht 672 (*open Fri–Mon 11–5; adm*). The house still belongs to the Van Loon family (who live in a small apartment next door) and offers the best example of all of Amsterdam patrician home life.

The patch where the Keizersgracht crosses Nieuwe Spiegelstraat is renowned for its antiques shops and art galleries. Known as the **Spiegelkwartier**, this is one of the two quarters in Amsterdam dedicated to one particular business (the only other one being the red-light district). Here you'll find top-quality antiques galore—shops crammed with elaborate clocks, solemn rows of carved wooden dressers and ornate gilded furniture. Enormous chandeliers hang at eye-level, and gold, silver and colourful gems shine at you from all sides. Tucked amongst all this grandeur, you can still find idiosyncratic little shops, obviously the domain of a single collector. Aalderink (Spiegelgracht 15) has a sparse but expertly selected range of oriental pieces and Africana. Thom and Lenny Nelis (Keizersgracht 541) sell curious and unmentionable medical antiques. Anneke Schat (Spiegelgracht 20a) makes delicate, sculpted jewellery inspired by spiders' webs and butterflies and much favoured by Dutch glitterati and the royal family. If your souvenir budget runs to multiple noughts you could pop into Elisabeth den Bieman de Haas for a little Chagall litho or bright modern oil from COBRA, the post-war expressionist movement (*see* p.49). Roel Houwink (Nieuwe Spiegelstraat 57) has one of those shops you could potter about in for ages—everything from musical boxes to escutcheons nicked from under the nose of a Prince of Orange. Kramers (Nieuwe Spiegelstraat 64) has tangles of old jewellery and trinkets, barrels of clay pipe bowls and a roomful of Delft tiles ranging from the 15th to 20th centuries and costing anything from the price of a sandwich to double your air fare.

The Prinsengracht

The Prinsengracht is the site of one of the most enduring symbols of Amsterdam—the spire of the Westerkerk. The **Westerkerk** (West Church) was consecrated in 1631. Its sober Protestant interior is brightened by large painted organ shutters showing a dancing King David and a voluptuous Queen of Sheba laden with gifts for Solomon. Rembrandt was buried here, but no one knows where the body is to be found. There's a flutter of academic excitement every so often, each time old bones are found, but it's most likely that the master's remains was crunched up during the digging of an underground car park. A memorial plaque has been put up near his son Titus's grave. The church tower, known as the Westertoren, built by (you guessed it) Hendrick de Keyser, is Amsterdam's highest (85m) and contains its heaviest bell (7500kg). The Westertoren has something of the significance to Amsterdammers that St Paul's has to Londoners. Sentimental songs are addressed to it, and you can only be a true Jordaaner (*see* below) if you were born in its shadow. In the 1940s a fervent engineer climbed out on to the top of the tower during a violent storm and, with the help of a theodolite, worked out that it swayed all of 3cm. During the summer months you can climb up rather more sedately for a rare view of Amsterdam from high up (*open April–Sept, Mon–Sat 10–4; adm*). At the top is the gaudily painted imperial crown of Maximilian of Austria. Amsterdam's merchants gained considerable international clout when, out of gratitude for support given to the Austro-Burgundian princes, he granted them the right to use the crown in the city coat of arms.

If you walk around the outside of the church you can see the house where Descartes lived when he was in Amsterdam (Westermarkt 6); the pink marble triangles of the Homomonument which commemorates gays killed in the concentration camps; and a sad little statue of Anne Frank, who wrote her diary just around the corner.

The Anne Frank Huis

The Anne Frank Huis is at Prinsengracht 263 (*open Sept–May Mon–Sat 9–5, Sun 10–5; June–Aug Mon–Sat 9–7, Sun 10–7; adm*). Anne Frank, the second daughter of German-Jewish immigrants living in Amsterdam, got her diary for her 13th birthday on 12 June 1942. Three weeks later her family were '*onderduikers*' ('divers')—in hiding from the Nazi occupying forces. They lived for two years in a small suite of rooms at the back of Anne's father's herb and spice business on the Prinsengracht. The windows had always been painted over to protect the herbs previously stored there, the entrance was hidden behind a hinged bookcase and, apart from four trusted office workers who supplied them with food, nobody knew they were there. Later they were joined by a dentist Fritz Pfeffer (whom Anne calls 'Dussel') and the Van Pelses ('Van Daans') and their son Peter. For two years they were cooped up in what became known as the Annexe, and Anne wrote in her diaries about life with the petulant and demanding Mrs Van Daan and her hen-pecked spouse, of the tiresomely childish Dussel, and of moments of joy and desperation within her own family. No one knows who betrayed them, but in August 1944 German police barged into the offices, walked straight up to the bookcase and demanded entry. All the hideaways, except Anne's father, died in concentration camps in Germany. The office cleaner found the diary in which Anne had written with astonishing lucidity about life in the 'Annexe' and about growing up. When it was given to her father, he found that she'd already began to edit it for publication. It appeared in 1947 with the title *The Annexe*, the one Anne herself had chosen. Now it's printed in over 50 languages and an estimated thirteen million copies have been sold. Well over half a million people visit the Anne Frank Huis annually. The house has been restored to its pre-war condition, giving a moving impression of what life was like for the families who hid there. In new premises next door you'll find an exhibition on Jews in Amsterdam and racial oppression.

Towards the eastern end of the Prinsengracht, south of Rembrandtplein, you'll find **Amstelveld**, a secluded square with a white wooden church and small Monday flower market, tucked away from the surrounding bustle. The recently restored 17th-century **Amstelkerk** has a popular left-wing preacher and is the one of the few churches in central Amsterdam that packs in a congregation. It isn't continuously open to the public, but sometimes stages chamber recitals. In front of the church, crossing the Prinsengracht, runs the Reguliersgracht, held by many to be the prettiest canal in town with its quiet gables and humpback bridges.

De Negen Straatjes

Crisscrossing the main canals, De Negen Straatjes ('The Nine Alleys') offer the most intriguing shopping in Amsterdam. **Huidenstraat** has trendy second-hand clothes stores and shops crammed with lamps and light fittings—from original Art Nouveau to bright and bulbous 1960s products. Pompadour at No.5 sells impossibly tempting hand-made chocolates. Across the Keizersgracht bridge in **Runstraat** is the Witte Tanden Winkel (White Teeth

Shop) for nothing but the tooth—psychedelic and electric toothbrushes, pastes galore, curious aids and sound clinical advice. Just the place to expiate your sins after Pompadour. All along the way, furniture from antiques shops tumbles out into the streets, though they're not always as cheap as the image suggests. **Wolvenstraat** has more second-hand clothes shops (one with Queen Mother hats) and a button shop (some in such shapes and sizes that their function is barely recognizable). **Berenstraat** is home to some of the younger, trendier art galleries. One, Animation Art: 'Name that Toon' sells storyboards and cels (the acetate originals from which cartoons are made) of everyone from Betty Boop to Winnie-the-Pooh. Hartenstraat has more fashion shops and another eccentric collector's outlet—this time vintage electronic equipment. The jolly naked illustrations of Eddie Varekamp that have found their way on to T-shirts and coffee mugs are on sale from his studio shop (No.30). Reestraat has a *poppendokter* (doll's doctor). Puppets hang from the ceiling, dolls of all sorts crowd the window and a disconcerting catalogue of dolls' faces hangs on the wall. Next door is a candle shop. Coloured, scented, sculpted, altar candles and erotic candles hang from the ceiling, are stacked on shelves or poked into odd candlesticks and elaborate candelabra—and they're not at silly prices.

Leidesplein and Around

On the outer edge of the 'Canal Belt', Leidseplein is Amsterdam's tourist vortex, with more than the usual complement of British boys in Union Jack shorts learning the strength of Dutch lager. Fire-eaters and itinerant musicians busk while your pockets are picked, though at night the atmosphere improves a little as the square becomes the festive hub of late-night transport. As a 17th-century traveller cautioned, 'Here be sure to furnish yourself with money.' The neon alleys leading off the square are lined with expensive and nasty restaurants and night-clubs with names like 'Cash'. Leidsestraat, the northern exit, is clogged with pedestrians and bicycles travelling on no particular side until, bells clanging, a yellow tram hurtles down the central rails scattering all. Mainly airline offices, 24-hour bureaux de change and shops selling clogs and Taiwan Delft, Leidsestraat is happily avoided.

On the southern end of the square, is the **Stadsschouwburg** (Municipal Theatre; *open nightly; backstage tours in summer daily at noon; adm; duration 1hr*). State theatres in Amsterdam were usually out in the sticks, and kept burning down. The first one on this site was built in 1774 (when Leidseplein was on the edge of town) and, after suffering the usual fate, was replaced by the present building in the late 19th century. The new building was designed by Jan Springer, the bohemian kingpin of Architectura et Amicitia, a wickedly unrestrained artists' society. Budget cuts put a stop to his more florid decorations, yet still the public disapproved of the result. Springer went into a sulk and virtually abandoned his career. The building has a small stage and the new Muziektheater on Waterlooplein has rather stolen its thunder, but it continues to host local and international productions.

Next door, the jutting balconies and odd protruding windows of the **American Hotel** are a Dutch interpretation of an original Art Nouveau design. The architect, W. Kromhout, is considered a forerunner of the fanciful Amsterdam School (*see* p.112). The writers and artists who once frequented the Café Américain (*open daily 10am–midnight*) have fled the tourist armies of the Leidseplein, but it's still worth a visit for the glass Japanese parasol lampshades and patterned windows that filter the hard Amsterdam light into a soft and playful kaleidoscope.

The inviting side streets, alleys and intimate canals of the Jordaan are lined with cosy cafés, curious shops and good restaurants. Jordaan comes from the French '*jardin*', but during the housing crisis in the 19th century this 'garden' on the outskirts of the city disappeared under rows of working-class housing. The houses were small, dark and close together and all the smellier industries (such as tanning) were banished to the Jordaan from the posher areas of town. Naming the streets after flowers didn't cheer things up much. Conditions were appalling, but the Jordaaners developed a pride and a culture akin to London's cockneys.

The true Jordaaner is born in the small patch bound by Prinsengracht, Brouwersgracht, Lijnbaansgracht and Looiersgracht, in the shadow of the Westertoren (*see* inside back cover map). The church tower is the symbol of the Jordaan. Jordaaners have their own accent and are renowned for a wry sense of humour and for being adept pigeon-fanciers. Everyone over the age of forty is known as '*ome*' or '*tante*'—uncle or aunt. (Until a decade or so ago, you could still be woken by Ome Hein, a professional 'waker-up', as he made his early morning rounds with a pet goat.) They're a rebellious lot. There have been a number of historical riots, including one in 1886 when police tried to put a stop to the gory-sounding pastime of 'eel-jerking'; and another when the council threatened to reduce the dole in 1934. Recently, traditional Jordaan life has been given a new edge by an influx of artists and music students. You're quite likely to be accompanied on your walk by strains of Mozart and will probably encounter odd art objects suspended over the street.

Lovers of curiosa and antiques should head for the area around **Looiersgracht**. At No.38 is the Rommelmarkt (literally 'rubbish market'), an indoor fleamarket that seems almost subterranean. Entering through a small street door, you seem to walk forever down a long, dim corridor lined with piles of old toys, tea caddies, zippo lighters, 1960s records and magazines. The further you penetrate, the more precious things become. You might even pick up some antique Japanese lacquerware or an Art Deco vase.

At the end of the canal you come to the **De Looier Indoor Antiques Market**, a collectors' and dealers' market pitched halfway between Rommelmarket junk and Spiegelkwartier splendour. Stallholders have a lively commercial spirit—they even have their own newspaper and weekly bridge drives. There are regular specialist fairs in this honeycomb of little stands selling furniture, glass, old lace and even older Delftware. Marking the northeastern corner of the Jordaan is the **Noordermarkt**. The square is quiet, and usually empty, but if you come back early on a Monday morning you'll find a crush of trendies, students and down-and-outs at Amsterdam's cheapest clothes market. The Noorderkerk was Hendrick de Keyser's last church and, as befits an old man, is solemn and austere with only the teeniest of spires.

The northern boundary of the Jordaan is formed by the **Brouwersgracht** (Brewers' Canal). This is quintessential Amsterdam; the canal's neat, gabled houses, humped bridges and shady towpaths feature in almost every brochure intended to lure you to the city. Yet the crowds that tramp up and down the grand canals seem to pass it by. There are no neon lights or noisy cafés. It's a quiet, residential canal for the hopelessly romantic. Most of the houses are converted warehouses. In the 17th century this canal, right at the harbour's edge, seethed with traders and reeked of fish and beer. Stockfish warehouses and no fewer than 24 breweries crowded its banks. Amsterdam had to import fresh water from the surrounding countryside to feed its industries and populace. Most of the long flat boats carrying this water entered the city along the Brouwersgracht, so breweries sprang up along the canal that afforded them the pick of the incoming supplies. Just off Brouwersgracht, the small square of the Herenmarkt is dominated by **Westindisch Huis** (West India House). The dumpy red-brick exterior dates from the 19th century, when it was rebuilt as a Lutheran orphanage. Nowadays it's an adult education college, but you can usually nip in for a glimpse of the 17th-century courtyard—the only remnant of the building's romantic past as headquarters of the West India Company. In the courtyard there's a memorial to Peter Stuyvesant, the notoriously grouchy peg-legged Governor of Nieuw Amsterdam—the Company's chief American trading post. In 1664 he surrendered the settlement to the British, who renamed it New York.

From the eastern end of the canal you can see the enormous copper dome of the old Lutherse Kerk (Lutheran Chuch). The church (also known as the **Ronde Lutherse Kerk**—Round Lutheran Church) was built in 1668 by Adriaan Dortsman, a leading light of the appropriately named Restrained Dutch Classicists. A careless plumber caused a fire which burnt it down in 1822; it was rebuilt the following year and was used as a church until the early 1930s, when dwindling congregations resulted in its closure. After some years of disuse, the church was converted into a conference hall for the hotel across the road, but in 1993 it burned down again. The gutted building cost ƒ4 million to restore and opened for business again in 1995. The round brick walls look impenetrable (conference delegates reach it through an underground tunnel).

The Museum Area

Museumplein

Amsterdam's (if not the nation's) greatest cultural institutions border Museumplein—the Rijksmuseum and Concertgebouw at either end, the Van Gogh and Stedelijk Museums up one side. Until recently Museumplein was bisected by a busy road nicknamed 'Europe's's shortest motorway', and was windswept, deserted and nasty. But dramatic re-landscaping in the late 1990s created a green and stylish spot with a long pool, a café and underground garages that suck up all the cars and coaches.

As you wander through the square, stop briefly to look at the Vrouwen van Ravensbrück memorial, a series of vertical steel slabs erected to commemorate the 92,000 women who died in concentration camps during the Second World War. The text translates as 'For those women who until the bitter end refused to accept fascism.' The flickering light and thumping sound emanating from the sculpture are intended as a beacon to call people to the monument and to continue the fight.

The Rijksmuseum

Open daily 10–5; adm exp, with free floor-plan. If there's a long queue at the ticket office, nip around the back to the entrance to the new South Wing, where there is usually hardly anyone waiting at all. There is an excellent guided tour to the museum on CD-ROM, obtainable on the shop level for ƒ7.50. You can walk around at your own pace, punching in codes to learn more about individual paintings and, if you wish, tapping ever deeper into more detailed background information. The CD comes with a printed suggestion of 15 paintings to see if you're in a hurry.

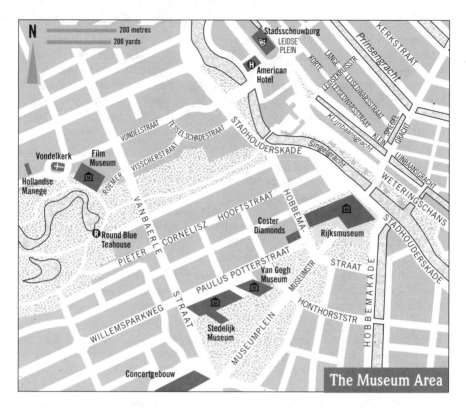

The Museum Area

The Rijksmuseum (National Museum, pronounced 'reyks-museum') was completed in 1885 to house the national collection of paintings and sculpture. The collection has evolved from a hoard of 200 paintings taken from the exiled Prince William V in 1798. First they had been gathered in the Huis ten Bosch palace in The Hague, and later were brought to the Trip brothers' mansion in Amsterdam. By the 1860s it was clear that the Trippenhuis was going to be too small for the growing collection. The quest for a new temple for the nation's art sparked off a conflagration of chauvinism, in-fighting and intrigue that would have impressed the Borgias. When the winners of an anonymous competition for a new museum design turned out to be German, the plan was rejected as 'non-Dutch'. Once a suitable Dutch architect was found in P. J. H. Cuypers (of Centraal Station fame) a new scandal emerged. The architect, project co-ordinator, government advisor and decorator were all Catholic. Protestant Holland scented popery and the building Cuypers produced was thought too extravagant and foreign to house the treasures of Dutch culture. What made it worse was that Cuypers, having had a more sober Romanesque plan accepted, managed, while building was in progress, to slip in more fantastical bits of a previously rejected Gothic plan. Good patriotic Calvinists found this mish-mash of styles deplorable. One critic railed: 'For two million guilders we now have the most sorry spec- · tacle of a building that anyone could have thought to call a museum.' In response to the gilding and plethora of sculptures, portraits and tiling depicting Dutch artists that adorns the outside walls, another critic compared the museum to 'a garishly decorated house of a rich parvenu'. Even the king pleaded a prior engagement on the day of the opening ceremony.

Ironically, Cuypers thought his red-brick and wood building with its clean, simple lines to be quintessentially Dutch, and today one would be inclined to agree with him. Like the Centraal Station on the other side of town, the Rijksmuseum was designed as a grand entrance to the city. (When it was built there were only fields beyond it.) A walkway through the middle of the building has bright bathroom acoustics that attract anything from opera-singing accordionists to steel bands. Though not as magical as the Centraal Station, 'De Rijks' is one of Amsterdam's most conspicuous landmarks, and has become a cultural icon. When it reopened after the Second World War the waiting queue of pallid, underfed Amsterdammers in slightly shabby formal dress stretched all the way down Stadhouderskade.

In the years following the completion of the Rijksmuseum in 1885 so many people left their complete collections to the museum that it had, almost immediately, to embark on a programme of expansion. Not all the additions have been happy ones. In 1906 a committee of artists and architects spent months fiddling about in a life-sized model of a hall intended to show off Rembrandt's *Night Watch*. They finally decided that light from the left, tempered by carefully placed curtains, would be ideal. It wasn't. The room was a disaster, ended up being used for minor exhibitions and earned the monicker 'De Puist' (the pimple).

All of Cuypers' ornate interior decorations have been removed and today the museum is a maze of whitewashed rooms. Prince William V's modest collection has become: 5,000 paintings, 30,000 sculptures and works of applied art, 17,000 historical objects, 3,000 works of Asiatic art and a million prints and drawings.

On the first floor, an archway leads to the **Gallery of Honour**. If your time is really tight, this is the one place to visit. It gives a good introduction to Golden Age painting, and houses the Rembrandt for which the museum is famous. At the far end, taking up the full wall, is Rembrandt's *Night Watch*.

Rembrandt

Rembrandt Harmensz. van Rijn (1606–69) was the son of a Leiden miller. When the poet Constantijn Huygens, who was also something of an art critic, visited Leiden in 1628, he went into raptures over Rembrandt's paintings (though he reprimanded the then unknown youth for his puniness and lack of manly exercise). A few years later Rembrandt upped sticks for the big city. He had made his mark in Leiden, and as the *burgemeester* wryly remarked: 'His portraits and other pictures pleased the citizens of Amsterdam, who paid him well for them.' And indeed they did. Wealthy burghers, trades guilds and companies of the civic guard all spent handsome sums to be painted by the fashionable young artist. His unromanticized portraits hit just the right note in rationalistic, post-Reformation Holland. Even his biblical and historical paintings have a truth and psychological rigour, especially in the faces, that seem to suggest direct experience of the world he's depicting. In 1634, already a rich and celebrated painter, he married heiress Saskia van Uylenburgh and five years later felt confident about paying a swingeing ƒ13,000 for a house in the Jewish quarter (*see* p.80). (This was where he had always wanted to live—he found Hebrew culture fascinating and preferred Jewish models for his religious painting.)

Saskia died in 1642, having just changed her will to leave everything to their infant son Titus, with the estate to be held in usufruct by Rembrandt for as long as he didn't remarry. The painter got round this by having a clandestine affair with Titus' nurse, Geertghe Dircx. Then, in 1649, he fell in love with a younger servant, Hendrickje Stoffels. Geertghe sued successfully for breach of contract. This came at a bad time. Rembrandt was receiving fewer commissions now—perhaps because of gossip about his domestic affairs, perhaps because he was becoming increasingly uncompromising in his work, or maybe he was just going out of fashion. He'd also spent far too much on paintings and the house. In 1656 he was declared bankrupt. The property that had been his home for some 20 years was sold, and he moved out to live on the Rozengracht with Hendrickje and Titus. They were going to try to revive his flagging fortune by working as his agents, but Hendrickje died within two years, followed by Titus in 1669, only months after he had married. Rembrandt was so hard up that he had to sell Saskia's tomb to pay for Hendrickje's funeral. When he himself died, he was buried in an unmarked grave in the Westerkerk.

The *Night Watch* was commissioned in 1642 by the militiamen of the Kloveniersdoelen (the Arquebusiers' Guildhall) to hang in their banqueting room alongside five other portraits of companies of the civic guard. It's officially called *The Company of Captain Frans Banning Cocq and Lieutenant Willem van Ruytenburch* and got its present title in the 19th century because ageing layers of varnish made it murky. For years it's had the reputation of being the work that signalled Rembrandt's decline. This is ill-deserved—he still had some of his most important commissions ahead of him. It is true though, that the 17th-century public didn't like it very much, and when it was moved to the Town Hall in 1715 the city fathers thought nothing of lopping a bit off the left-hand side so that it would fit on the wall: two of Captain Cocq's militiamen disappeared forever.

Today, together with *The Syndics*, it's considered the prize of the Rijksmuseum's collection. It was usual to paint group portraits in fairly static compositions, giving each member equal prominence. Rembrandt, however, paints the company in a flurry of movement, as if about to set off on a march. Rich clothes and a wonderful collection of plumed and pointed hats all add to the sense of grandeur and motion (this is all pure invention—the guards' uniforms were in reality rather dull, and they never marched). A little girl in a luminous gold dress, possibly the company mascot, looks bewildered by all the activity. (The rather surreal touch of a dead chicken tied to her waist is an allusion to the militia's coat of arms.) The captain and his lieutenant, in fine clothes, dominate the scene. The rest of the company look far less important—which is possibly why the painting was initially unpopular: they had after all each paid their *f*100, and deserved the same billing.

When the controllers of the Drapers' Guild (the 'Staalmeesters', or 'Syndics') commissioned Rembrandt to paint their portrait in 1662, they were determined not to make a similar mistake, and stipulated a more traditional composition. Rembrandt obeyed, yet still managed to create a work that brims with life. The Syndics look up from their table, and the viewer has the odd sensation of having just walked into the room and disturbed them at work. It's one of the finest group portraits ever painted—Kenneth Clark acclaims it as 'one of the summits of European painting'—and seems to be the image picture librarians most reach for to evoke old Holland.

As you wander through the Gallery of Honour, keep an eye open for three more of Rembrandt's paintings: *The Jewish Bride* (1667), a glowing, tender portrait of a couple, no longer all that youthful, but very much in love; a rather depressed, world-weary *Self-portrait as the Apostle Paul* (1661); and *St Peter's Denial* (1660), showing a very troubled, down-to-earth apostle. Other paintings in the Gallery of Honour may change from time to time, but you can probably see **Nicholas Maes'** delicately detailed *Old Woman at Prayer* and work by one of Rembrandt's better-known pupils—**Ferdinand Bol**. Massive *penschilderijen* ('pen paintings', rather like etchings) of naval battle scenes by Willem van de Velde I are also on show.

The other halls on the left wing of the first floor take you off on a chronological journey through Dutch painting. In Rooms 201–6 you'll find works from the Middle Ages and the Renaissance (which reached the Netherlands a century later than Italy).

You'll probably want to save your energy for the Golden Age, but as you pass through the early rooms have a look at **Geertgen tot Sint Jans'** brightly detailed *Holy Kinship* (1485), crammed with emblems and symbolic references and his *Adoration of the Magi* (1490), set against an intricate backdrop of ruined landscapes, processions and misty forests. *The Seven Works of Charity* (1504), instructive panels by the **Master of Alkmaar**, have survived attacks by iconoclasts and creeping damp, and still preach their catalogue of worthy acts. **Lucas van Leyden**'s *Adoration of the Golden Calf* (1530) is suitably riotous and a good example of the way Dutch Renaissance painters introduced realistic landscape settings for mythological scenes. The youth trying hard not to break the egg on the tavern floor in Pieter Aertsen's *Egg Dance* (1557) prefigures the scenes of everyday life that were to be such a feature of the Golden Age. The **Dutch Mannerists**, who worked in Haarlem between 1580 and the 1620s, get a good showing; Cornelis Cornelisz.'s enormous *Fall of Man* (1592) teems with animals mythical and domestic. In Karel van Mander's *The Magnanimity of Scipio* (1600), the 3rd-century BC Roman hero nobly refuses the offer of a beautiful captive for his slave and returns her to her betrothed.

Rooms 207–36 are filled with paintings from the 17th century, the '**Golden Age**' not only of Dutch art but of the Netherlands' political and economic might. Intense realism and the naturalistic rendering of domestic and everyday life are the hallmarks of the Golden Age. There are precise, calm interiors, minutely detailed still lifes, wild taverns and salacious brothel scenes. Homely Dutch mothers and their *onnozele schaapjes* (innocent lambs) take the place of the Madonna and Child, and you'll see businessmen and civic guards rather than generals and fantastical battle scenes. As you walk around the collection you'll see more of Rembrandt and his pupils, but there are a number of other artists particularly worth searching out.

Frans Hals' happy and rather cheeky-looking *Wedding Portrait of Isaac Abrahamsz. Massa and Beatrix van der Laen* (1622), and the florid *Merry Drinker* (1628–30)—which seems as though it has been dashed off with swift brushstokes and scratches in the wet paint—testify to his greatness as a portrait-painter. **Pieter Saenredam**'s church interiors are so still, and he pays such close attention to architectural shapes, that they seem almost abstract, Pieter de Hooch—especially in *Woman and Child in a Pantry* (1658) and *Women beside a Linen Chest* (1663)—is a master of quiet family scenes. Light from the busy outside world streams in through a door or window in the background, while in the spotless rooms with their symmetrical black and white floor tiles all is order and calm—though the impish children seem just on the verge of disrupting it.

A somewhat sadder *schaapje* can be seen in **Gabriel Metsu**'s touching, yet unsentimental *Sick Child*. **Jan Steen** gives quite another idea of family life. He used his experiences as a tavern-keeper to create scenes of such jolly domestic upheaval—as in *The Merry Family* (1670)—that the Dutch still use the expression 'a Jan Steen household' for any chaotic but cheerful home. You'll also find still lifes which, at the beginning of the century, are sober arrangements of herring, bread and cheese, but later overflow with ornate tableware, full-blown flowers and juicy fruit at its *toppunt* (literally: top-point)—the last moment of perfection before decay. **Abraham van Beyeren**'s 1665 painting shows fat peaches, seafood, leaking melons and a toppled silver candlestick in meticulous detail. Look out also for **Gerard ter Borch**'s exquisite fabrics—poor little *Helena van der Schalke* (1648) is weighed down by her fine silk dress and in *Gallant Conversation* the young woman's silver gown shimmers. (The conversation wasn't really that gallant—the man holding up his hand in gentle admonition was originally offering her a coin. A pious owner painted it out.)

Skim as fast as you like through the rest of the collection, but don't miss the Vermeers (Room 221a). Only 30 works by **Johannes Vermeer** (1632–75) exist; the Rijksmuseum has four of them. He had a passion for light and his paintings seem translucent. Light from a window reflects off a white wall, a jug, or softly glowing fabric. The tranquil *Kitchen Maid* (1658) and *Woman Reading a Letter* (1662–3) are totally without stylistic artifice, yet come close to perfection. In quiet, everyday scenes, Vermeer captures a sense of eternity.

If you walk through the rooms in numerical order you'll end up back in the Gallery of Honour. From here you can go downstairs for a coffee. Before you do, have a look in Room 248, tucked away behind the film hall. Here you'll find the small Italian Collection with some chubby pink Rubens, Carlo Crivelli's elegant tempera *Mary Magdalene* (1485–90) and Piero di Cosimo's warts-and-all portraits of a Florentine architect and his cauliflower-eared father (1485).

It's probably a better idea to come back another day to see the rest of the museum, but if time is short refresh yourself as best you can in the museum café and head back up the stairs, this time to the right wing of the building, devoted to sculpture and applied art.

The museum's collection of **sculpture and applied art** includes ceramics, china, glass, furniture, costumes, lace, tapestries, jewellery and silver from the Middle Ages to the 20th century, and can be utterly overwhelming. On a first visit the best idea is to give yourself a gentle overview. In the rooms leading off the entrance hall (Rooms 238–42), you'll find some of the best pieces in the collection. Ten 15th-century bronze figures, poised in graceful attitudes of mourning, have been filched from the tomb of Isabella de Bourbon in Antwerp. There's a tiny portable altar, carved in gold and encrusted with enamel, that some lucky nun used for her private devotion in the Abbey de Chocques in France in the 16th century. Look out also for Adriaen van Wesel's busy and energetic oak carving of *The Meeting of the Three Magi* (1475–7). A little further on, in Room 245, you can see Late Gothic German carvings of *Christ and the Last Supper*, still with some original polychrome and gilding.

If you have a taste for camp, head straight for Room 251a and Wenzel Jamnitzer's extraordinary *Table Ornament*, made for the city of Nuremberg in 1549. Mother Earth stands, one hip cocked, in a rockery of flowers, lizards and shrimps (all silver casts of real specimens) and supports on her head an enormous birdbath of cherubs rampant, scrolls, snakes and more flowers. All this is surmounted by yet another posy of enamelled silver foliage. Its ornate gilded wood and leather carrying case is displayed alongside.

The collection of **Delftware** (Rooms 255–7) has some prize polychrome as well as more traditional blue and white pieces. The people of Delft first started making cheaper imitations of the
Chinese porcelain brought back by the Dutch East India Company in the 17th century. (Now
souvenir shops sell imitation Delftware made in Taiwan.) Among the usual plates and cups
you can see a functioning Delftware violin and towering tulip pagodas with space for forty
stems (which, in the 17th century, would have cost a fortune to fill).

Back downstairs (in Room 164) you can see two exquisite early 18th-century **doll's houses**—
collectors' pieces assembled by the lady of the house, rather than toys. The museum is full of
choice life-size furniture too, but it's rather coldly presented and, unless you have a specialist
interest, the canal-house museums earlier in this chapter will probably appeal to you more—
though do keep an eye open for the rich **Gobelin tapestries** (Room 165) and an ornate oak
table-leaf veneered with tortoiseshell and inlaid with a mass of birds, monkeys, fruit and putti
worked in copper, brass and mother-of-pearl. If you appreciate good porcelain, the **Meissen
collection** (Rooms 170–71) is one of the best in the world. An alchemist in the German town
of Meissen, near Dresden, discovered the secret of Chinese porcelain manufacture while
trying to make gold for the king, and the pieces subsequently produced in the area have been
collectors' items for centuries.

The **South Wing** houses a small but carefully selected **costume and textile collection** (in
Room 15) and **18th- and 19th-century art**, including bright pastels by the Swiss artist Jean-
Etienne Liotard (1702–89)—mostly of aristocrats and socialites. The best 19th-century work is
by painters of two movements from the second half of the century. The three Maris brothers
were leading artists of the **Hague School** (nicknamed the 'grey' school after its heavy, cloudy
skies). Jacob painted beaches and townscapes, Matthijs portrayed romantic fairytale scenes and
Willem seemed preoccupied with ducks. Anton Mauve's pearly grey *Morning Ride along a
Beach* (1876) is characteristic of the movement. The **Amsterdam Impressionists** are well
represented by George Breitner, who liked to paint Amsterdam in the rain, and Isaac Israëls,
whose brighter pictures are closer to the work of the French Impressionists.

Downstairs in the South Wing, you'll find the **Asiatic Art Collection**. Three hundred years of
Dutch trade connections have resulted in a glittering stash of treasures from the East. You can
see lacquerwork, ceramics and textiles from Japan, Javanese sculptures, and religious works
from China and India. A small, bronze dancing Lord Shiva (the Hindu god of creation) from
the 12th century and an elegantly relaxed Chinese Buddhist saint, the Bodhisattva
Avalokitesharva, from the same period, make the trip across to the South Wing worthwhile.

In the **Rijksprentenkabinet** (Print Room) exhibition hall, on the ground floor near the
museum café, you can see temporary exhibitions from a vast collection of prints, drawings and
watercolours by the likes of Rembrandt, Dürer, Goya and Canaletto. To see works from the
collection not on view, you need written permission (from the Director, Jan Luykenstraat 1a).

On the ground floor of the left wing of the main building, you'll find the **Dutch History
Collection**. The history collection comprises paintings, documents and memorabilia dating
from the Middle Ages to the Second World War. There's an emphasis on ships and sea battles,
but the presentation is not exciting. If you have the time, pop in for a look at some of the more
amusing curiosities—like a gorgeous copper crown with glass jewels sent as a bribe to an
African king by the 17th-century Duke of York (via the Dutch naval hero Admiral de Ruyter), or
the grand but diminutive jackets worn by the toddler Prince William V.

The Van Gogh Museum

The Rijksmuseum Vincent Van Gogh (National Vincent Van Gogh Museum; *open daily 10–6; adm f12.50*) has really cornered the Van Gogh market with 200 paintings, 500 drawings, a collection of works by Van Gogh's contemporaries, the letters from Vincent to his brother Theo, Vincent's collections of Japanese woodcuts and 19th-century engravings, a press archive dating from 1899—and publishing copyright for the lot. The museum was completed in 1973 and is based on an initial drawing by the influential Dutch architect, Gerrit Rietveld (*see* p.52), who died before working the plan through. Brave efforts by later architects to realize his rather sketchy ideas produced a hard-edged and unsympathetic building. But in 1999, a new wing by renowned Japanese architect Kisho Kurokawa gave the museum the sort of proud architectural profile it deserves.

Works from the permanent collection are displayed in the old part of the museum; the Kurokawa wing is used for temporary exhibitions and houses the darkened Print Room, where you can find Van Gogh's drawings and studies, and trace some of his influences—sketches by friends, pictures he copied and his collection of Japanese prints and magazine engravings. The selection on display changes frequently, but you can usually follow his development through some rather conventional Dutch landscapes, with all the expected perspectives, and studies of gnarled hands and heavily jowled peasant faces to the wild movement of *Women Dancing* (1885). Millet's *Labours of the Field* and woodcuts by Hiroshige and Kesai Yeisen clearly had an influence on some of Van Gogh's better known oils. The museum has an exceptionally good library, where you can view photographs of Vincent's letters to Theo. Training courses, and all sorts of activities to help working artists, are held regularly. (Details are available from the museum.)

Vincent van Gogh was born in 1853 in the tiny village of Zundert, near the Belgian border. We have an image of him as a wild, schizophrenic bohemian; a simpleton, out of touch with the world and reliant on his younger brother's handouts. This isn't the full truth. He came from an old Dutch family of clerics, naval officers and gallery owners. Though he was constantly at odds with his relations, and indeed offended almost everyone he met, he was in many ways part of the Establishment. He spoke three languages fluently, had a wide knowledge of European art and had the business acumen and connections needed to organize two exhibitions of friends' work in Paris. He signed himself 'Vincent' because he thought his surname, difficult for foreigners to pronouce, would be bad salesmanship. (You say it with two guttural 'g's—'fun HGoHG'). Even the money he got from his art-dealer brother he excused as a business arrangement—an advance on the money Theo would one day make selling his work. Yet all his life he was desperately lonely, dogged by a sense of failure and frustrated by how few people appreciated his art. Towards the end he was beset by bouts of madness which left him exhausted and depressed. He was acutely sensitive to his surroundings. The colours, people, light or weather in one environment would become loathsome to him and the need to move would become consuming. Suddenly he'd up sticks and go—to the sun, to the city, to the country. These moves would often be reflected in a change in his work, so it's interesting to approach the paintings with some knowledge of what was going on in Van Gogh's life at the time.

Vincent's first job, at the age of 16, was as an assistant with the art dealer Goupil & Cie in The Hague. In 1873 he went to work at the London branch and was impressed by Constable, Turner and especially the Pre-Raphaelite John Everett Millais. An unhappy love affair made him grumpy at work. He began to be rude to customers about their taste, was shuttled between London and Paris and finally, despite family connections (his uncle was a partner in the firm), dismissed. Still obsessed by his English rose, he returned to Britain as a teacher, but was soundly rebuffed. She married someone else and he went back to Holland to work in a bookshop. He still didn't know what he wanted to do with his life.

But in May 1877 it all suddenly seemed clear: following in his father's footsteps, he set off for Amsterdam to study theology. Greek and Latin proved an uphill struggle and he was entirely defeated by algebra; after less than a year he went to a crammer for evangelists in Brussels, where mathematical aptitude was not a prerequisite. But he couldn't preach either. Yet again the family pulled strings. The Brussels Evangelist Committee reluctantly sent him to prove his worth among the coalminers of the Borinage—a wasteland in south Belgium. After seven months he was dismissed for over-zealous involvement with the poor.

He stayed on in a hovel for another year, almost starving to death, and began to draw. He was 26 and had found his direction. His younger brother, Theo, rescued him and started to pay him the monthly allowance that was to be Vincent's only income for the rest of his life.

Van Gogh was largely self-taught, though he spent a brief period studying perspective and anatomy in Brussels in 1880. The following year he fell in love with his widowed cousin, Kee Vos. He walked to Amsterdam from his parents' home in south Holland, stormed into her father's house on the Keizersgracht and held his hand over a candle yelling, 'Let me see her for as long as I can hold my hand in the flame.' But Kee had fled. Van Gogh left without seeing her and with a hole burned into his flesh. The incident caused a family row; he was thrown out of home and went to The Hague. Here he met members of the Hague School of painting, a movement characterized by muddy colours and gloomy skies. He was given lessons by one of its leading members, Anton Mauve (a cousin by marriage), and was also much influenced by Jozef Israëls' earthy studies of peasants. He was especially friendly with a young painter called George Breitner, who later became known as one of the best Amsterdam Impressionists. They discovered a mutual interest in Zola and together drew the street life in the seedier parts of town. An uncle who had commissioned 12 views of the city was horrified by Vincent's unconventional approach and refused to pay up. The relationship with Mauve grew tense when Van Gogh began to reject the older painter's advice, and family relations soured on a wider scale when it became known that he was living with the prostitute Sien Hoornik 'in order to reform her'.

In September 1883 Van Gogh suddenly left The Hague for the countryside of Drenthe in the north of Holland. He had begun to paint in oils, but still with a muddy Dutch palette. The good people of Drenthe thought him a dangerous lunatic and a tramp, and refused to pose for him—so this became a period of landscapes with small figures in the distance. After a few months, loneliness drove him to a reconciliation with his parents and he went back south to live with them in Nuenen. Weavers and peasants in the surrounding Brabant farmland were his dominant motif. The period culminated in the dim glow and gravy browns of *The Potato Eaters* (1885). Van Gogh loved this 'real peasant picture'—he felt you could smell the bacon, smoke and potato steam, and that the rough hands that dipped into the dish were the same hands that had dug the earth.

In *The Old Church Tower at Nuenen*, the tower stands crooked and solitary in a flat, empty churchyard. A few crows flutter against the overcast sky. Van Gogh painted it in May 1885, a few months after his father had been buried there, and just before it was demolished and all the wood—including the graveyard crosses—sold to peasants. His father had been an unpopular preacher in a declining sect. *Open Bible, Extinguished Candle and Book* (1885) has been seen as Vincent's homage to their difficult relationship. Next to the huge Bible and snuffed candle (a convention for death) is a French novel—something his father would not have allowed in the house.

Margot Begemann, a neighbour, took poison after her family refused permission for her to marry Vincent. She survived, but Vincent got the blame and the village turned against him. He went to Antwerp, studied Rubens, covered his walls with Japanese prints and enrolled in the academy—which he left a few months later without ever learning of the academy's decision to demote him to the beginners' class. He then went to Paris. The first Theo (who was working there for Goupil & Cie) heard of the move was a note brought by a messenger asking him to meet Vincent in the Louvre. Vincent moved into Theo's tiny apartment, but was such a chaotic and irritating flatmate that Theo had to find somewhere bigger, with a separate studio space for his brother. The first few canvases in Paris (such as *View over Paris*, 1886) still use the Dutch browns and greys. But when Theo introduced him to a few Impressionist friends, the shock of their fresh, bright canvases changed Vincent for life. At first the colour creeps in gradually (*Woman Sitting in the Café du Tambourin*, 1887) but soon he is copying the flat colours of the Japanese prints and painting some of the familiar bright self-portraits. He began to long for harder light and a less hectic milieu than Paris could offer. Writing to his sister Wil about *Self-portrait at the Easel* (1888), he draws her attention to his sad expression. He's had enough of Paris and wants the sun. He gives himself pinkish-grey skin against a greyish-white wall, his tightly drawn features contrast with a bristly, unkempt, bright red beard. On the palette he holds are all the colours of the painting except this fiery orange of the beard.

On 20 February 1888 Vincent escaped to the Mediterranean warmth of Arles in the south of France. Here in the famous 'Yellow House', which he shared for a while with Gauguin, his best known works were painted. It is hard to believe that the raucous yellows and bright reds and blues of *Harvest at La Crau* were painted only three years after *The Potato Eaters*. Look closely at one of the versions of *Sunflowers*. Between the greens and yellows are bright streaks of ice blues, mauves and reds—colours you never notice in the reproductions. Portraits of the postman, Roulin, and his wife are drenched in sun and colour. Even the *Night Café* has a bright, steamy heat. The solitary *Sower at Arles* works under an enormous yellow orb in a green and pink sky. The most ordinary things around him evoke intense response. *Vincent's Bedroom at Arles* is filled with a brilliant light but the smooth paintwork, the mauves and blues of the walls have a calming effect. (The green splodge under the chair is the result of a botched repair job after the painting was damaged in transit to Theo.)

Van Gogh was very excited by Gauguin's arrival on 20 October 1888 and went to great pains to furnish his room comfortably. The money to do this, of course, came from Theo. *Gauguin's Chair* shows a piece Vincent bought for his friend (elaborate in comparison with his own). On the seat are novels intended to indicate Gauguin's spirituality and modernism. A candle burns as well as the gas light, to suggest Gauguin's fiery nature. Together they visited nearby towns such as Les Saintes-Maries-de-la-Mer, where Vincent painted *Boats on the Beach*. The small red, green and blue boats had reminded him of flowers. He paints them with the flat colours and definite lines of a Japanese print, while the sea eddies and swirls with a shimmering complexity of colouring.

Gauguin's stay was not a happy one. The two artists had tempestuous arguments. After a particularly violent dispute on Christmas Eve, Vincent threatened Gauguin with a razor, then slashed off his own right ear and presented it to a prostitute who had complimented it. Gauguin left for Paris. Another nervous crisis followed Van Gogh's recuperation, and he was voluntarily admitted to the asylum of St-Paul-de-Mausole at Saint-Rémy. Paintings from this period—usually of fields around the asylum, the hospital garden or of individual trees and flowers—are in softer hues. In February 1890 Vincent painted *Branches of an Almond Tree in Blossom* for Theo's newly born son—blossom-laden branches stand out against an eggshell-blue background.

By May he felt well enough to leave the asylum, though he could only bear Paris for three days. He travelled to Auvers-sur-Oise where an eccentric art-lover, Dr Gachet, promised to keep an eye on him. But Vincent became more and more overwrought: his colours became harder, brush strokes more violent. In *Crows in the Wheatfields* (July 1890) it seems difficult for the birds to fly into the thick, dark sky. A path curves and goes nowhere. One of his last paintings, *Roots and Tree Trunks*, has even more disorientating perspectives and thick layers of paint in unexpected colours. The painter seems completely self-engrossed, and the viewer is quite alienated.

On 27 July Vincent went into the fields and shot himself, but he bungled even this. He staggered back to the inn where he was staying and died on 29 July, in Theo's arms. After a short illness, Theo himself died six months later, at the age of 32. The brothers are buried side by side in the churchyard at Auvers-sur-Oise.

Dedication, or desperation, drove Theo's widow—Johanna van Gogh-Bonger—to promote the works stacked all over her apartment. The art world began to take notice. In 1891 there was an exhibition in Brussels, followed by numerous others all over the Netherlands and in Paris. Paintings started to fetch high prices and national museums added Van Goghs to their collections. After Johanna's death in 1925 her son, Vincent's namesake, took over the collection and in 1931 put it on permanent exhibition in the Stedelijk Museum in Amsterdam. To prevent the break-up of the collection after his death, the Van Gogh Foundation was formed in 1960 and set about building the present museum. With three members of the Van Gogh family on the board of the foundation, there's a feeling that it's still very much a family concern—and Vincent, once the black sheep, is again part of the Establishment.

The Stedelijk Museum of Modern Art

The Stedelijk Museum ('Municipal Museum'; *open daily 11–5; adm*) is a solid 19th-century red brick building with fussy plaster decorations and spiky gables. A row of rather haughty architects stares down at you from niches on the first floor. The widened entrance and glass box extension at the back were part of a drive in the 1950s to make art more accessible: the guiding principle was that a museum loses its sense of mystery when works can also be viewed from the street. A good idea—if the blinds didn't have to be drawn every afternoon against the damaging sunlight.

Don't be deceived by appearances. It's a bright, lively museum of modern art. You'll find not only conventional paintings, but all sorts of applied art (designer chairs, feather hats and gaudy teapots) and work by less established artists. As you queue for your ticket, the person in front may just as likely be a professor of art history as some painter's proud mother.

The museum owes its existence to two benefactors. Sophia Augusta de Bruyn, the eccentric dowager of Jonkheer (Lord) Lopez Suasso, spent as little as she could on clothes (scandalizing Amsterdam society by wearing the same dress more than once). Instead she amassed as many jewels, trinkets, curios (and especially clocks) as she could. When she died, she left everything to the City of Amsterdam. There was so much that the council felt obliged to build a museum to display it all. At the same time the wealthy Vereeniging tot het Vormen van eene Openbare Verzameling van Heedendaagsche Kunst (Society for the Formation of a Public Collection of Contemporary Art) or VvHK, was looking for a home.

The city council and the 'society with the long name' (as it was understandably nicknamed) got together and the museum opened in 1895. It wasn't until the early 1970s that the last of Sophia Augusta's bric-a-brac was dispersed to specialist museums and the Stedelijk became devoted exclusively to modern art.

Successive directors have left their imprint on the collection, but it was the imagination, energy and skill of Willem Sandberg—'part poet, part artist, part designer, part administrator, part magician'—that between 1945 and 1963 established the Stedelijk as one of the world's leading modern art museums. He built up an important collection and held a series of notable, usually controversial, exhibitions. In 1949 there were fisticuffs in the foyer at the opening of the first COBRA exhibition. (COBRA was a group of artists from Copenhagen, Brussels and Amsterdam whose colourful, childlike painting was the first to provoke the response that 'a three-year-old could do better'.) Though that's not happened again, daring new acquisitions still spark off public uproars.

Space is limited, so only a small portion of the collection is shown at any one time. Outside the summer months (May–September) you may even find that much of the museum is taken over by a special exhibition, though present museum policy is to show the core of the permanent collection on a more stable, long-term basis. A plan of what is currently on view is available from the information desk (to the left of the entrance).

You'll find whatever is being exhibited of the **permanent collection** up the wide marble staircase, on the top floor. In 1972 the large **Van Gogh** collection, which had been kept at the Stedelijk, moved next door to its own museum. Because Van Gogh is considered so important to modern art, a few paintings were left behind. *La Berceuse* (The Cradle) was inspired by a story Gauguin told Van Gogh about fishermen who pinned prints of their patron saint—Stella Maris (Maria, Star of the Sea)—to the cabin wall. Van Gogh felt that a portrait of Madame Roulin (a postman's wife), holding a cord for a rocking cradle, would be ideal for such a print. He imagined the seamen 'would feel the old sense of being rocked come over them and remember their own lullabies'. It's a pity that the painting isn't hung the way Van Gogh suggested—as a triptych with sunflower paintings on either side. Don't miss the paintings by **George Breitner**, Van Gogh's contemporary and drinking partner. In *De Dam*, a view of Dam square, he captures that special Amsterdam light in a way that makes the exact time of year, even the time of day, immediately recognizable. Keep an eye open also for his highly patterned, exotic *Woman in a Red Kimono* (in reality a hat shop assistant).

The museum has a good collection of modern art classics. You'll probably find Manet's picture of a barmaid (staring at you saucily from under a crystal chandelier), a study for his famous *Bar at the Folies-Bergère*. There are some gentle Cézanne landscapes and a whole range of **Picassos**—from bright early collages to nudes from his Blue Period. One wall is sure to be filled by **Matisse**'s vast paper cut-out *The Parakeet and the Mermaid*, done towards the end of his life when his eyesight was too poor for painting, and painstakingly restored in 1996. You'll find at least one of **Kandinsky**'s vivid Improvisations—paintings where he used colour to represent the sounds of various musical instruments—and some rather good **Chagalls**.

The 1960s are well represented by **Warhol** screen-prints, **Roy Lichtenstein**'s comic strip blow-ups and **Bruce Nauman**'s neon light.installations, and the museum comes right up to date with works by some of the best living European and American artists.

The high point is the museum's collection of the Russian artist **Kazimir Malevich** and the Dutch movement, *De Stijl*. Side by side, these two collections show how abstract art began and we see the gradual disappearance of any reference to outside reality. The visionary director of the museum, Willem Sandberg, was responsible for tracking down the Malevich collection, unearthing a treasury of works that had been forgotten in a cellar in Germany for three decades. Malevich had left the entire contents of an exhibition for safe-keeping with a friend in Beieren, but was subsequently never allowed to leave Russia. He died in 1935, so there the cache remained (under a pile of rubble after the war) until Sandberg swooped down and bought it in the late 1950s. The museum has a complete range of his work, from early Impressionist pieces, through a Cubist period to the completely abstract—solid shapes of colour (oblongs, squares, triangles) on a white background. Malevich composes these shapes at such angles that the paintings seem full of movement.

At around the same time (1917) *De Stijl* artists were coming up with very similar work. The best known is that of **Piet Mondriaan** (he dropped the last 'a' to appear French, but the Dutch prefer the original). His *Compositions* of vertical and horizontal black lines with blocks of primary colours, so shocking at the time, now appear on everything from oven gloves to shampoo bottles. When Theo van Doesburg (co-founder of De Stijl) after ten years of recti-linear painting produced a Contra-composition, in which he daringly tilted his lines through 45°, Piet left the movement in a huff. They were never reconciled, though Mondriaan later took up the challenge by tilting his canvas through 45° and keeping the lines vertical.

In the Print Room, halfway down the main staircase, you could find anything from a Toulouse-Lautrec poster to Mapplethorpe's startling close-up photographs of male nudes. Keep an eye open for the innovative work of Dutch photographer Cas Oorthuys, and Roland Topor's blackly comic cartoons. Work not on display can be viewed by appointment in the study-room.

Most of the ground floor is given over to travelling exhibitions and applied art. The small door to the left of the ticket office leads to rooms of odd-shaped furniture, gaudy ceramics and lumpy mats. There's a video art room under the stairs, and the glass box extension at the back of the building occasionally displays work (often dire) by contemporary Amsterdam artists. Two installations on the ground floor shouldn't be missed. The *Appelbar* (through a door to the right of the information desk), adorned with murals of colourful birds, fish and children, is the work of the COBRA artist Karel Appel. It was used as a café until the opening of the present restaurant in 1956. The commission was offered to Appel as a palliative after a débâcle at the Town Hall in 1951: a mural in the canteen, commissioned by the Building Department, had to be boarded over when the Catering Department insisted that it would put people off their food. Edward Kienholz's *Beanery* is a near-life-sized version of a poky Los Angeles bar. You can wander about in the dim light, examining the bric-a-brac. Rusty music scratches away in the juke-box. There's a murmur of conversation. A couple sit at the bar. Someone has passed out in the corner. A waitress clears the remnants of a disgusting meal. But all the faces of the figures are clock-faces, and as you're the only thing that moves it is a surreal and rather disorientating experience. Luckily, the real bar (bright and airy) is just across the corridor. (Unlike the *Appelbar*, the *Beanery* is not a permanent installation, so sometimes disappears into storage or off on tour.)

The Concertgebouw

The Concertgebouw at the southern end of the square was designed by A. L. van Gendt (who was one of the collaborators on the Centraal Station design) and completed in 1888. It is solid Dutch neo-Renaissance; no frivolity is to be found here—indeed, the few urns and obelisks he included in the design either never went up for lack of funds, or have fallen off through lack of funds. The twin staircase towers are intended to harmonize with Cuypers' Rijksmuseum across the way (more out of toadyism than artistic integrity—Cuypers headed the committee that chose the design). Busts of Beethoven, Bach and Sweelinck (Holland's one claim to musical fame) grace the façade. The gilded lyre on top is a 1960s replacement of the original (which fell off). The entrance is no longer through the front, but through a shiny glass extension built in 1988 as part of a complete renovation of the building, which had been subsiding dangerously. The portico, classical shapes and colouring of the extension mean that it does fit in reasonably well and it certainly meets the general manager's stipulation that if there was to be a new front door, he didn't want to have to hang an 'Entrance around the Corner' notice on the old one.

In the 1870s Amsterdam, always a city with metropolitan aspirations, found itself without a concert hall and with Brahms's admonition ringing in its ears: '*Ihr seid liebe Leute aber schlechte Musikanten*' (You are lovely people but awful musicians). The government maintained that art was not its business, so it was a committee of private citizens that raised the money, bought some cheap land outside the city limits next to an evil-smelling candle factory and commissioned Van Gendt (more for his figures than his design). Van Gendt prided himself on being a salesman rather than an artist and was completely unmusical. It is ironic that he should have produced a concert hall with possibly the best acoustics in the world. The area soon became very fashionable. The candle factory was replaced by ostentatious mansions and every Thursday the streets would be crammed with the carriages of season-ticket holders.

Under the baton of conductors like Mengelberg (who was sacked for his Nazi sympathies in 1945 after 50 years' service) and Haitink, the resident Royal Concertgebouw Orchestra has become world-famous. If you're passing on a Wednesday, pop in for a free '**lunchconcert**' (*12.30pm, through it's a good idea to be there by 12*). These are usually recitals given in the Kleine Zaal (Small Hall—a chamber music room upstairs), but if you're lucky you might catch the RCO itself in open rehearsal in the Grote Zaal (Big Hall—the main auditorium).

At the turn of the century there was a garden behind the Concertgebouw. On summer afternoons it would rustle with silk as Amsterdam's élite gathered for outdoor concerts. Those (literally) outside the charmed circle would have to crush around the railings. In 1922 the garden was sold to developers to raise money for a pension fund for the orchestra, and disappeared behind a housing development. If you walk a short way up J. Verhulststraat and look back you'll get the only view now available of the little gilded mermaid blowing her trumpet on top of the Kleine Zaal.

Beyond Museumplein

Almost next door to the Rijksmuseum, on the corner of Hobbemastraat, is **Coster Diamonds** (*open daily 9–5; adm free*). Jews fleeing persecution in Antwerp set up the diamond-polishing industry in Amsterdam in the 16th century. Roaring trade with South Africa established it in the 19th century. (Diamond-cutters would light their cigars with a *f*10 note, more than the average weekly wage.) The city is still a focus for diamond-dealing and processing. What this means in practical terms is that you can buy the gems for half the price you'd pay in London or New York. All over the city factories invite you in to see the craftsmen at work in order to lure you into their salerooms.

Coster Diamonds is one of the biggest. The 'Koh-I-Noor' (Mountain of Light), one of the prize gems in the British crown jewels, was cut here, and there's a glassy replica in the exhibition hall. Smart, uniformed hostesses conduct you on a short tour through the cutting and polishing works (done with whizzing discs coated with diamond dust and olive oil) and then propel you past a room temptingly labelled 'Self-Service' (it turns out to be a café) into the jewellery shop. It's an interesting ten minutes, though if you want to buy it might be worth shopping around.

A block or two away from Museumplein is **Pieter Cornelisz. Hooftstraat**, Amsterdam's most chic shopping street, named after a 17th-century poet. It's one of the few streets in the city where you can confidently window-shop without fear of stepping in dog turds. There are a few exotic delis, certificated Delft porcelain at Focke & Meltzer (No.65) and some elegant, but dull, cafés. Mostly it's clothes: shops for the hip toddler or the fashion-anxious adolescent. If you're past voting age then things range from well-cut classics to the outré (well, almost). All the favourite names (Armani, Gucci, Hamnett) can be found. Some (like MaxMara and Stephane Kelian) have their own shops. P. C. Hooftstraat and Van Baerlestraat, which crosses it further up, are also home to some of the better Dutch designers—Edgar Vos, Rob Kroner and Sissy Boy.

Around the Vondelpark

During the so-called 'Second Golden Age' at the end of the 19th century, when the butter market was turned into Rembrandtplein and the neighbourhood around the museums was being developed as an upmarket residental area, some local burghers got together to create the Vondelpark to commemorate the poet Joost van Vondel.

Joost van Vondel

Joost van Vondel (1582–1674; pronounced in the way an old English army officer might say 'fondle') is proclaimed the Dutch answer to Shakespeare. He excelled in ornate poems in celebration of public events, clocking up over a thousand lines for the opening of the Town Hall alone. The lack of action in his dramas is notorious: he went in for static pictorial representations accompanied by long flowery descriptions of anything exciting. His play *Gijsbrecht van Amstel* is a Dutch literary classic. It's said that one of the scenes inspired Rembrandt's *Night Watch*. By all accounts the Master would have had quite enough time to paint it during the performance. From humble beginnings in his father's busy hosiery shop on the edge of the red-light district, Vondel built up a considerable reputation and a small fortune. The former counted for little in mercantile Amsterdam when his son squandered the latter. At the age of 70 he had to go back to work in the city pawnbrokers. He was sacked after 10 years' service for writing poetry in office hours and finally, in his eighties, was granted a state pension. He died at 92 of hypothermia, and suggested his own epitaph:

> *Hier ligt Vondel zonder Rouw,*
> *Hij is gestorven van de kou.*

> *Here lies Vondel, without regret [or unmourned],*
> *He was killed by the cold.*

It's a large park by Amsterdam standards and J. D. Kocher's informal English landscaping gives it calm, graceful lines and wide perspectives. Curved tree-lined avenues, irregularly shaped lakes and ponds, little furrow-like paths through shrubberies, hidden gardens and wide stretches of lawn attract Amsterdammers from all over the city—especially at weekends. A lone accordionist sits on a bench and plays for the ducks. Refugee guitarists from South America play heartrending tunes, homesick for a stronger sunlight. Jugglers meet to learn, practise and show off. There's a party atmosphere whenever the sun shines, and in the summer the festivities go on well into the night with concerts, theatre performances and an open-air cinema. On holidays (especially Queen's Day) enjoyment reaches carnival pitch.

There are a number of dainty bridges, a few sculptural surprises and some odd architecture to catch your eye. As you enter the park, you can see, across the pond, one of the more attractive examples of Nieuwe Zakelijkheid (Functionalist) architecture: H. J. Baanders' **'t Ronde Blauwe Theehuis** (Round Blue Teahouse), a cross between a pagoda and a flying saucer that seems to hover over the water. Across the way Vondel himself, in badly fitting laurels, looks gouty, prosperous and entirely oblivious of the Muses playing about his ankles. His ornate pedestal was made in 1867 by P. J. H. Cuypers (architect of the Centraal Station and Rijksmuseum).

The pavilion near the main entrance to the park was designed in 1881 by P. J. and W. Hamer, and is now the **Netherlands Film Museum** (no exhibition—cinema shows from the archive only, details published in listings magazines). The first director, Jan de Vaal, was a voracious but secretive collector. He hoarded his treasures and seemed wary of the outside world. The result was that not many people bothered about the film museum until the dynamic duo—director Hoos Blotkamp and film buff Eric de Kuyper—took over in the late 1980s and discovered an archive of world significance. Funding was secured, the building was revamped, the long process of cataloguing begun (unearthing such gems as hand-coloured silent movies) and the occasional screenings were boosted to three times a day. There are all sorts of special events and films are shown in the original language. On summer Saturdays there are free screenings on the terrace (around 10pm), when you can buy a beer and have a giggle at Charlie Chaplin or Abbott and Costello. The main hall is worth a peek: its interior is from Amsterdam's first cinema, the Cinema Parisien built in 1910. The Parisien had declined ungracefully into a porn pit when the daughter of the original owner heard, in 1987, that it was about to be gutted by the hotel next door. Armed with coffee flask and screwdriver she went to rescue the interior (still intact after a 1930s redecoration) and, aided by the Monuments Trust, the old atmosphere was bottled and transferred to the Film Museum. The **library** (*open Tues–Fri 10–5, Sat 11–5; adm free*), with a good selection of magazines and reference works and a stash of posters and publicity material, is in the building alongside the pavilion.

The grand 19th-century Gothic of the **Vondelkerk** (Heilige Hartkerk) fills a tiny oval in Vondelstraat, which runs parallel to the park. The architect P. J. H. Cuypers was highly respected for his churches, and this is one of his best. Unfortunately it's been converted to offices, so the interior is lost. The houses at Nos.73–9 Vondelstraat were also designed by Cuypers. The tiled tableaux on the wall show the architect, the mason and the jealous critic. The motto translates as: 'Jan conceives it, Piet realizes it, Claes tears it apart. Oh, who cares?'

Further up Vondelstraat, at No.140, through the arch and up a long passage lies one of Amsterdam's best kept secrets. As you walk up towards the black door at the end of the passage, you'll notice a clue—the earth and cumin-musty smell of horses. Open the door and immediately you are in the vast, light and eerily silent **Hollandse Manege** (*open daily, usually from 10am–midnight*). The architect, A. L. van Gendt (who also designed the Concertgebouw), was influenced by the Spanish Riding School in Vienna. The beautifully plastered interior, with horses' heads worked into the classical design and elegant, open iron roofing, comes as a complete surprise. The one marked 'Tribune' leads to a balcony overlooking the arena. Sawdust muffles all sound and the occasional sharp command from the instructor is all that breaks the thick silence. The door marked 'Foyer' takes you to a café that runs the width of the building. It has the relaxed grandeur of a palace stables. You can see the horses in the arena through glass doors all up one side of the café—and the drinks are the cheapest in town.

The Port of Amsterdam

The Western Islands

The Western Islands, in the old Western Docks beyond Central Station, are man-made. They're close together, criss-crossed by canals and connected by little wooden bridges. There's an eerie sense of isolation, even though they are nowadays very much part of the mainland. In the 17th century Amsterdam burst beyond the boundaries that had contained it for generations. More and more land was created by draining off water into new canals. The area of the city increased by nearly 40 per cent. The poet Vondel wrote some histrionic verse in praise of the achievement (as was very much his wont), using the sort of hyperbole usually reserved for military victories. Travellers marvelled at the size and number of the warehouses. Buildings shot up all over the new islands, and were immediately filled with tobacco, salt, tin, wine, draperies, spices, copper, furs, gold—almost any commodity that could realize a profit.

On **Bickerseiland** (Bicker's Island, named after the original developer), modern concrete apartment blocks with bright red and blue window frames line one side of the narrow walkway. The other side is a jumble of houseboats. Rafts, tugs, canal boats, barges—anything that floats (and some things that almost don't) have been commandeered to solve Amsterdam's chronic housing problem. In the 1950s, when the canal transport industry went into an almost terminal decline, skippers were only too pleased to offload their craft on the oddballs who wanted to live on the water. By the 1970s there were around 800 legally licensed moorings and countless illegal ones. The council outlawed all newcomers and granted an amnesty to over a thousand of the unlicensed boats that were already occupied. Recently, moves have begun again to get rid of them.

Their occupants were allowed (like those on the legal boats) to connect up to the water and electricity supplies. Arrangements for the latter are alarmingly Heath Robinson. Wonky home-made poles hold up yards of black flex as it snakes along the canalside and between the boats. Wet washing flutters from these improvised clothes lines. Originally houseboats were the domain of the weird and rebellious, but now lawyers and stockbrokers sun themselves on deck and talk for hours about waterproofing techniques. One boat even houses a community of nuns. Streetnames like 'Sailmaker's Street' and 'Blockmaker's Street' are all that's left of the shipbuilding yards for which Bickerseiland was renowned. (It was also famous for its dogs. There were so many that the local church had to employ two dog-chasers to keep the aisles free during services.) Most of the island is taken up by soulless 1970s housing estates. At

The Port of Amsterdam

Zeilmakerstraat 15, in one of the few buildings to escape post-war redevelopment, you'll find the **Amsterdams Beeldhouwers Kollektief** (Amsterdam Sculptors' Collective; *open Thurs–Sun 1–5*). The sixty members (some of the city's best young sculptors among them) keep the gallery well supplied. Exhibitions change frequently. Most work is on sale, and not all of it is of a size to preclude taking it home in your overnight bag.

Realeneiland is named after Jacob Real, the original owner. Ahead of you as you cross the bridge on to the island is a neat little row of 17th-century houses. Jacob Real's own, rather modest house (now a restaurant) is at the end. He was a fervent Catholic. The gold-painted coin on the gable stone commemorates the treasures he saved from the iconoclasts by smuggling them out of a monastery in the nick of time. Real's surname (also the name of a coin) afforded an appropriate pun, and the house became known as '**De Gouden Reael**'. There's a tang of tar and varnish in the air. The diligent occupants of the rather stately row of boats on the dockside seem perpetually involved in maintenance.

Hidden in the middle of the Western Islands, **Prinseneiland** is the best of all. Its little lanes are a mish-mash of architectural styles. Tumbledown warehouses crumble quietly next to smart, sharp-edged new apartments. Tall, carefully restored façades grace the canal. The island is perfumed by freshly sawn timber from the working boatyard. There's seldom any traffic. All you hear is the sound of sawing, workmen calling to each other and (to jolt you back down to earth) pop music from their ghetto-blasters. The bridge at the eastern end of Galgenstraat used to afford a fine prospect of the city's Golgotha ('Galg' means 'gallows'). The curious were not always afforded a view of the whole process. Offenders were often executed in the city centre. The heads, sometimes with the heart stuffed into the mouth, were posted on the city wall and only the discarded bits ended up on the grassy mound near the Galgenbrug.

Around Haarlemmerplein

On the busy square of Haarlemmerplein, some way west of Central Station, stands the massive **Willemspoort** (a.k.a. Haarlemmerpoort), a neoclassical gatehouse built for the entrance of King William II in 1840. The masons botched the rather special *trompe-l'œil* effect that has to be achieved to keep the perspectives right: the central columns appear to taper rather suddenly at the top. It's never been a popular structure. At a town council meeting at the turn of the century it was saved from demolition by only four votes. If you walk through the gate you'll see four small rectangles set into the second pillar on the left. They mark the position of the old *stokmaat*, the measure by which horses were judged large enough for military service. It was used right up to the First World War.

Over the past few years the streets leading to the square, **Haarlemmerdijk** and **Haarlemmerstraat**, have developed into one of the quirkiest shopping quarters in town. New Age stores, junk shops, galleries, zany boutiques and ethnic gift shops all contribute to the appeal. Among the more curious is Beune's confectioners at No.156. If you take them your photograph, they'll reproduce it in icing on the cake of your choice. The result is a white slab with a sombre sepia image, rather like a Portuguese tombstone. There's a chess and go shop (No.147) and a shop selling hand-woven Tibetan tiger rugs. A church by the 19th-century grand-father of modern Dutch architecture, P. J. H. Cuypers, has been converted into offices. Towards the end of the street you'll have to concentrate hard not to miss De Groene Lanteerne which, at 128cm wide, claims to be the world's narrowest restaurant.

Going East

Skirting the top edge of inner Amsterdam, going east from Central Station you come to the **Scheepvaarthuis** (Shipping House), built in 1916 (on the site of the place where the first Dutch fleet set sail for the East Indies) as the offices for six big shipping companies. After serving as the headquarters of the municipal transport authority during the 1980s and most of the 1990s it was closed for renovation, and will probably reopen as a hotel. It was the first building designed by the team of architects (Van der Meij, Kramer and De Klerk) who became known as the Amsterdam School, a sort of fantastical Dutch Art Nouveau movement. Nothing escapes decoration. The building comes to a prow-like point crowned by a statue of Neptune. He waves his trident while his wife Salicia takes the wheel. Four female figures represent the points of the compass. The walls are encrusted with unflattering reliefs of sea heroes. Doors, stairs, window frames and any wall space left are patterned with appropriate images—wave forms, sea horses, dolphins, anchors, seals and ship's wheels. The roof line is a cheval-de-frise of moulded lead. It's as if you're viewing the building in a distorting mirror: there's hardly a smooth surface in sight. The maritime motifs continue inside with filigreed metalwork ornamentation, beautiful stained-glass skylights and windows and much of the original furniture (also designed by the architects). Doorknobs, lamps, wall-panels, floor patterns all reflect the theme. No detail is missed.

Farther along Prins Hendrikkade you come to the eye-catching **New Metropolis Science & Technology Centre** (*open Tues–Sun 10–6, Sat open until 9pm; adm f24, after 4pm f14, under-17s f16*), featuring all sorts of interactive equipment in a giant ship-shaped museum designed by Italian architect Renzo Piano. Across the water is the **Nederlands Scheepvaart Museum** (Maritime Museum), built as an admiralty warehouse in 1655 (*open Tues–Sun 10–5; adm f14.50*). It's a wonder the building's still upright: workers were bribed with *drinkgelt* (drinking money) and finished it in just nine months and fourteen days. The new warehouse had a system of cisterns and sprinklers to put out fires and an army of rat-catching cats with their own office and keeper. The museum's main attraction—a full size replica of the *Amsterdam*, one of the VOC's ships—is moored outside (occasionally it pays visits to other ports). You can see the captain's cabin, have a look at his tiny loo then descend into the ship's murky maw where up to 200 sailors would live for months at a stretch. Back in the museum you can see a cutaway of an 1840s outrigger and the ostentatiously gilded Royal Barge used for state occasions and for paddling visiting dignitaries around the canals. You can also climb up to the Second World War room to peer out at Amsterdam through a periscope. The rest of the museum comprises room after room of maps, navigational equipment from previous eras, and models and pictures of ships. Everything is informatively labelled in Dutch and English, giving you a good introduction to the history of Dutch seafaring. The 'Time Voyage' multimedia show takes you a step further, portraying—with smoke machines, movies, slide shows and special effects—how unjolly it was to be a tar in the 17th century. In an unmarked room in the cellar a man sells model kits of awesome complexity (*Thurs–Sat only*).

Across the bridge to the right is the **Kromhout Museum** (*open Mon-Fri 10–4; adm f3.50*), one of Amsterdam's oldest shipbuilding yards, and one of the few to survive the 19th-century decline in the trade. It had a new lease of life in the 20th century when it produced the diesel engine used by most Dutch inland craft. In the 1960s it moved to larger premises and the old yard became a museum. Some boat building and restoration still goes on, but rows of diesel engines form the bulk of the exhibits. It's very much a place for the enthusiast.

The Plantagebuurt

The elegant, wide streets of the **Plantage** ('Plantation') district east of Waterlooplein were once a bushy parkland where Amsterdammers would lounge about on feast days, or go on long evening walks. At the end of the 19th century this was flattened by rows of showy neoclassical houses with outrageous colonial embellishments (pineapple pinnacles, exotic festoons, negro figurines propping up the beam ends). Many of the wealthier Jews moved into the grand new houses and by the 1920s it was the suburb of the Jewish élite. In 1897 the **Hollandse Schouwburg** (Holland Theatre) at Plantage Middenlaan 24, after a false start as an operetta theatre, became the home of the Nederlandsche Toneelvereeniging (Dutch Drama Society)—the company that propelled Dutch theatre into the 20th century. Because of the large number of Jews in both the audience and the theatre group itself, the occupying forces during the Second World War renamed it the Joodsche Schouwburg (Jewish Theatre). In 1942 it was designated an assembly point for Jews waiting to be deported. People were kept in the darkened building for days and then herded on to trains bound for Westerbork and then on to the death camps at Auschwitz and Sobibor. Understandably, after the war no one much wanted to use the Hollandse Schouwburg as a theatre again; in the 1960s it was declared a memorial to the deported Jews who never returned. Today only a secluded memorial garden lies behind the façade. Every year on 4 May (Remembrance Day) the city keeps a two-minute silence at 8pm to commemorate those who died in the war.

Nearby is the **Desmet Cinema**. During the war, German Jewish refugees staged theatre and cabaret here. The shows were so good that even the Nazi officer in charge of deportation would slip in to watch. Across the way is the **Wertheimpark**, the last remaining patch of the old Plantage gardens. At the entrance, two sphinxes with lanterns on their heads glower from the top of disproportionately large gateposts. Most of the park seems taken up by a fountain in memory of A. C. Wertheim (1832–97), a philanthropic banker who lived out his motto: 'Be a Jew in the synagogue and a human being in society', by being available in his office for an hour every morning to anyone, Jew or gentile, who needed to appeal to his charity. In one corner of the park, built over an urn of ashes brought back from Auschwitz, is a monument to Jews who perished in the concentration camps. Smashed mirrors lie flat on the ground: a symbol that the Earth can no longer reflect Heaven without distortion.

Just a little nearer to town, the **Hortus Botanicus** (*Botanical Gardens; open 1 April–1 Oct, 9–5 on weekdays and 11–5 other days; from 1 Oct to 1 April it closes at 4pm; adm f7.50*), was originally an apothecaries' herb garden in a marshy corner of the Plantage. It was later inundated by tropical plants pillaged by the Dutch East India Company, and has ended up with one of the biggest botanical collections in the world. A coffee shrub cultivated at the Hortus was presented to Louis XIV in 1714. Its seeds were used to initiate the cultivation of coffee in South America. A century later the gardens narrowly survived Louis Bonaparte's attempt to turn them into a zoo. The animals arrived before any cages had been built and the orangery became a volatile dormitory for wolves, lions, monkeys and porcupines. Tranquillity was restored when, after the king's untimely departure from the Netherlands, a relieved directorate put the animals up for auction. During the first half of this century, the gardens' biggest attraction was the massive Victoria Amazonica water lily. People would queue for hours on the one night of the year when it flowered, and—so the stories go—could stand, three at a time, on the broad lily pads. The sturdy plant survived this abuse, but not the demolition of its greenhouse in the 1960s. For decades there was no Victoria Amazonica at the Hortus, but in the 1990s a new greenhouse was built, and the giant lily once more has pride of place. The Hortus is a tranquil spot, a pocket-sized patch of green that's not really part of the tourist circuit. It won't take you long to nip in and see the ancient varieties of tulip, visit the world's oldest pot plant, warily observe the cabinet of flesh-eating plants, enjoy the tropical climes of the glass-domed palm house or the balmy air in the new three-climate hothouse. Then you can cool off with a fruit juice in the Orangery.

Along the Amstel

On the Amstel river just south of its crossing with Prinsengracht is a lively classical building with a cornice of jesters and grinning clowns. This is the **Royal Carré theatre**, built as a circus for Oscar Carré in 1887. Until 1875, Amsterdam had held an annual fair in September. It was a three-week beanfeast that engulfed the entire city with balls, celebrity performances, sideshows and circuses. One of these was Carré's, which King Willem III had granted the honorary title of 'Royal Dutch'—the equivalent of an official 'By Appointment' stamp. But the revels had grown a little too unleashed for the tastes of the Protestant patricians, and the city council declar-ed that the 'Kermis' of 1875 was to be the last. Despite rioting in the streets (which destroyed much of the original mauve 17th-century glass in canal-house windows), their edict was carried out and Amsterdam lost its annual wassail. But Carré decided he was going to stay. He built a 'temporary' wooden circus tent beside the Amstel and, when the council wasn't looking, erected a stone façade. Outraged city fathers declared that he should take it down, but Carré fought on tenaciously throughout the 1880s, and eventually got his way. The striking building you see today was built within months as the circus's permanent home. Now it hosts mainly musicals, but the best time to see its circular plush interior is when it reverts to being a circus over the Christmas holiday.

A little way up the river you can see the **Magere Brug** ('Skinny Bridge'). It was built in the 17th century for two spoilt young maidens who were too lazy to walk the long way round from their house in Kerkstraat to their stables across the river. A public outcry prevented its being replaced by a steel bridge in 1929, but the old structure was rotting and today's delicate white wooden swing bridge is a replica.

De Pijp

The area just south of the Singelgracht, east of Museumplein, is known as De Pijp (The Pipe) for the long thin passages that run between the 19th-century tenement houses. Once a slum, it's now a lively neighbourhood populated by artists and immigrant communities. The main north–south street is Ferdinand Bolstraat, but the streets seem to get brighter, busier and nosier as you get closer to the **Albert Cuyp Market**, where it all explodes into a kaleidoscope of colour and a press of eager shoppers that stretches for over a kilometre. Eating seems to be an important reason to be here. Between the piles of silk, gaudy modern clothes and cheap shoes, boxes of dried herbs and teas, people slip raw herrings down their throats, guzzle home-made chocolates, queue for freshly cooked waffles, taste farm cheese and stock up on fish, fruit and vegetables for even greater feasting at home.

The **Heineken Brewery Museum** (*guided tours only: Mon–Fri 9.30 and 11am,1pm and 2.30pm Saturdays in July and Aug also noon and 2pm; allow 2 hours; adm f3, which goes to charity*) on the corner of Ferdinand Bolstraat and Stadhouderskade is the birthplace of Heineken beer. The brewery, established here in 1867, stopped production on this site only a few years ago when Amsterdam began to drink more than the brewery could produce. Now smart guides lead you through the stables (old dray horses *in situ*) and past huge copper vats. You learn how beer is made and how the Heineken family made its fortune. The real purpose of the visit for many people, however, seems to be the free beer at the end of the tour.

Amsterdam School Architecture and the New South

The Nieuw Zuid (New South) was created by the architect H. P. Berlage (1856–1934), the father of modern Dutch architecture (*see* p.51), after a new law had revolutionized Amsterdam housing conditions. In 1915–17 he drew up a plan of wide avenues and narrow side streets that reflected the 17th-century canals. He died before he could implement it, and his work was taken on with even greater enthusiasm by Michel de Klerk and Pieter Kramer, architects of what became known as the Amsterdam School. De Klerk was a working-class wunderkind headhunted from primary school to begin work with the city's leading architectural firm at the age of 14. He and Kramer set out to design buildings that were, in his words, 'sensationally shocking'. They were successful. When the Nieuw Zuid was finished nobody wanted to live there. The area eventually became a ghetto for Jews fleeing persecution in Germany. (The Frank family lived on Merwedeplein before going into hiding.) In the past few years there's been a revival of interest in the Amsterdam School. Houses, bridges and even public lavatories are being declared national monuments.

In reacting against their sober, rational Dutch predecessors, the Amsterdam School produced an idiosyncratic cross between Old Dutch and Art Nouveau, which has led to some quirky and amusing, but also rather beautiful building. You can see why they're sometimes called the 'Gaudís of the North'. Their whimsical brick buildings are instantly recognizable by the curves and bulges of their façades. The buildings are constructed around a reinforced concrete frame, so the bricks can do what they like. The pleats and folds earned the movement's work the nickname *schortjesarchitectuur* (apron architecture). Decorative, polychromatic, almost sculptural brickwork is used lavishly. Odd parabolic and trapeziform windows and angulated carved doors contrast startlingly with the general symmetry of the buildings. Stone and brick sculptures are integrated into the building's design, especially at corners and on bridges. In the Nieuw Zuid these are usually the gnome-like mythical figures by Hildo Krop (1884–1970).

You can see prime examples of Amsterdam School in the area around **Burgemeester Tellegenstraat**, a patch of streets and squares designed entirely by Kramer and De Klerk. In 1918 the housing association **De Dageraad** (Daybreak) gave the young men free rein to design the neighbourhood. Strikingly curved staircase towers, wavy rooftops, jutting sharp-edged windows and fancy coloured brickwork are the results of this freedom from restriction. The buildings are wonderful to look at, but residents complain their furniture doesn't fit in the odd-shaped rooms. The two crescents of Burgemeester Tellegenstraat are completely symmetrical. Look at the lettering in the doorways. You'll occasionally even find corresponding lettering on one side reflected in mirror image on the other.

spectator sports

The Amsterdam **football** team, Ajax, is one of the best and most popular in the country. Important matches have even been known to cause the city council to adjourn sessions. Ajax won European Cups three times in the 1970s, and managed again in 1995. If you want to see the team for yourself, head for their flashy new home, the Amsterdam ArenA, ✆ 311 1333, next to the Bijlmer metro station in Amsterdam South East. A good **ice hockey** team (S IJ S Amsterdam 89) plays at the Jaap Edenhal rink, Radioweg 64, ✆ 694 9652, from Oct to Feb. The local **basketball** team, Canadians Amsterdam, is one of the best in the country. They play at the Apollohal, Stadionweg, ✆ 671 3910. Fans of **American football** might be lucky enough to catch an Amsterdam Admirals, ✆ 465 0550, home game at the Amsterdam ArenA or at the old Olympic Stadium.

do-it-yourself

The 1980s health mania hit Amsterdam as soundly as it did other major cities in the Western world, and has persisted into the 1990s. You can find a number of well-equipped **gyms and fitness centres** around town. Two of the best are: Splash, Looiersgracht 26–30, ✆ 624 8404 (*open daily 7am–midnight; weights, machines, sauna, steam, massage and aerobics; f35 per day/f65 per week/f135 per month all inclusive*) and Garden Gym, Jodenbreestraat 158, ✆ 626 8772 (*open Mon, Wed, Fri 9–11, Tues and Thurs 12–11, Sat 11–6.30 and Sun 10–5 mainly, though not exclusively, for women; weights, dance, sauna, solarium, massage, self-defence; day pass f15, with sauna/shower f22.50, sauna only f17.50*). Sauna Deco, Herengracht 115, ✆ 623 8215 (*open Mon–Sat 11–11, Sun 12–6 adm f17.50 before 2pm, or f25 per day*) is an exhilarating experience. You sweat away those extra inches in a stylish Art Deco interior rescued from a famous 1920s Parisian department store.

Swimming pools in Amsterdam are clean, well-maintained and supervised. They often have small bars or coffeeshops at the water's edge so you can top up the calories after a swim. Opening times are complicated, with periods set aside for club and naked swimming, so phone first. The Marnixbad, Marnixplein 9, ✆ 625 4843 (*adm f4.50*) has waterslides and a whirlpool. The Mirandabad, De Mirandalaan 9, ✆ 642 8080 (*adm f7*) has tropical temperatures, a pebble beach and a wave machine. There's an outdoor pool for good weather and a slide and whirlpool. The Zuiderbad, Hobbemastraat 26, ✆ 679 2217 (*adm f4.5*) is just a plain, rectangular pool of water for swimming quietly up and down in. It was built at the beginning of the century and still has most of its original features, including some beautiful tile work and a neat perimeter of wooden changing cubicles opening on to the edge of the pool.

Walking and **cycling** are national pastimes, and the canals and cycle paths make both a joy. If you want an uninhibited jog, head for the Vondelpark or the Amsterdamse Bos. The Amsterdam Tourist Board can offer suggestions for cycling or walking tours (*see* p.61 for bicycle hire). They will also be able to give you information on the **Grachtenloop** ('canal run'), Amsterdam's equivalent of the London Marathon. One Sunday early in June thousands of people come together to spend the best part of the day jogging set distances up and down the main canals.

If you're lucky you may be in Amsterdam in a year when the canals freeze over, and everyone whizzes around the city on **skates**. (Be careful, though, the ice can be thin and sometimes doesn't freeze under bridges.) If you don't have your own skates, head for Jaap Edenhal, Radioweg 64, ✆ 694 9652, a large indoor rink where you can hire skates for ƒ9 (you'll need your passport or a ƒ100 deposit).

If bats, rackets and balls are your forte, you'll find **squash** and **indoor tennis** courts at the Frans Otten Stadion, Stadionstraat 10, ✆ 662 8767 (*open Mon–Fri 9–11, Sat 9–8, Sun 9–10; tennis ƒ37.50 per hour/ƒ50 after 5pm, squash ƒ30/ƒ37.50 per hour; racket hire ƒ5*). There are 36 tennis courts, most of them outdoor, at the Amstelpark, Koenenkade 8, ✆ 644 5436 (*open daily 8am–11pm; indoor courts ƒ35 per hour, outdoor courts ƒ30; racket hire ƒ5*). Squash City, Ketelmakerstraat 6, ✆ 626 7883 (*open Mon–Fri 8.30–midnight, Sat and Sun 8.30–10; ƒ17.50 for 45 minutes after 5pm Mon–Fri and on Sun, ƒ13.50 before 5pm and on Sat; racket hire ƒ5*) also has a weights room and sauna for players to use. For **table tennis** enthusiasts, there's the Table Tennis Centre Amsterdam, Keizersgracht 209, ✆ 624 5780 (*open Sun 1–7.30pm, Mon 2–6pm, Tues–Sat 2pm–1am; ƒ12.50 per table per hour*).

As gentler form of relaxation, you might try a little **billiards**, **snooker** or the pocketless Dutch variation called ***biljart*** (countless volunteers willing to explain the rules and offer advice around every table). You'll find all three played at the Biljartcentrum Bavaria, Van Ostadestraat 97, ✆ 676 4059 (*open daily 11am–1am; snooker ƒ10 per hour until 2pm, then ƒ15*). The Snookercentrum de Keizer, Keizersgracht 256, ✆ 623 1586 (*open Mon–Thurs and Sun noon–1am, Sat noon–2am; ƒ8.50 per hour before 7pm, then ƒ12 for pool and ƒ15 for snooker*) is in a 17th-century canal house. The tables are in private rooms and you can phone down to the bar for drinks.

Amsterdam ✆ *(020–)*   **Shopping**

> *What is there that's not found here*
> *Of corn; French or Spanish wine*
> *Any Indies goods that are sought*
> *In Amsterdam may all be bought*
> *Here's no famine—the land is fat.*

Constantijn Huygens, 17th-century Dutch poet

Amsterdam's prosperity in the Golden Age turned it into an exotic emporium mundi. The little shops below the decorative *uithangborden* (painted signs) were crammed with Nuremberg ceramics, Lyons silk, Spanish wines, mysterious Egyptian potions and an abundance of local pastries, cheeses, linen and boots. When Marie de Médicis made her grandiose entry into Amsterdam in 1638, the first thing she did when she had a moment's spare time (amidst the lavish ceremonies celebrating her arrival) was to swoop down on the Amsterdam shops where, apparently, she haggled with the adept confidence of someone reared in a marketplace.

Amsterdam's markets, boutiques and eccentric speciality shops are still one of the city's greatest allures. The only barriers against your absolute financial ruin are the inconvenient opening hours. Calvinism wins over tourism—despite the recent relaxation of laws governing shop hours, you'll find very few places at all open on a Sunday. Many shops also stay closed on Monday mornings, if not for the whole day. However, most stay open late on Thursday nights.

after-hours shopping

Amsterdam night shops include **Baltus**, Vijszelstraat 127, **Big Bananas**, Leidsestraat 76, with big price tags and rude assistants, and **Heuft's First Class Nightshop**, Rijnstraat 62, for late-night oysters and champagne. In addition to these, the **Albert Heijn Supermarket** on Koningsplein is open 10–10 Mon–Sat and noon–6 on Sunday. It is a conventional supermarket with normal prices. Some larger stores in the city centre (such as **Hema** and **De Bijenkorf**) are now also open on Sunday afternoons.To locate a late-night pharmacy contact an information service on ✆ 694 8709.

antiques

The Rokin (the street running from the Dam to Muntplein) was once the traditional stretch for antique dealers. Now there are only a few crusty die-hards here—the sort of shop where you have to comb your hair and ring a bell before they let you in. These days the most stylish, outlandish and enticingly chaotic treasure-troves are to be found in the Spiegelkwartier (*see* p.86) and around the Looiersgracht.

bicycles

Macbike, Mr Visserplein 2. Second-hand bikes. Parts, repairs and sympathy when your machine falls to bits or the front wheel gets caught in the tram lines.

't Mannetje, Frans Halsstraat 35. Tandems, three-wheelers and other curious designs, as well as repairs.

books

Good antiquarian bookshops pop up all over the city, but especially around the university at the southern end of the red-light district. New books in English are usually quite expensive in Amsterdam.

American Book Center, Kalverstraat 185. After W.H. Smith's, the best stock in town of English fiction and non-fiction, magazines and children's books.

Architectura & Natura, Leliegracht 44. Just what it says, with an impressive collection of books on Amsterdam.

Atheneum, Spui 14–16. Stamping ground of the city's intelligentsia. Good selection of magazines and English non-fiction.

The Book Exchange, Kloveniersburgwal 58. Essential in this town of outrageous prices.

La Carte, Utrechtsestraat 110–12. Maps, streetplans and guide books.

The English Bookshop, Lauriergracht 71. Carefully selected range, with some second-hand.

Intertaal, Van Baerlestraat 76. Everything you need to learn Dutch or to teach English.

Lankamp & Brinkman, Spiegelgracht 19. Children's books in English.

Lambiek, Kerkstraat 78. Cheery comic shop. Collectors' pieces and a cartoonists' gallery.

Robert Premsela, Van Baerlestraat 78. Art books a cut above the museum shops.

De Slegte, Kalverstraat 48–52. Discount and antiquarian megastore.

Waterstones, Kalverstraat 152. Large well-stocked branch of the British chain.

Foto Amsterdam, Rokin 22. Official dealer for all the big names.

Superfoto, Leidsestraat 80, and around town. Colour film ready in an hour.

Ruad Foto, Jan Toroopstraat 47. Cameras, computers and camcorders to hire.

clothes

You will find tasteful, well-cut clothes in fine fabrics at much lower prices than in other capitals. The second-hand clothes shops attract stall-grubbers from around the globe. **P. C. Hooftstraat** and **Van Baerlestraat** are the corridors of high fashion—here you'll find international labels as well as Dutch designers.

Cora Kemperman, Leidsestraat 72. Slightly off-the-wall yet supremely stylish.

Edgar Vos, P. C. Hooftstraat 134. Nifty suits for the high-powered businesswoman.

Fever, Prinsengracht 192. Hot little numbers for hot little people.

Sissy Boy, Van Baerlestraat 15. Middle-of-the-road elegance at fast-lane prices.

Rob & Rik, Runstraat 30. Leatherwear from functional to fetish.

Tothem, Nieuwezijds Voorburgwal 149. Swimsuits and sexy underwear for men.

La Culotte, P. C. Hooftstraat 111. Pricey, sensuous silk lingerie.

Clubwear House, Herengracht 265. Clubwear for the brave and the beautiful.

For children's clothes there's **Bam Bam**, Magna Plaza, Nieuwezijds Voorburgwal 182, where there's treasure-trove for trendy toddlers, and **Oilily**, P. C. Hooftstraat 133, for tiny tots whose mums and dads have big pockets.

Clusters of second-hand shops rub elbow patches with each other in the zigzag of lanes from Huidenstraat to Hartenstraat. You could also try **Hans en Grietje**, Overtoom 255, for ethnic and colonial bits and bobs, and **Petticoat**, Lindengracht 99, for Fifties retro, hats, shawls and cufflinks, and zooty underwear.

department stores

De Bijenkorf, Dam 1. 'The Beehive'—aptly named. Bustling shop with a wide range of good quality merchandise, and no pretensions to being Harrods.

Hema, Kalvertoren, Kalverstraat (and all around town). The Dutch Woolworth's or five-and-dime—but all in good taste. An excellent one-stop shop to stock up on essentials.

Metz & Co., Keizersgracht 455. Liberty prints, stylish kitchenware and design-museum furniture. Superb view of Amsterdam from the glass-walled café on the top floor.

Delftware, clogs and gifts

Rinascimento Gallerie d'Arte, Prinsengracht 170. Old and new Delftware (the real thing, not souvenir shop tat). Watch the designs being painted on by hand.

De Klompenboer, Nieuwezijds Voorburgwal 20. Clogs and other wooden goodies carved on the premises. Also pewter and lace.

diamonds

Shop around but stick to established dealers. You can watch diamonds being cut in a number of shops, including **Coster Diamonds**, Paulus Potterstraat 2–6, **Rokin Diamonds**, Rokin 12, and **Van Moppes**, Albert Cuypstraat 2–6.

food

Look out for two kinds of **bakery**. A *warme bakker* sells breads and biscuits and a *banketbakker* sells pastries and all the wonderful creamy things that the doctor forbids. Many also sell hand-made chocolates. Try **Runneboom**, 1e van der Helststraat 49, for delicious ryebread, Greek village loaves, healthy wholemeals and crispy white rolls, **Hendrikse**, Overtoom 472, with tarts and cream cakes fit for Queen Beatrix, and closer to the centre of town, **C. O. Hotkamp**, Vijzelgracht 15.

In the better **cheese** shops you'll be given a sliver to taste before buying. Choose from mild *jong* (young), or the more tangy *belegen* (matured) or *extra belegen*. **Arxhoek**, Damstraat 19, has a large selection, especially of farm cheeses. **Pasteuning Deliwijn**, Willemsparkweg 11, is a traditional Italian deli with a good selection of wines. **A Taste of Ireland**, Herengracht 228, sells British provisions for the homesick; and the chain **Natuurwinkel**, Weteringschans 133, and all around town, provides everything from organic vegetables and wine to vitamins and tofu-burgers.

Albert Hein is the most popular chain of supermarket. You'll find branches on Waterlooplein, Koningsplein and Vijzelstraat. The largest—the one behind the Royal Palace—is also open on Sundays.

For tea and coffee, go to **Keizer**, Prinsengracht 180, with wondrous aromas and odd utensils in an early 19th-century setting; or **Geels & Co**, Warmoesstraat 67, the city's oldest tea and coffee specialist, in the middle of the red-light district.

De Bierkoning, Paleisstraat 125, a cosy shop behind the palace, sells glasses of all shapes and around 750 brands of bottled beer. **Hart's Wijnhandel**, Vijszelgracht 3, has a wide range of wines and spirits.

markets

Albert Cuyp Markt, Albert Cuypstraat, *Mon–Sat 9–4.30*. Foodstuffs, clothes and hardware (*see* p.111).

Bloemenmarkt (Flower Market), Singel, between Muntplein and Koningsplein, *Mon–Sat 9–6*. Amsterdam's floating flower market (*see* p.76).

Boerenmarkt, Noordermarkt, *Sat 10–3*. Organic produce, ethnic crafts.

Lapjesmarkt, Westerstraat, *Mon 7.30–1*. Bargain clothes and spectacular fabrics.

Lindengracht, *Sat 9–4*. Small general market, but the best.

De Looier Indoor Antiques Market, Elandsgracht; *Mon–Thurs 11–5, Sat 9–5*. Mid-price antiques market. There's also a *rommelmarkt* (junk market) just around the corner.

Nieuwmarkt, *May–Sept, Sun 10–5*. Good quality antiques in the shadow of a medieval city gate and weighing house.

Noordermarkt, *Mon 7.30–1.30*. Pile upon pile of junk. Get there early for a treasure hunt.

Oudemanhuis Book Market, Oudemanhuispoort, *Mon–Sat 10–4*. A dim alley smelling of musty binding and yellowing paper.

Stamp Market, near Nova Hotel, Nieuwezijds Voorburgwal 276; *Wed, Sat 11–4*. Grizzled collectors swap stamps, currency, medals and esoteric jokes.

Waterlooplein; *Mon–Sat 10–4*. Amsterdam's famous fleamarket.

Amsterdam abounds in idiosyncratic speciality shops: old family businesses, outlets for some personal obsession or the fantasies of quixotic visionaries. Here are but a few:

De Beestenwinkel (The Animal Shop), Staalstraat 11. Stuffed bunnies, tiger puppets and teddy bears to put your pyjamas in.

Brillenwinkel, Gasthuismolensteeg 7. Classic spectacle frames, from Mahatma Gandhi to Dame Edna.

Condomerie Het Gulden Vlies, Warmoesstraat 141. Condom as consumer item.

Joe's Vliegerwinkel, Nieuwe Hoogstraat 19. Kites weird and wonderful.

Hangmatten Maranón, Singel 488–90. Bright and breezy hammocks.

P. G. C. Hajenius, Rokin 92–6. Tobacconist with famed house-brand cigars.

The Head Shop, Kloveniersburgwal 39. Accessories for dope devotees.

Kitsch Kitchen, 1e Bloemdwarsstraat 21. Gaudy plastic goodies, brightly patterned enamel bowls and curious kitchen implements.

Knopenwinkel, Wolvenstraat 14. Buttons of all shapes and periods.

Kramer, Reestraat 20. Candles and candlesticks—ethnic to high altar.

Klamboe Imports, Prinsengracht 232. Mosquito nets—the best way to ward off the pests.

Olivaria, Hazenstraat 2a. An entire shop devoted to olive oil; there's even a tasting bar.

Poppendokter, Reestraat 20. Dolls and parts of dolls.

Vlieger, Amstel 34. Pencils, pigments and piles of inspiring paper.

Waterwinkel, Roelof Hartstraat 10. Over 100 types of mineral water from around the world, and mud from the Dead Sea.

De Witte Tanden Winkel, Runstraat 5. Champagne-flavoured toothpaste and toothbrushes, toothbrushes, toothbrushes.

Amsterdam ℂ (020–)   ### Where to Stay

It's a summer Friday afternoon. The Amsterdam Tourist Board information office opposite Centraal Station is brimming with hopeful weekenders looking for accommodation. But by 4 o'clock Amsterdam is full. Frustrated visitors are being despatched to surrounding towns like Leiden or Haarlem—pretty towns, and commuting is swift and cheap, yet this is always going to be second-best.

The truth is, to relish Amsterdam you need to stay right in the centre, preferably on a canal, and to do that you should book a hotel room well in advance—two to three weeks at least, more in the summer or over holiday weekends. There is, of course, always the chance of catching a cancellation, and some hotels do keep back a room or two until the last minute; if you cannot book in advance, try calling the hotel direct just before noon—the witching hour between check-out and check-in—and try your luck.

As Amsterdam is such a compact city, hotels in this list are graded by price rather than area. Nearly all of them are within easy walking distance of the main tourist sites, and have been chosen because of their pleasant atmosphere, location or historical significance. An asterisk ★ indicates hotels that are especially recommended.

American Hotel, Leidsekade 97, 1017 PN, ✆ 556 3000, ✆ 625 3236 (*luxury*). An Art Deco extravaganza overlooking the thronging Leidseplein. The café downstairs was once the meeting place for Amsterdam's literati.

★Amstel Hotel Intercontinental, Professor Tulpplein 1, 1018 GX, ✆ 622 6060, ✆ 622 5808 (*luxury*). A gracious and sedate hotel on the banks of the Amstel. If you're stuck for transport you can use the hotel's motor yacht or limousine.

Blakes, Keizersgracht 384, 1016 GB, ✆ 530 2010, ✆ 530 2030 (*luxury*). Style diva Anouska Hempel brings her touch to a grand canal house. Bedrooms range from voluptuous to Buddhist minimalist. Guests are rich and famous. Well, rich anyway.

★Hotel de l'Europe, Nieuwe Doelenstraat 2–8, 1012 CP, ✆ 531 1777, ✆ 531 1778 (*luxury*). An elegant 19th-century hotel in the grand old style. Knocks spots off the Doelen down the road.

The Grand Amsterdam, Oudezijds Voorburgwal 197, 1001 EX Amsterdam, ✆ 555 3111, ✆ 555 3222 (*luxury*). The Grand Amsterdam was built as an inn in 1578, then used as Admiralty Headquarters, and finally served as Amsterdam's city hall (from 1808 to 1988). Many fine 1920s interior fittings remain (including the Wedding Room in which Queen Beatrix plighted her troth), but some people are put off by the proximity of the red-light district.

Grand Hotel Krasnapolsky, Dam 9, 1012 JS, ✆ 554 9111, ✆ 626 1570 (*luxury*). Right in the centre of town. Very grand from the outside, and inside a mix of period charm and all mod cons.

★Hotel Pulitzer, Prinsengracht 315–31, 1016 GZ, ✆ 523 5235, ✆ 627 6753 (*luxury*). Twenty-four canal houses linked up to form a warren of oak-beamed rooms. There's a peaceful garden and a magnificent 18th-century restaurant.

Amsterdam Hilton, Apollolaan 138–140, 1077 BG, ✆ 710 6005, ✆ 710 6000 (*luxury*). Modern building in the south of the city, not in the centre.

Hilton International Schiphol, Herbergierstraat, 1118 ZK, ✆ 710 4000, ✆ 710 4080 (*luxury*). Part of Schiphol complex around the airport. Shuttle bus from airport.

Seven One Seven, Prinsengracht 717, 1017 JW, ✆ 427 0717, ✆ 423 0717 (*luxury; special weekend rates*). Superb, antique-filled suites on one of the smartest canals in town. The owners have aimed at creating a relaxed, homey atmosphere—albeit an extremely chic and well-appointed home.

Hotel Ambassade, Herengracht 335–353, 1016 AZ, ✆ 626 2333, ✆ 624 5321 (*expensive*). Eight converted houses, dotted about with antiques and with a magnificent breakfast-room overlooking the canal.

Golden Tulip Doelen Hotel, Nieuwe Doelenstraat 24, 1012 CP, ✆ 554 0600, ✆ 622 1084 (*expensive*). One of Amsterdam's oldest hotels, though fading in grandeur. Rembrandt painted the *Night Watch* here in 1642.

★Dikker & Thijs Fenice Hotel, Prinsengracht 444, 1017 KE, ✆ 626 7721, ✆ 625 8986 (*expensive*). Plum in the middle of it all, in a hectically lively area of town. Modern furnishings in a 100-year-old shell.

Jan Luyken Hotel, Jan Luykenstraat 58, 1071 CS, ✆ 573 0730, ✆ 676 3841 (*expensive*). Smart, efficient business hotel in quiet area near the Concertgebouw.

★Schiller Karena Hotel, Rembrandtplein 26–36, 1017 CV, ✆ 554 0700, ✉ 626 6381 (*expensive*). The downstairs café was once the meeting place of actors and artists. The hotel itself is smart, comfortable and overlooks a lively square.

Acca International, Van de Veldestraat 3a, 1071 CW, ✆ 662 5262, ✉ 679 9361 (*moderate*). Modern, functional hotel near the main museums.

Hotel Acro, Jan Luykenstraat 44, 1071 CR, ✆ 662 0526, ✉ 675 0811 (*moderate*). Sparkling, simple, if a little soulless. Set in the quiet museum district.

Hotel Agora, Singel 462, 1017 AW, ✆ 627 2200, ✉ 627 2202 (*moderate*). The owner is interested in fine furniture—and it shows. Rooms overlooking the canal or back garden are the best.

Hotel Amsterdam Prinsengracht, Prinsengracht 1015, 1017 KN, ✆ 623 7779, ✉ 623 8926 (*moderate*). Friendly, all mod cons and canal views. The décor is a little bland.

Hotel Belga, Hartenstraat 8, 1016 CB, ✆ 624 9080, ✉ 623 6862 (*moderate*). Unpretentious, family-run hotel in a quaint shopping alley.

★Het Canal House, Keizersgracht 148, 1015 CX, ✆ 622 5182, ✉ 624 1317 (*expensive–moderate*). Stunning converted canal houses, filled to the brim with the owner's carefully chosen antiques. The hotel has the feel of a tastefully (if grandly) decorated private home, and it has a lift (quite a rarity in these historic houses).

★La Casaldó, Amsteldijk 862, 1079 LN, ✆ 642 3680, ✉ 644 7409 (*moderate*). Romantic houseboat with a waterside terrace and just four rooms, all individually decorated. It's on the outskirts of town, so a car or bicycle is a good idea.

★Hotel De Filosoof, Anna Vondelstraat 6, 1054 GZ, ✆ 683 3013, ✉ 685 3750 (*moderate*). Each room is named after a well-known thinker, and decorated accordingly. The hotel can arrange consultations with one of Holland's practising philosophers.

Hotel Orlando, Prinsengracht 1099, 1017 JH, ✆ 638 6915, ✉ 625 2123 (*moderate*). Canalside house with just five rooms, individually decorated in a modern style.

Owl Hotel, Roemer Visscherstraat 1–3, 1054 EV, ✆ 618 9486, ✉ 618 9491 (*moderate*). Smart family hotel with garden. In the museum neighbourhood.

★Quentin Hotel, Leidsekade 89, 1017 PN, ✆ 626 2187, ✉ 622 0121 (*moderate*). Popular with musicians playing at De Melkweg around the corner. Posters of past (now famous) residents adorn the walls. Spotless, tastefully decorated and good views over the canal.

★Hotel Seven Bridges, Reguliersgracht 31, 1017 LK, ✆ 623 1329, no fax (*expensive–moderate*). The most charming of the small hotels. Beautifully decorated rooms—and breakfast served in bed.

Hotel Toren, Keizersgracht 164, 1015 CZ, ✆ 622 6033, ✉ 626 9705 (*moderate*). Seventeenth-century canal house with high moulded ceilings, and antiques scattered among the modern furniture.

Hotel Washington, Frans van Mierisstraat 10, 1071 RS, ✆ 679 6754, ✉ 673 4435 (*moderate*). Large 19th-century house on a peaceful avenue near the Concertgebouw. Room furnishings are simple but tasteful, and there's a small back garden.

★Hotel Wiechmann, Prinsengracht 328–30, 1016 HX, ✆ 626 3321, ✉ 626 8962 (*moderate*). Carefully converted canal houses with an air of old world charm, and a noble breakfast-room.

Hotel De Admiraal, Herengracht 563, 1017 CD, ✆ 626 2150, @ 623 4625 (*inexpensive*).
Friendly owner, views over two canals, and a good breakfast.

Hotel Adolesce, Nieuwe Keizersgracht 26, 1018 DS, ✆ 626 3959, @ 627 4249 (*inexpensive*). Cheerful, simple hotel with a sunny breakfast-room. A good one if you have children, as it is one of the few establishments that genuinely welcomes them.

Hans Brinker, Kerkstraat 136, 1017 GR, ✆ 622 0687, @ 638 2060 (*inexpensive*). Prides itself on its no-frills good value and central situation.

Hotel Brouwer, Singel 83, ✆ 624 6358, @ 520 6264 (*inexpensive*). A gem. Canal house with rooms tastefully done up with lovely old furniture.

Hotel Engeland, Roemer Vischerstraat 30, 1054 EZ, ✆ 689 2323, @ 685 3148 (*inexpensive*). The English representative in a quaint row of 19th-century houses built to show seven different national architectural styles.

Hotel de Harmonie, Prinsengracht 816, 1017 JL, ✆ 625 0174, @ 622 8021 (*inexpensive*). Bright, jolly, family-run hotel.

Hotel Hoksbergen, Singel 301, ✆ 626 6043. @ 638 3479 (*inexpensive*). No-nonsense knotty pine, some canal views, clean rooms and friendly management.

Hotel Impala, Leidsekade 77, 1017 PM, ✆ 623 4706, @ 638 9274 (*inexpensive*). Clean, laid-back hotel with young crowd.

Hotel Prinsenhof, Prinsengracht 810, 1017 JL, ✆ 623 1772, @ 638 3368 (*inexpensive*). Quiet, thoughtfully decorated hotel with friendly management.

Hotel de Westertoren, Raadhuisstraat 35b, 1016 DC, ✆/@ 624 4639 (*inexpensive*). Well-kept, if a little noisy.

bed and breakfast

Amsterdammers do not seem much taken by B&B. When you do find private accommodation, it probably won't be all that much cheaper than a room in a small hotel.

Bed and Breakfast Holland, Theophile de Bockstraat 3, 1058 TV, ✆ 615 7527, @ 669 1573, has a number of B&Bs on its books. *Prices range from f95 for a minimum 2-night stay and there is a f20 booking fee per reservation. Advance bookings only.*

hostels

The two official International Youth Hostel Federation hostels are **Vondelpark**, Zandpad 5, 1054 GA, ✆ 589 8999, @ 589 8955; and **Stadsdoelen**, Kloveniersburgwal 97, 1011 KB, ✆ 624 6832, @ 639 1035. *Members f28 per person (incl. breakfast); non-members f33; sheet hire f6.25.*

There are also **Arena**, 's Gravesandestraat 51, 1092 AA, ✆ 694 7444, @ 663 2649, an erstwhile seedy hippy Sleep-Inn, now considerably smartened up and attracting a friendly crowd of backpackers, *double room f135, dormitories from f27.50, bedding f5*; ★**Eben Haezer Christian Youth Hostel**, Bloemstraat 179, 1016 LA, ✆ 624 4717, @ 627 6137, a spotless, not oppressively religious and the best value of the lot. *f27.50, including breakfast and bed linen, no membership required, lockers available*; and **The Flying Pig Park**, Vossiusstraat 46, 1071 AJ, ✆ 400 4187, @ 470 5159, friendly crowd, clean dorms, free lockers and a cosy café beside the Vondelpark, *dorm beds from f26.50 per person, double room f120.*

The following list is a very personal selection from the hundreds of good restaurants Amsterdam has to offer. An exploratory wander around the Jordaan, through the alleys that criss-cross the canals (from Reestraat to Huidenstraat), or along Utrechtsestraat will reveal even more. Restaurants are listed in three areas. '**Central**' refers to the semi-circle bounded by the three main canals. The **Jordaan** is the area in the west of the city, just beyond the canals. Restaurants in the north, south and east will be found under '**Further Afield**'.

Amsterdam is very much a cash city. Many smaller restaurants don't accept **credit cards**, and there's an air of reluctance about those that do. Even some of the larger establishments don't like plastic—so it's always a good idea to check in advance. Feasting Amsterdammers and hungry tourists fill up most good restaurants pretty quickly, so it's wise to reserve a table by telephone.

Really good, inexpensive foreign food can be found in foreign-national snack bars. Try **Bird** (Thai; Zeedijk 77), **Kismet** (Turkish; Albert Cuypstraat 64), **Maoz** (Israeli falafel; Reguliersbreestraat 45), **Riaz** (Surinam; Bilderdijkstraat 193).

Central

Excelsior, Hotel l'Europe, Nieuwe Doelenstraat 2–8, ✆ 531 1705 (*expensive*). Grand without being pompous. Waiters in tails bring you *haute cuisine* classics or the very best in new Dutch cooking, and there's a superb view over the Amstel. Dress: jacket and tie.

Koriander, Amstel 212, ✆ 627 7879 (*expensive*). The view is even more sublime than from the Excelsior, but the menu and décor more down-to-earth. The *gezellig* atmosphere and no-nonsense (yet imaginative) fare are a great attraction to artistes from the nearby Opera House. *Open till midnight; closed Sun/Mon.*

Sichuan Food, Reguliersdwarsstraat 35, ✆ 626 9327 (*expensive*). Proud possessor of the first Michelin star awarded to a Chinese restaurant in the Netherlands. There are aperitifs made from flowers, sautéed oysters with tangy sauces, lobsters and fish cooked in ways that local western restaurants are beginning to imitate.

De Silveren Spiegel, Kattengat 4–6, ✆ 624 6589 (*expensive*). The building, all Delft tiles and cosy corners, dates from 1614. The visionary chef comes up with such dishes as guinea fowl with rose petal sauce, and uses prime local ingredients, such as lamb from the North Sea island of Texel (where the creatures frolic freely and eat wild herbs). Service is personal and friendly.

't Swarte Schaep, Korte Leidsedwarsstraat 24, ✆ 622 3021 (*expensive*). Up a steep staircase in a 300-year-old building you'll find oak beams, antiques, superb wines, an eclectic cuisine and passing members of the Dutch royal family.

De Utrechtsedwarstafel, Utrechtsedwarsstraat 107, ✆ 625 4189 (*expensive*). Igor works single-handedly in the kitchen, Hans is front-of-house. Igor is a culinary whizz, and Hans an expert on wines. There's no menu, just a grid offering three, four or five courses, at a simple, medium or gourmet level. Wine is included in the price. You pick your level, tell them if there is anything you prefer not to eat, and wait to be surprised.

Igor comes out to tell you about the meal; Hans chats about the wine, tailor-making choices as you go along. It's like going to dinner at a friend's, who just happens to be a heavenly cook and have an enviable cellar. *Closed Sun/Mon.*

D'Vijff Vlieghen (The Five Flies), Spuistraat 294–302, ✆ 624 8369 (*expensive*). An intriguing conglomeration of antique-filled rooms in a wonky 17th-century inn. It gets its name from the original owner, Jan Vijff Vlieghen. In the 1950s and 1960s it was frequented by the likes of Orson Welles, Benjamin Britten, Jean Cocteau and Walt Disney. These days the restaurant rests on its laurels, and doesn't give good value.

Van Harte, Hartenstraat 24, ✆ 625 8500 (*moderate*). Modest, yet an excellent kitchen. Berries and wild mushrooms in the sauces, tender meats and charming service.

Vasso, Rozenboomsteeg 12–14, ✆ 626 0158 (*moderate*). Fresh pasta and fine Italian food in a restaurant that has the lively atmosphere of the kitchens of a faded palazzo.

1e Klas, Platform 2B, Centraal Station, ✆ 625 0131 (*moderate*). Well-prepared (though not wildly adventurous) Dutch fare in the beautifully restored First Class restaurant.

De Compagnon, Guldehandsteeg 17, ✆ 620 4225 (*moderate*). Down an alley in the red-light district, and through a green door, you'll find a series of tiny rooms, perched on top of each other, filled with antique bric-a-brac, and with views across the little harbour on the Damrak. It is an unexpected find, romantic and intimate—but sadly one of those restaurants where the atmosphere outdoes the cuisine, which is run-of-the-mill Franco-Dutch.

Hemelse Modder, Oude Waal 9, ✆ 624 3203 (*moderate*). Haunt of writers. Before you get to the divine chocolate mousse that gives the restaurant its name ('Heavenly Mud'), try some of the fish or vegetarian dishes. *Closed Mon.*

Kort, Amstelveld 2, ✆ 626 1199 (*moderate*). Freshly prepared food with simple sauces. Somewhere for the health-conscious gourmet. Quiet terrace on the water's edge, and a coolly rational Wiener Werkstätte interior.

Krua Thai, Spuistraat 90a, ✆ 620 0623 (*moderate*). After much audible campery in the kitchen, spectacular dishes issue forth. The hot-and-spicy beef salad is unbeatable, and the stuffed chicken wings divine.

Maison Descartes, Vijzelgracht 2, ✆ 622 4936 (*moderate*). In the depths of the French cultural institute, surrounded by the Delft tiles of a 17th-century Dutch kitchen, you can enjoy regional French cuisine. Menus change nightly.

Memories of India, Reguliersdwarstraat 88, ✆ 623 5710 (*moderate*). Top-class Indian cuisine in curious sub-continental post-modern surrounds. Sit between copper palm trees and stubs of marble column and enjoy fried pomfret, chicken with cinnamon and cardamom sauce, or searing curries. Run by the same family who own the renowned Khan's restaurant in London.

Pier 10, De Ruyterkade Steiger 10 (behind Centraal Station), ✆ 624 8276 (*moderate*). A little wooden hut, once a shipping line office, right on the end of a pier in the IJ. Watch the boats chug past as you devour scrumptious Dutch/French food.

Saturnino, Reguliersdwarsstraat 5h, ✆ 639 0102 (*moderate*). Trendy Italian restaurant on the city's main gay street. You can pop in for a pasta, or linger for a full meal. The atmposhere is glitzy, but the food has a wholesome home-made touch.

Sluizer Visrestaurant, Utrechsestraat 45; and **Sluizer**, Utrechtsestraat 41–3, ✆ 622 6376 (*moderate*). Two adjacent trendy restaurants, evocative of the thirties with marble-topped tables and fringed lamps. Both are usually packed, and the fish restaurant especially has a good reputation. Both open till midnight.

Tujuh Maret, Utrechtsestraat 73, ✆ 427 9865 (*moderate*). All too often an Indonesian rijsttafel turns out to be a series of bowls of barely distinguishable spicy gunge, served with piles of rice. But here you can treat yourself to a flavoursome feast. The soto ayam (chicken broth) has a fine bouillon base, and the different chicken and meat dishes are just that: different. You can enjoy beef in a mild sauce of soya and nutmeg, or a zippier version cooked with red peppers and tamarind; chicken as a tangy curry, or with a gentle coconut sauce.

Turquoise, Wolvenstraat 22–24, ✆ 624 2026 (*moderate*). A bizarre combination of wood-panelled Art Nouveau décor and Turkish cuisine. Under Tiffany lamps, beside cherubs rampant, you can tuck into a feast made up of different starters or try such main courses as chicken breast with cheese and garlic. Warm, homey service.

Le zinc...et les dames, Prinsengracht 999, ✆ 622 9044 (*moderate*). A converted 17th-century warehouse, adorned with portraits of women. The clientele may all seem under 25 and on their first date, but the French cuisine is robust and tasty, with dishes from various regions and wines-by-the-glass to match. *Closed Mon.*

Zuid Zeeland, Herengracht 413, ✆ 624 3154 (*moderate*). Specializes in fish dishes from Belgium and the south of Holland, but also meat dishes with a French and Japanese influence. *Closed Sat, Sun.*

Anda Nugraha, Waterlooplein 339, ✆ 626 6046 (*cheap*). Tasty home-cooked Indonesian food. *Rijsttafel f45 for two people.*

Axum, Utrechtsedwarsstraat 85–87, ✆ 622 8389 (*cheap*). Authentic Ethiopian cuisine—which means a giant communal pancake and a few sizzling pots of stews and curries. Toss on some salad and yoghurt sauce, add a spoon of stew, and roll up mouth-sized bites with your fingers. Appropriately ethnic décor and utterly charming service.

Balthazar's Keuken, Elandsgracht 108, ✆ 420 2114 (*cheap*). Every Wednesday Alain Parry and his cousin Karin have breakfast together, and decide the week's menu. The kitchen takes up a third of the room, and diners crowd around a few small wooden tables, three nights a week. You take pot luck, though there's a fish-or-flesh choice for the main course. Starters are usually meze-style and might include cockles with ginger and parsley or a red-pepper salad with anise pepperoni. For a main course you may have buttery pink salmon in a crackly coat of nori, scattered with crisp-fried green asparagus, served with sepia risotto and a perky anchovy sauce. *Open Wed–Fri.*

Bird, Zeedijk 77, ✆ 420 6289 (*cheap*). Tiny Thai snack bar with a kitchen one end, a trendy crowd squashed around a few tables, and tantalizing Thai cuisine.

De Blauwe Hollander, Leidsekruisstraat 28, ✆ 623 3014 (*cheap*). Cheap and cheerful, if rather heavy, Dutch cooking.

Casa di David, Singel 426, ✆ 624 5093 (*cheap*). Wooden beams and canalside charm give this pizzeria a special edge. The food is good too. The pasta is made on the premises and there is an excellent array of antipasti. The pizzas are cooked in a wood-burning oven and are fragrant and crusty.

Centra, Lange Niezel 29, ✆ 622 3050 (*cheap*). Busy, garish, cafeteria-like atmosphere, and the best Spanish food in town.

Et Alors, Nes 35, ✆ 421 6056 (*cheap*). Run by two sisters in the heart of the alternative theatre district. Suzanna serves at table, while Sandra slaves single-handedly in the kitchen. Dedicated Francophiles, they have decorated their small restaurant with a comfortable clutter of old furniture picked up on treks through France. It's all for sale, even the plates you eat off. The cuisine, of course, is French—unpretentious fare, with a cared-for, home-cooked touch.

Goodies, Huidenstraat 9, ✆ 625 6122 (*cheap*). Arty hangout that sells good sandwiches and salads by day, and pasta by night.

Haesje Claes, Spuistraat 273–5, ✆ 624 9998 (*cheap*). Touristy, but unhurried. Folksy Old Dutch interior, solid tasty Dutch food, lots of salad and vegetables.

Keuken van 1870, Spuistraat 4, ✆ 624 8965 (*cheap*). Began as a soup kitchen in 1870. Punks, pensioners and passing backpackers come in for enormous, tastily cooked meals for under ƒ17. *Kitchen closes 8pm weekdays, 9pm Sat–Sun.*

Pancake Bakery, Prinsengracht 191, ✆ 625 1333 (*cheap*). The best pancakes in town.

La Place, Rokin 162, ✆ 620 2364 (*cheap*). A great salad bar, fresh pastas and grilled meats cooked while you wait. Most of the ingredients are organic, you sit in one of a honey-comb of rooms in an atmospheric 17th-century building.

Rose's Cantina, Reguliersdwarsstraat 38, ✆ 625 9797 (*cheap*). Crowds of Bright Young Things, tasty Tex-Mex food and lethal margaritas.

Song Kwae, Kloveniersburgwal 14, ✆ 624 2568 (*cheap*). The place to go for Thai food when you've been unable to squeeze into Bird (*see* above).

Surinam Express, Halvemaansteeg 18, ✆ 622 7405 (*cheap*). Tiny sandwich shop off Rembrandtplein with seeringly authentic Surinamese food—spicy vegetable and tangy curry fillings. But you can order fuller meals too, and eat at a counter along the wall.

d'Theeboom, Singel 210, ✆ 623 8420 (*cheap*). Georges Thubert scorns rip-off prices and culinary pretension. He runs his restaurant, in a converted canalside warehouse, in classic French style, and offers excellent value and fine cooking.

Upstairs Pannekoekhuis, Grimburgwal 2, ✆ 626 5603 (*cheap*). Teeny pancake parlour suspended above a bustling lane.

Woeste Walmen, Singel 46, ✆ 638 0765 (*cheap*). Run by squatters, who have decorated a large canal-house parlour with quirky flair and who come up with food that they have enjoyed cooking. The menu changes daily, and there is usually one meat and one non-meat option for the main course. *Open Sat and Sun only.*

The Jordaan

Christophe, Leliegracht 46, ✆ 625 0807 (*expensive*). The atmosphere can be a little frigid, but Algerian-born Jean-Christophe Royer comes up with superb French cuisine enlivened by zesty north-African flavours, which makes up for all.

De Luwte, Leliegracht 26, ✆ 625 8548 (*moderate*). Candlelight, wooden tables and chairs, subtle *trompe l'œil* scenes on the walls, and windows looking on to a small canal make for a romantic evening. Delicious meals with fresh (often organically grown) ingredients and tangles of salad complete the picture.

Speciaal, Nieuwe Leliestraat 142, ✆ 624 9706 (*moderate*). Many say the best Indonesian restaurant in town.

Stoop, 1ᵉ Anjeliersdwarsstraat 4, ✆ 639 2480 (*moderate*). Small, busy restaurant with an open kitchen and an all-embracing cuisine. Try home-made beef pastrami salad with ginger-and-yoghurt dressing, or Peking duck with a chutney of aubergines and figs.

Ristorante Toscanini, Lindengracht 75, ✆ 623 2813 (*moderate*). Cavernous, rowdy and very Italian. A gastric and sensual delight, but service is exceeding slow. Bring a pack of cards. *Closed Tues.*

Caramba, Lindengracht 342, ✆ 627 1188 (*cheap*). Lively South American restaurant where an arty crowd consumes tortilla and gets poleaxed by vicious margaritas.

De Eettuin, 2ᵉ Tuindwarsstraat 10, ✆ 623 7706 (*cheap*). Forests of greenery, generous Dutch portions and a modest salad bar.

Moeders Pot (Mother's Cooking), Vinkenstraat 119, ✆ 623 7643 (*cheap*). Meat and ten veg cuisine. A one-person affair run by a huge hairy man who must have 'mother' tattooed somewhere under his white T-shirt.

Further Afield

Beddington's, Roelof Hartstraat 6–8, ✆ 676 5201 (*expensive*). Austere décor, but sumptuous meals by a chef who combines culinary experience from Derbyshire, the Far East and the summits of French haute cuisine. *Closed Mon.*

Ciel Bleu, Okura Hotel, Ferdinand Bolstraat 333, ✆ 678 7111 (*expensive*). God's-eye view of Amsterdam from the 23rd floor of one of the city's lone tower blocks. The cuisine is appropriately *haut. Dress: jacket and tie.*

Vis aan de Schelde, Scheldeplein 4, ✆ 675 1583 (*expensive*). Minimalist décor, no muzak, subdued conversation, and above all a gentle hand in the kitchen. Fish comes perfectly cooked: tuna with just a tinge of pink, meltingly soft monkfish. The chef's imagination roams free without running rampant. For a starter try marinated salmon with asparagus steeped in vanilla and orange.

Yamazato, Hotel Okura, Ferdinand Bolstraat 333, ✆ 678 7111 (*expensive*). Supreme Japanese cuisine, from the appropriately named 'Emperor's Menu' to the smallest sushi, all exquisitely presented on lacquered platters and in hand-made bowls, brought to you by waitresses in kimonos..

Yoichi, Weteringschans 128, ✆ 622 6829 (*expensive*). Amsterdam's oldest Japanese restaurant, and still up there with the best. Traditional décor, traditional food, traditional high prices.

Basak, Frans Halsstraat 89, ✆ 664 9534 (*moderate*). Unassuming Turkish restaurant lit by multicoloured glass lanterns, and serving tasty casseroles as well as the usual grills. Everything comes with heaps of fresh salad.

La Brasa, Haarlemmerdijk 16, ✆ 625 4438 (*moderate*). One of the more intimate of the Argentinian grills. Very much a place for carnivores: hairy cowhide seats and juicy beef on a wood grill.

De Gouden Reael, Zandhoek 14, ✆ 623 3883 (*moderate*). A 17th-century house on a quayside in the Western Islands. Renowned for its French provincial cuisine.

Griet Manshande, Keerpunt 10, ℗ 622 8194 (*moderate*). Hidden in a corner of a modern housing estate on the Bickerseiland. Choose your meal from the daily selection in the vitrine—anything from classic coq au vin to roast skate with beurre noir. The service is friendly and the cooking subtle and skilled.

De Groene Lanteerne, Haarlemmerstraat 43, ℗ 624 1952 (*moderate*). The narrowest restaurant in the world—in places just a doorway wide, run by a couple who are becoming renowned for their hearty French fare.

Bodega Keyzer, Van Baerlestraat 96, ℗ 671 1441 (*moderate*). Writers and musicians have been coming here for nearly a century to eat smoked eel and fresh sole. (The Concertgebouw is right next door.) *Closed Sun; open till midnight.*

Kilimanjaro, Rapenburgerplein 6, ℗ 622 3485 (*moderate*). A tabletop tour of Africa, Begin with a delicious fish soup from Guinea, then crocodile from Senegal, or a spicy Tanzanian red snapper curry.

De Knijp, Van Baerlestraat 134, ℗ 671 4248 (*moderate*). Near to the Concertgebouw. Fresh oysters are a speciality. *Open till midnight.*

The Movies, Haarlemmerdijk 159, ℗ 626 7069 (*moderate*). Crowded restaurant attached to an old Art Deco cinema offers 'Cuisine Sauvage'—challenging concoctions such as red bass with kumquats.

De Ondeugd, Ferdinand Bolstraat 15, ℗ 672 0651 (*moderate*). Just minutes' barrow-trundle from the Albert Cuyp market. The fish and vegetables are alarmingly fresh. Try the goose liver on apple compôte, Thai soup or grilled swordfish with tomato *beurre blanc*. Main dishes come with frites and mayonnaise—but here the mayo is home-made and the chips hand-hewn and delicious.

Sparks, Willemsparkweg 87, ℗ 676 0700 (*moderate*). Friendly neighbourhood brasserie, with a small garden courtyard and understated décor. Amsterdammers in the know come here to savour Sander van Ommeren's inspired Mediterranean-influenced cooking. Start with marinated octopus with rocket and artichoke crème, then try a brochette of lamb with sea lavender, bulgur pilaf and thyme-lavender gravy.

De Witte Uyl, Frans Halsstraat 26, ℗ 670 0458 (*moderate*). Big tables, comfortable chairs, a carefully chosen wine list, and a menu of imaginative medium-sized dishes. Just the place to come with a group of friends, order a few bottles, and share the food. *f80.*

Witteveen, Ceintuurbaan 256–58, ℗ 662 4368 (*moderate*). Peter Greenaway meets Zeffirelli. Vast red, black and gilt interior; dressed-up waiters, and tables smothered with white linen. Folk from the neighbourhood, looking a little stiff and uncomfortable in their Sunday best, tuck in the napkins and sit down to some of the best traditional Dutch cooking in town.

Zabar's, Van Baerlestraat 49, ℗ 679 8888 (*expensive–moderate*). It doesn't look much from the outside—a tatty jalousie and plants squashed up against the window. But inside you'll find a cheery crowd of Amsterdammers enjoying flavourful food from all over the Mediterranean region, from Moroccan lamb casserole to crunchy Greek halva. And it's just a few minutes' walk to the Concertgebouw.

Arena, 's Gravesandestraat 51, ℗ 694 7444 (*cheap*). Backpackers and assorted budget travellers chomp their way through stews and other tummy-filling fare in café-like surrounds. The occasional cloud of hashish smoke wafts by.

Kong Kha, Rijnstraat 87, ℗ 661 2578 (*cheap*). Small, bustling restaurant and take-away, where you'll find authentic Thai home-cooking. A bit out of the way, but well worth a short ride on the number 4 tram. The *tod man plaa* (fishcakes) are delicious, and the *tom kha kai* (chicken and coconut soup) is sweet and soothing to the palate, a perfect contrast to some of the more fiery main dishes.

Riaz, Bilderdijkstraat 193, ℗ 683 6453 (*cheap*). Great Surinamese curries, which you can order with rice or roti—a pancake in which you roll up your food then eat with your fingers.

De Vrolijke Abrikoos (The Jolly Apricot), Weteringschans 76, ℗ 624 4672 (*cheap*). Pastel shades, pine tables and bio-dynamic ingredients combined with subtlety and flair. Try giant roast mushroom with a creamy sauce, delicate oriental soups, or bass with a robust tomato sauce. In good weather you can sit at tables in the back garden. *Closed Tues.*

Waroeng Asje, Jan Pieter Heijestraat 180, ℗ 616 6589 (*cheap*). Surinamese/ Indonesian takeaway with a few tables for eating-in, near the Vondelpark. The *soto soep* (spicy meat-and-veg soup with a bowl of rice alongside, *f7*) is a meal in itself.

vegetarian

Bolhoed, Prinsengracht 60, ℗ 626 1803 (*cheap*). Exotic Thai statues, quirky lamps and candelabra, bright colours (but soft lighting) make a far remove from clichéd knotty pine. The cuisine has a Mexican touch, and is imaginative and tasty. There are vegan dishes available, fish too, and the daily special three-course menu (*f30*) is excellent value.

Golden Temple, Utrechtsestraat 126, ℗ 626 8560 (*cheap*). Simple décor, but tasty food with strong Indian flavours. Vegan options.

De Waaghals, Frans Halsstraat 29, ℗ 679 9609 (*cheap*). Vegetarian cuisine with organic ingredients and international influences. Try the Tunisian bean casserole, or coconut and aubergine soup—though flavours are sometimes subtle to the point of blandness.

Zest, Prinsenstraat 10, ℗ 428 2455 (*moderate*). Trendy restaurant in fusion mode, but offering good vegetarian choices. Try Thai risotto with sugarsnap beans and mushrooms.

Restaurants that put special effort and imagination into the vegetarian options on the menu are: **Hemelse Modder** (Central); **Woeste Walmen** (Central); **De Luwte** (Jordaan); **De Vrolijke Abrikoos** (Further Afield); **Griet Manshande** (Further Afield).

late night

Of the restaurants listed above, a few keep their kitchens open until midnight: **Bodega Keyser** (Further Afield), **De Knijp** (Further Afield), **Koriander** (Central), **Sluizer** (Central), and **Saturnino** (Central). The downstairs **Diner** at the Holland Casino is open until 2am and serves good food. You don't have to buy a casino ticket to get in. **Bojo** (Lange Leidsedwarsstraat 51) is an Indonesian restaurant open until 2am during the week and until 5.30am on Fri and Sat. **Maoz** (Reguliersbreestraat, near Tuschinski Cinema) serves scrumptious falafel and salads on the street all through the night. **Gary's Late-Nite Bagel Shop** (Reguliersdwarsstraat 53) sells genuine New York bagels, cheesecake and muffins until the wee hours.

Cafés are at the centre of an Amsterdammer's social life. Wooden floors and furniture, and walls stained by years of cigarette smoke, have inspired the name '**brown café**'. Here you can have a drink or just a coffee, nibble snacks or plough through hefty Dutch meals. But most of all you sit and talk, or while away the time leafing through the day's papers or glossy magazines. There's seldom any grating background music—though in friendly neighbourhood bars the clientele may burst into song. Whether it's in a tiny café supported by a handful of locals, or a stylish new bar with an arty crowd, you'll find that Amsterdammers create an atmosphere where they can relax and feel both *uit* and *thuis* ('out' and 'at home').

The term 'café' covers a wide range of establishments. At one end of the spectrum are the poky **bars**, where you go to knock back a few beers (with the odd *jenever* chaser); you might also be able to buy snacks. At the other end you'll find enormous, airy grand cafés and *eetcafés* (*see* p.17). Some rather startling newcomers made an appearance during the 1980s: the designer bars are the complete antithesis of the brown café—hard metal furniture, bright light and colours and loud music—but are now very much part of the Amsterdam scene.

Café-crawling is the best way to discover Amsterdam: between museum visits, on rainy afternoons, on long, hot summer evenings. There are nearly 1,500 cafés to visit, and you're sure to rootle out a few favourites for yourself—but here is a list of a few special ones to help you on your way. Most cafés close at 1 or 2am over weekends. They begin opening their doors around 11am, though some don't get it together until 3 or 4pm.

An asterisk (*) indicates cafés particularly recommended for their food. The letters after the address give you some indication of where the café is: C—the central area bounded by the main canals; J—the Jordaan and northwestern Amsterdam; S—south and southeast of the centre.

cafés

*Aas van Bokalen, Keizersgracht 335 (C). Arty brown café.

In 't Aepjen, Zeedijk 1 (C). A '*rariteitencafé*', crammed with antiques.

*Américain, American Hotel, Leidseplein (C). Splendid Art Deco grand café.

*Eetcafé Van Beeren, Koningsstraat 54, ✆ 622 2329. Quiet neighbourhood café with an imaginative chef.

*Belhamel, Brouwersgracht 60 (J). Art Nouveau décor on a pretty canal.

De Blaffende Vis, Westerstraat 118 (J). Cheery Jordaan café.

Cul de Sac, Oudezijds Voorburgwal 99 (C). Tucked away down a side alley—one of the few really good bars in the red-light district.

Dantzig, Zwanenburgwal 15 (C). Attractive corner of the ugly new Stadhuis. A grand café that frequently fills with wedding parties.

De Druif, Rapenburg 83 (near Maritime Museum) (C). Dates from 1631.

Dulac, Haarlemmerstraat 118 (J). Fantasy grand café, inspired by the French fairytale illustrator Edmund Dulac.

*De Duvel, 1ᵉ van der Helststraat 59–61. Busy café with a large terrace near the Albert Cuyp market.

Eik en Linde, Plantage Middenlaan 22 (near Zoo) (C). Local brown café with mixed, arty crowd.

Eland, Prinsengracht 296 (C). Traditional brown café.

*Engelbewaarder, Kloveniersburgwal 59 (C). Writers gulp down pasta and scribble away on wooden tables. Heated discussions about art and life echo from the corners.

*1ᵉ Klas (First Class), Platform 2B, Centraal Station. Lose yourself in the great age of rail travel.

De Gijs, Lindengracht 249 (J). Tiny two-tier bar with an edge of Jordaan eccentricity.

Gollem, Raamsteeg 4 (C). Home of a hundred (or more) beers.

*De Groene Olifant (The Green Elephant), Sarphatistraat 510 (S). Huge windows flood this cosy bar with light. The folk are friendly and the food delicious.

Het Hok, Lange Leidsedwarsstraat 134 (C). A refuge from the hordes on Leidseplein. Filled with quiet people playing chess.

Hollandse Manege Café, Vondelstraat 140 (S). Overlooks an exquisite 19th-century riding school arena.

Hoppe, Spui 18–20 (C). Dates from 1670. These days it's an after-work watering hole.

*Huyschkamer, Utrechtsestraat 137 (C). Trendy café in a former male brothel.

De IJsbreker, Weesperzijde 23 (S). Attached to Amsterdam's leading venue for serious contemporary music, with appropriate background sounds. Tranquil riverside terrace.

*De Jaren, Nieuwe Doelenstraat 20 (C). Light and airy. Home of the arts and media set.

Karpershoek, Martelaarsgracht 2 (C). Claims to be Amsterdam's oldest café (this is challenged by Café Chris).

De Kat in de Wijngaert, Lindengracht 160 (J). Quiet and friendly Jordaan café.

Koophandel, Bloemgracht 49 (J). Converted warehouse that only begins to fill up around midnight, then throbs till dawn.

*Kort, Amstelveld 2 (C). Modern café with a quiet canalside terrace.

*De Kroon Royal Café, Rembrandtplein 17 (C). Historic meeting place of variety artistes and their agents, with a view over Rembrandtplein.

Luxembourg, Spui 22–24 (C). Grand café that attracts well-heeled office workers.

*Het Molenpad, Prinsengracht 653 (C). A brown café that sometimes crams a live jazz band into one corner. A smoky, dreamy place to while away a Sunday afternoon.

Nol, Westerstraat 109 (J). Outrageously kitsch Jordaan bar. Locals, gangsters and astonished visitors get swept into uproarious sing-songs.

L'Opera, Rembrandtplein 19 (C). Sedate Art Deco café on a bustling square.

Papeneiland, Prinsengracht 2 (C). Built in 1642, with a secret passage to the house across the canal.

De Prins, Prinsengracht 124 (C). Pretty canalside pub popular with students.

*Van Puffelen, Prinsengracht 377 (C). Sawdust on the floor, and cherubs on the ceiling. A good restaurant at the back, a terrace on a barge on the canal in front, and a very smart clientele.

Rooie Nelis, Laurierstraat 101 (J). A Jordaan institution. Bursting with Jordaaners and visitors all having a good time.

*Rosereijn, Haarlemmerdijk 52 (J). Cosy brown café with a good selection of magazines and cheap, tasty food.

*Schiller, Rembrandtplein 26 (C). Cosy Art Deco bar tucked away from the rumpus of Rembrandtplein. Excellent cuisine.

't Smalle, Egelantiersgracht 12 (J). An 18th-century *proeflokaal* converted into brown café. Gets packed most evenings.

De Tuin, 2e Tuindwarsstraat 13 (J). Dim light, board games and a twinge of eccentricity. All the ingredients of a classic brown café.

Twee Prinsen, Prinsenstraat 27 (C). Heated terrace and a friendly Jordaan crowd who profess great rivalry with the 'yuppies' at the Vergulde Gaper on the opposite corner.

Twee Zwaantjes, Prinsengracht 114 (C). Electric organ music, accordions and big ladies with big voices from the Jordaan will make any visit unforgettable.

*Vertigo, Vondelpark 3 (S). Wonderful terrace on Vondelpark for good weather, cosy cellar under the Film Museum for bad.

*De Waag, in the old Waag (Weighing House) on Nieuwemarkt (C). Vast café, decorated with medieval austerity and lit entirely by candles.

Welling, J. W. Brouwerstraat 32 (C). Traditional brown café convenient for the Concertgebouw.

De Wetering, Weteringstraat 37 (C). A real log fire in winter and an ancient television that is used only for crucial football matches.

Wildschut, Roelof Hartplein 1–3 (S). Art Deco interior and noisy, smoky but none the less popular terrace.

designer bars

Esprit, Spui 10 (C). Plate-glass and aluminium showcase for the trendy.

Krull, Corner of 1e van der Helststraat and 1e Jan Steenstraat (S). Friendly café near the Albert Cuyp market.

*Morlang, Keizersgracht 451 (C). Brittle trendier-than-thou atmosphere, but good food.

*Het Land van Walem, Keizersgracht 449 (C). Friendlier than the Morlang next door, with a bigger terrace and a garden at the back.

Schuim, Spuistraat 189 (C). Shop-window café that fills up with students during the day, and at night artsy types who admire their friends' paintings on the walls.

Seymour Likely Lounge, Nieuwezijds Voorburgwal 250 (C). Real creation of a fictitious artist, and one of the trendiest spots in town.

Proeflokaalen (see p.18)

(see p.18)

De Admiraal, Herengracht 319 (C). Enormous, with comfy chairs—stretches the definition somewhat.

De Drie Fleschjes, Gravenstraat 18 (C). More traditional *proeflokaal*. Some nearby offices have their own marked barrels.

Het Proeflokaal, Pijlsteeg 31 (C). Delightfully cramped and crooked old *proeflokaal* with a range of flavoured *jenevers* and sticky liqueurs.

Backstage Boutique, Utrechtsedwarsstraat 65–7 (C). The zaniest coffeeshop in town.

Granny, 1e van der Helststraat 45 (S). Near Albert Cuyp market. Some of the best *appelgebak* in town.

Greenwoods, Singel 103 (C). Real English afternoon tea for the homesick. The owner is most frequently seen up to her elbows in flour making the next batch of scones or sponge cake.

Pompadour, Huidenstraat 12 (C). Refined hand-made chocolates in a splendid setting.

Puccini, Staalstraat 17 (C). Irresistible cakes and outrageous chocolates near the Waterlooplein fleamarket.

Reibach, Brouwersgracht 139 (J). German specialities, such as wickedly alcoholic fruit from the Rumtopf jar, and a view over a beautiful canal.

smoking coffeeshops

The Bulldog, Leidseplein 13–17/Oudezijds Voorburgwal 90 (C). Oldest but also the most commercial.

Rusland, Rusland 16 (C). Privately owned, intimate and relaxedly scruffy.

Pink Poffertje, moored at southern end of Oude Schans (C). Cosy boat that even sells marijuana beer.

Prix d'Ami, Haringpakkersteeg 5 (C). Deeply respectable-looking branch of a chain of coffeeshops.

Amsterdam ✆ (020–)   **Entertainment and Nightlife**

Amsterdam's nightlife centres on cafés. They offer everything from a quiet evening over the backgammon board to jolly sing-songs in just about any language you choose. There are even some cafés where you can dance, though a handful of good nightclubs serve those who really like to bounce and sweat. The more genteel spectator entertainments are quite accessible to foreigners. Films are usually shown in their original language, with Dutch subtitles; there's a strong tradition of highly visual theatre, and many performances in English; the new Muziektheater provides a venue for touring opera and dance companies and Amsterdam has high international status in the various music worlds. Up-and-coming British rock bands test the water here; there are some good jazz festivals, and recent immigration has upped the quality of salsa and Latin American music. The acoustically superb Concertgebouw attracts leading classical artists and conductors, and there's a very healthy contemporary music scene.

listings information

The various listings magazines will guide you through the maze. The tourist office publish a monthly *What's On In Amsterdam* (ƒ4, available at Amsterdam Tourist Board and around town). The free monthly **Uitkrant** (from Amsterdam Tourist Board, AUB (*see* p.63), libraries, museums and theatres) is more comprehensive and although it's in Dutch, fairly easy to follow. An even better bet (though also in Dutch) is the *PS Weekend* supplement to *Het Parool*. *Shark/Queer Fish* (ƒ2.50 from larger newsagents) is a twice-monthly guide to trendy Amsterdam, focusing mainly on clubs and with a strong gay slant. *Oor* (available from newsagents) is the Dutch equivalent of NME, the British rock music newspaper. Both the Amsterdam Tourist Board and the AUB booking office can reserve tickets. The AUB also has an up-to-the-minute 'What's On' noticeboard (good for pop music) and a few rainforests' worth of leaflets. If you're on line, access *www.aub.nl* for up-to-the-minute information on shows and exhibitions, and a bookings service too; or call Uitlijn on ✆ (0900) 0191.

cinema

You'll find most of the multi-screened commercial cinemas in the area around Leidseplein, where they offer pretty standard fare. The six-screen Tuschinski must be a hot contender for the most beautiful cinema in the world and is worth a visit no matter what's showing.

Desmet, Plantage Middenlaan 4, ✆ 627 3434. Ornate Art Deco cinema used by a Jewish cabaret company in the early years of the Second World War. These days known for its imaginative mini-festivals and weekend gay screenings.

Netherlands Film Museum, Vondelpark 3, ✆ 589 1400. Frequent changes of programme, usually with something from the museum's unique and extensive archive—such as tinted silent movies (*see* p.105).

Kriterion, Roeterstraat 170, ✆ 623 1708. Cult American movies and erotic French late-nights.

The Movies, Haarlemmerdijk 161, ✆ 638 6016. Some of the programming verges on the mainstream, but the 1920s interior is a delight and there's a vibrant café/restaurant.

Rialto, Ceintuurbaan 338, ✆ 675 3994. Good on retrospectives, science fiction, animation and children's films.

De Uitkijk, Prinsengracht 452, ✆ 623 7460. Amsterdam's oldest cinema (dating from 1913) squashed into an even older canal house. It features a white grand piano that has long since tinkled its last notes, but is too big to be removed.

See also **De Melkweg**, 'Multimedia Centres' below.

theatre

Two local English-speaking companies compete with foreign touring productions for the Amsterdam audience. The In Theatre presents small-scale productions, usually upstairs in a converted prop room at the Stadsschouwburg, and Boom Chicago offers improvised comedy in their own supper theatre next door. The Nes (off Damstraat) and the banks of the Amstel are traditionally Amsterdam's theatreland, but these days no old warehouse, factory or stable is safe from troupes of eager actors.

If you want to go to the theatre, the best thing to do is check the listings magazines for touring companies—but here's a short list of venues where you're most likely to find good work in English.

't Fijnhout Theater, Jacob van Lennepkade 334, ✆ 685 3755. A popular theatre with English-language touring companies.

Koninklijk Theater Carré, Amstel 115–25, ✆ 622 5225. Built for a circus—a function it still performs over the Christmas period when Dutch children regard a visit as de rigueur. It's the home of most big Amsterdam musicals, but more off-the-wall performances slip into gaps in the programme.

Felix Meritis, Felix Meritis Building, Keizersgracht 324, ✆ 626 2321. A descendant of the Shaffy, which was at the forefront of the avant-garde during the 1970s and 1980s, and housed in a building with a rich cultural past, the Felix Meritis is still a place to catch exciting new work.

De Stadsschouwburg, Leidseplein 26, ✆ 624 2311. Amsterdam's municipal theatre. The programme includes not only a wide range of national productions but also visiting international companies. There's a good theatre bookshop near the main entrance.

See also **De Melkweg**, 'Multimedia Centres' below.

dance

Bellevue, Leidsekade 90, ✆ 624 7248. Often host to modern dance touring companies.

Frascati, Nes 63, ✆ 626 6866. A venue for more established modern dance.

Muziektheater (Stopera), Waterlooplein 22, ✆ 625 5455. If you want to see something in this new opera house, ballet may be the best choice as the acoustics are iffy (*see* below).

classical music

AGA Zaal and Yakult Zaal, Damrak 213, ✆ 627 0466. Home to the Netherlands Chamber Orchestra and the Netherlands Philharmonic respectively. Beautifully converted concert halls in the old Beurs van Berlage (*see* pp.67–8).

Concertgebouw, Concertgebouwplein 2–6, ✆ 671 8345. The Grote Zaal (Large Hall) has perfect acoustics and is used for orchestral concerts and occasionally for visiting pop stars and jazz bands. Nervous students from the Sweelinck Conservatorium across the road make their professional débuts in the Kleine Zaal (Small Hall). There are free lunchtime concerts on Wednesdays (*see* p.103).

De IJsbreker, Weesperzijde 23, ✆ 693 9093. A deservedly famous centre for contemporary music. It brings out its own news-sheet and offers a stimulating programme of local and international composers and improvisers.

Muziektheater (Stopera), Waterlooplein 22, ✆ 625 5455. Home to the national ballet and opera companies, but subject of one of the biggest architectural and property development controversies of the century, and of angry complaints by musicians and audience alike about the bad acoustics (*see* p.79). It does, however, have an attractive, cosy auditorium—rare for a modern theatre.

De Rode Hoed, Keizersgracht 102, ✆ 638 5606. Varied programmes in a converted church.

Scan the listings magazines to find out about church concerts at the Oude Kerk, the Nieuwe Kerk, the Engelse Kerk and the Waalse Kerk.

rock and pop music

Akhnaton, Nieuwezijds Kolk 25, ✆ 624 3396. Recording studios, rehearsal facilities and a forum for much of the liveliest new music, hip-hop, Latin and other ethnic bands.

Amsterdam ArenA, Arenaboulevard 1, ✆ 311 1333. Sports stadium that is the venue for visiting megastars.

Arena, 's Gravesandestraat 51, ✆ 694 7444. The old hippy Sleep Inn has undergone a transformation into one of the trendiest music and dance venues in town.

Cruise Inn, Zeeburgerdijk 272, ✆ 692 7188. Flotsam and jetsam from the 1950s shake, rattle and roll in an old wooden clubhouse.

Korsakoff, Lijnbaansgracht 161, ✆ 625 7854. A venue for headbanging post-punks, which nods towards heavy metal and gothic teeny-boppers.

Paradiso, Weteringschans 6–8, ✆ 626 4521. An Amsterdam institution. A gloomy looking church that has been converted into a bright and buzzing venue for good music— anything from big rock names to jazz, African, Latin and even contemporary classical. Prices range from free entrance to around ƒ20 and starting times are usually between 9 and 11pm.

See also **De Melkweg**, 'Multimedia Centres', and 'Nightclubs' below.

jazz, Latin and folk

Jazzcafé Alto, Korte Leidsedwarsstraat 115, ✆ 626 3249. Live jazz every night in a cosy brown café tucked away in a brash touristy street.

De Badcuyp, 1ᵉ Sweelinckstraat 10, ✆ 675 9669. Neighbourhood café-cum-arts centre in a converted bathhouse, and a lively venue for jazz and salsa.

Bimhuis, Oudeschans 73, ✆ 623 1361. The city's major jazz venue plays host to visiting artistes and the cream of the locals, and has free sessions on Mondays and Wednesdays.

Brasil Music Bar, Lange Leidsedwarsstraat 70, ✆ 626 1500. Live Samba and a gyrating throng of Latin expatriates.

Casablanca, Zeedijk 26, ✆ 625 5685. Café hosting mainstream and standards bands, with the occasional jam session.

Jazz Cruise, tour starts at Rijksmuseum, Saturdays, April to Nov; 8pm and 10pm, ✆ 623 9886. An hour and a half of jazz on a canal boat, with beer, wine and cheese thrown in for good measure.

Maloe Melo, Lijnbaansgracht 163, ✆ 420 4592. Enduring, if somewhat poky, blues café.

Meander, Voetboogstraat 3, ✆ 625 8430. Lively café where, on alternate nights, students and their kind swing to salsa, bop to funk and chill out to jazz.

Mulligan's, Amstel 100, ✆ 622 1330. Rousing Irish sing-a-longs.

Odeon Jazz Kelder, Singel 460, ✆ 624 9711. Trad jazz in an intimate atmosphere.

Rembrandt Bar, Rembrandtplein 3, ✆ 623 0688. The Rembrandt Bar plays Dutch folk music. But for a real knees-up and noisy accordion rather visit Café Nol or De Twee Zwaantjes (*see* 'Cafés', p.129).

Rum Runners, Prinsengracht 277, ✆ 627 4079. Glitzy Caribbean bar/restaurant with live Latin bands on Sunday afternoons and early evening.

Soeterijn, Linnaeusstraat 2, ✆ 568 8500. The city's top venue for music from Africa, Indonesia, Eastern Europe and the Middle East.

nightclubs and dancing

The commercial discos (complete with chart music, plastic palm trees, expensive drinks and posses of drunken men) cluster around Leidseplein. What follows is a list of places for those with rather different tastes. Most venues close at 4am (5am over weekends). You should tip the doorman as you leave (about ƒ5), and avoid using cabs cruising outside. Legal cabs will be found at a nearby rank—or the club may phone for one for you.

Dansen bij Jansen, Handboogstraat 11, ✆ 620 1779. A bit like a Students' Union bop. You usually need to prove membership of a college or university to get in. Frequent theme and fancy-dress nights.

Escape, Rembrandtsplein 11, ✆ 622 1111. A cavern of a place that has shed its commercial image to become a hyper-trendy club, complete with shops and even a hairdresser.

Mazzo, Rozengracht 114, ✆ 626 7500. Comfortable club with a good atmosphere and an excellent range of music, often live with local bands.

Odeon, Singel 460, ✆ 624 9711. Multi-roomed venue in a converted canal house, but often overpopulated by adolescent tourists.

Scandals Lounge, Reguliersdwarsstraat 13, ✆ 422 6220. Glitzy hip and garage.

Sinners in Heaven, Wagenstraat 3, ✆ 620 1375. Weird 'n' wonderful décor; world-famous-in-Holland clientele.

Soul Kitchen, Amstelstraat 32, ✆ 620 2333. The sort of music that thirty-somethings can understand and dance to, in a friendly refreshingly untrendy atmosphere. No under 25s allowed.

Trance Buddha, Oudezijds Voorburgwal 216, ✆ 422 8233. Young New Age crowd with appropriate soundtrack.

West Pacific, Haarlemmerweg 8, ✆ 488 7778. Fun, hip dance-café that is part of an arts complex in an old gasworks.

See also **De Melkweg** below.

multimedia centres

De Brakke Ground, Nes 45, ✆ 626 6866. Attractive venue for Flemish art and performance. Dance programmes are especially worth catching.

De Meervaart Centrum, Meer en Vaart 1, ✆ 610 7498. A modern arts centre that stages a good variety of film, theatre, dance and music (both classical and jazz).

De Melkweg, Lijnbaansgracht 234a, ✆ 624 1777. Converted from an old dairy in the 1960s, De Melkweg (Milky Way) has lost its old hippie image, and emerged as a vibrant centre for the arts. The theatre has an imaginative programme and plays host to companies from around the world (performances are often in English). There is a small cinema that shows films from mainstream to cult; and a concert hall that stages excellent African and South American bands, and acts as a venue for a lot of up-and-coming rock groups. At weekends, when the bands have finished, an alternative disco takes over. The coffeeshop was one of the first where the sale of marijuana was tolerated by the authorities. If you're going to use the centre a lot, it's a good idea to take out membership (*f*15, valid three months) which gives you considerable discount on admission prices.

Amsterdam RAI, Europaplein 12, ✆ 549 1212. A business congress centre which frequently houses large concerts and touring musicals. It is also the venue for KunstRAI, an annual fair of contemporary art.

Westergasfabriek, Haarlemmerweg 8–10, ✆ 681 3068. Amsterdam's most recently opened arts centre is in a converted gasworks. It's home to the Toneelgroep Amsterdam and is the European base for the Cirque du Soleil. Visiting shows are usually in an experimental vein. Every night after 11pm the chairs in the café are moved aside and the customers bop until late.

In the heady social upheaval of the 1960s and 70s, when pixie-hatted members of the Gnome Party held protest meetings on the Dam and troupes of hippies camped out in the Vondelpark, Amsterdam's lesbians and gays joined in the frolic. Homosexuality had been decriminalized in 1811, but the gay community wanted a city free of the petty prejudices and subtle discrimination they ran up against in day-to-day life. In many ways they succeeded. Today Amsterdam is known as the Gay Capital of Europe. Gay bars and cafés, though often in clusters, aren't in ghettos. Nobody bats an eyelid if two men kiss or hold hands in public. The city was quick off the mark in coping constructively with HIV, the council housing department gives gay couples the same status as married heterosexuals, and in 1987 the world's first memorial to persecuted lesbians and gays, the Homomonument, was unveiled.

There are gay bars, clubs, hotels, bookshops and restaurants all over town. You'll find most of the heavier leather bars lurking up the north end of **Warmoesstraat**, ribbons of coffeeshops, restaurants and bars along **Kerkstraat** and **Reguliersdwarsstraat**, a jolly throb of clubs and pubs along the **Amstel** off Rembrandtplein, and scores of local cafés. Despite accusations that the Amsterdam gay scene is stagnating, gay tourists flock to the city. Over weekends, the hunk at the end of the bar is more likely to be a computer programmer from South London than a local lad. Many Amsterdammers respond to this invasion by staying at home, venturing out on Thursdays and Sundays when the occupying forces are thinner on the ground. The atmosphere, though, is friendly and welcoming. Most gay venues distribute free **maps of gay Amsterdam**, leaflets and free magazines (such as *Rainbow*) giving you an idea of what's on about town; though word of mouth is often the best way to find out what the evening might have in store.

Here is an idiosyncratic selection of places to go; some are well known but others are quirky, local establishments, out of the tourist maelstrom.

cafés, coffeeshops and restaurants

Backstage Boutique (a.k.a. 'The Twins'), Utrechtsedwarsstraat 75; *open Mon–Sat 10am–6pm*. Not exclusively gay, but with an atmosphere of stratospheric camp that shouldn't be missed.

Café Secret, Kerkstraat 346; *open Sun–Thurs 9pm–3am, Fri–Sat 9pm–4am*. Cosy café that sometimes has live entertainment.

COC, Rozenstraat 14; coffeeshop *open Wed–Sat 1–5pm*. Spartan but amiable haven in Amsterdam's lesbian and gay 'culture centre'.

Downtown, Reguliersdwarsstraat 31; *open daily 10–8*. A friendly day-time coffeeshop, popular with tourists and locals, in one of Amsterdam's gay streets. It serves food and has a sprawl of pavement tables on sunny days.

Getto, Warmoesstraat 51; restaurant/café *open Wed–Sat noon to 1am, Sun noon–midnight; closed Mon and Tues*. A young, friendly crowd and good food make this one of the most popular recent additions to the gay scene.

Le Monde, Rembrandtplein 6; *open daily 8am–midnight*. Tiny, cheery snack café with a terrace on Rembrandtplein.

La Strada, Nieuwezijds Voorburgwal 93; *open daily noon–1am.* Brown café with good food and friendly staff, popular with local lesbians.

Reibach, Brouwersgracht 139; *open daily 10–8, but closes 6pm Oct–Mar.* Trendy café with a Germanic edge, great cakes and a pleasant, small terrace on one of Amsterdam's most tranquil canals.

bars

Amstel Taveerne, Amstel 54; *open daily 3pm–1am, to 2pm at weekends.* Beer mugs and bric-a-brac hang everywhere. Dutch reproductions on the walls. Dutch originals around the bar. A provincial pub in the middle of the city with sing-alongs and good cheer (all Dutch).

April, Reguliersdwarsstraat 37; *open daily 2pm–1am.* More than double its previous size (and more attractively designed) after a 1996 renovation. Popular with young Amsterdammers during the week. Over the weekend tourists swell numbers until the bar bursts into a street party.

Argos, Warmoesstraat 95; *open Mon–Thurs 9pm–3am, to 4pm at weekends.* Amsterdam's oldest leather bar sweats with bikers' jackets, cowboy chaps and denim. As you wander into the dimmer recesses, what the gay guides coyly term 'action' becomes quite lively.

Havana, Reguliersdwarsstraat 17; *open daily 4pm–1am, to 2am at weekends.* Comfortable café/bar with an exhausting constellation of beautiful people. There's a small dance floor upstairs, so you can pop up for an early bop.

Casa Maria, Warmoesstraat 60; *open Sun–Thurs noon–1am, Fri–Sat noon–2am.* In the heart of the red-light district. A jukebox full of uproarious kitsch, a gregarious Spanish owner, and a picture window that offers the best people-watching possibilities in town.

Montmartre, Halvemaansteeg 17; *open daily 4pm–1am, to 2am on Fri and Sat.* Dancing barmen, original 1920s décor, loud music and a tight squeeze.

Le Shako, 's Gravenlandseveer 2; *open daily 9pm–2am, to 3am at weekends.* A miniscule bar that attracts students, writers, academics and a good load of local scruffs. Cheap beer on Tuesdays and free snacks on Thursdays.

clubs

COC, Rozenstraat 14. Amsterdam's Gay Centre runs a disco on Friday nights (*10pm–2am*) which attracts a local crowd and ingénues from the provinces.

C'ring (or Cockring), Warmoesstraat 96; *open daily 11pm–4am, to 5am on Fri and Sat.* Steamy, sweaty, swarming venue for emergency sex.

Exit, Reguliersdwarsstraat 42. April's busy disco-sister.

De Trut, Bilderdijkstraat 165; *open Sun 11pm–4am.* A trendy, but relaxed and pose-free club with a wide range of music, a (mainly) young crowd and a mix of lesbians and gay men. The Trut is in the cellar of what was once one of Amsterdam's biggest squats. The entrance is unmarked, but if you turn up between 11 and midnight, you'll see where to go. Often the club gets so full you have to wait for someone to leave before you're allowed in.

accommodation

Hotels are forbidden by law to discriminate against gay couples, but here's a selection of specifically gay places to stay. The prices are for a double room with shower in season, with breakfast included. (Addresses are given with the Amsterdam postcode.)

Amsterdam House Hotel, 's Gravelandseveer 3, 1011 KM, ✆ 624 6607, ✉ 624 1346 (*inexpensive*). Friendly canalside hotel just minutes from gay hotspots.

International Travel Club/ITC, Prinsengracht 1051, 1017 JE, ✆ 623 0230 (*inexpensive*). Quiet hotel overlooking one of Amsterdam's finest canals.

Jordaan Canal House, Egelantiersgracht 23, 1015 RC, ✆ 620 1545, ✉ 638 5056 (*moderate–inexpensive*). Beautifully situated, exclusively gay 17th-century canal house.

Hotel New York, Herengracht 13, 1015 BA, ✆ 624 3066 (*moderate*). Swish hotel with all mod cons, hiding behind three 17th-century canal houses at a tranquil end of Amsterdam's grandest canal.

GIS Apartments, Keizersgracht 33, 1015 CD Amsterdam, ✆ 625 0071, offers furnished apartments *from f150–250 per night.*

Many of Amsterdam's best 'straight' hotels are sympathetic places to stay, and many are gay-owned. See especially the Quentin Hotel (which has a large lesbian clientele), Seven Bridges Hotel and Hotel Engeland under 'Where to Stay'.

lesbian Amsterdam

Lesbians are not as well catered for as gay men in Amsterdam, but there's a lively, friendly scene in places such as:

Sarah's Grannies, Kerkstraat 176; *Mon–Sat 9am–6pm.* Offers good Dutch meals in a relaxed atmosphere. Not exclusively gay, but popular with local women.

Café Saarein, Elandsstraat 119; *open Mon 8pm–1am, Tues–Thurs and Sun 3pm–1am, Fri and Sat 3pm–2am.* A cosy local café, currently the citadel of Amsterdam's lesbian life.

Café Vive-la-Vie, Amstelstraat 5; *open daily noon–1am, to 2am at weekends.* Sociable crowd in a vaguely Art Deco bar with music that increases in volume as the night wears on.

COC (see under 'clubs' above) holds a house-oriented women-only disco on *Saturdays from 8pm–2am.*

You II, Amstel 178, *open Thurs to Saturday 11pm to 5am; Sunday 4pm to 1am.* More of a disco than Vive-la-Vie, and less heavily house than COC. Much-needed hip, yet pretty, relaxed lesbian meeting place.

other attractions

If the sun's shining, the place to be is **Zandvoort**, on Amsterdam's gay beach. Zandvoort is not the forgotten patch in the dunes that such places usually are, although it's a bit of a trek to reach it. There are two gay bars (Eldorado and Sans Tout) on the beach. Both are open from 8am until midnight. You can get there by train from Centraal Station (about 30mins, frequent trains right through the day). Once you get to the beach, walk south along the promenade and then on past the 'Naakt Strand' (nudist beach) for about 5km.

There's a **gay cinema** every Saturday and Sunday at Desmet, Plantage Middenlaan 4a, ℗ 627 3434. It shows a selection of popular and independent films and attracts a local crowd.

You can spend hours browsing around **gay bookshops** like Intermale, Spuistraat 251—mostly for men—or Boekhandel Vrolijk, Paleisstraat 135, which has a wide selection of literature, biographies and non-fiction of interest to lesbians and gay men. The American Discount Bookshop, Kalverstraat 185, has a good gay section.

Mandate, Prinsengracht 715 (*open Mon–Fri 11am–10pm; Sat noon–6pm, Sun 2–6pm; daily membership f18, six visits f63*) is a well-equipped **gay gym** with a busy coffee bar; and the notorious Amsterdam saunas are Thermos Day, Raamstraat 35 (*open Mon–Fri noon–11pm, Sat and Sun noon–10pm; adm f30*) and Thermos Night, Kerkstraat 60 (*open daily 11pm–8am; adm f30*).

information

COC is Amsterdam's lesbian and gay social centre (Rozenstraat 14, ℗ office 626 3087/information ℗ 623 4079; *open Mon–Thurs 9–5; for disco and coffeeshop hours, see* 'Clubs' and 'Lesbian Amsterdam' above).

Gay and Lesbian Switchboard (℗ 623 6565; *open 10am–10pm*) gives information and advice in English.

Day Trips from Amsterdam

Just 15 minutes by train from Amsterdam, Haarlem has a cosy, provincial atmosphere quite different from the capital—but it's by no means dull. You'll find hordes of friendly cafés, the much-painted St Bavo's church, tiny *hofjes* tucked behind over-the-top public architecture, Holland's oldest and most intriguing museum and an important collection of paintings by Frans Hals. Haarlem acts as an overflow for students who have accommodation problems in Amsterdam and Leiden, and this gives the town a youthful, carefree air.

Getting Around

Most of the tourist sights are within easy walking distance, but your *strippenkaart* (*see* p.8) will be valid on bus trips.

Tourist Information

The VVV tourist office is outside the railway station, open Mon–Sat 9–6; © (0900) 616 1600, and can supply you with maps and public transport information.

Around the Grote Markt

Most people arriving in Haarlem head straight for the **Grote Markt** (Market Square) and the imposing Gothic **Grote of St Bavokerk** (Great or St Bavo's Church; *open Mon–Sat 10–4; Sept–March 10–3.30; adm*). The view across the square hasn't changed much over the centuries, and on a quiet morning you feel you could be looking at one of Gerrit Berckheyde's 17th-century paintings of the church. The interior is bright and painted white. A gleefully ostentatious Baroque organ upstages even the soaring Gothic arches. It was built by the Amsterdammer Christian Muller in 1738, and is said to be one of the biggest in the world. Clusters of musical putti and graceful maidens cling to the pipes. Handel, Mozart and Albert Schweitzer have all had a go on the ivory and tortoiseshell keyboard. Before you leave, have a look at the fading tapestry designs painted on the columns at the side of the church and fluid lines of a marble relief by The Hague sculptor Xavery: Poetry and Music paying homage to the town patroness. In the centre column of the Brewers' Chapel (near the south transept) two little lines mark the heights of past Haarlem residents: Giant Cajanus (2.6m/8ft 8ins) and Paap (94cm/37ins).

Outside the church is a statue of **Laurens Coster**. Local legend has it that while he was carving his lover's name in a tree trunk, a letter fell into the sand. He was inspired by the imprint to invent printing. Though Haarlem is proud of him today, his contemporaries took him for a sorcerer and drove him out of town. He went to live in Germany—which might explain why the rest of the world believes that printing began with Gutenberg.

The oldest part of the **Stadhuis** across the square is a 14th-century hunting lodge built for the Count of Holland. It's been altered and expanded over the years, and the present complex incorporates a medieval monastery. During office hours you can have a look at the old heavy-beamed **Gravenzaal** (Count's Hall). On the south side of the square is the relentlessly ornamented **Vleeshal** (the former Meat Market, built in 1602). Sacheverell Sitwell remarked that we should 'regard it less as a building, than as Dutch cabinet work on a most capricious scale'. The cellar houses a small **Archeological Museum** (*open Wed–Sun 1–5; adm free*) displaying local finds from prehistory onwards.

Just off Grote Markt, above a clock shop once owned by the Ten Boom family is the **Corrie Ten Boom House** (Barteljorisstraat 19; *open Nov–March Tues–Sat 11–3; April–Oct Tues–Sat 10–3.30; adm by donation*). The Ten Boom family offered refuge to Jews in the Second World War in a cupboard-like hideaway, which the Gestapo never found—even though they once spent nearly a week living in the house, hoping to starve out any *onderduikers* (literally 'under-divers' *see* pp.36–7). Most of the Ten Boom family were active in the Resistance and perished in concentration camps, but Corrie returned, and told the story in a book, *The Hiding Place*.

Hofjes

Haarlem is renowned for its *hofjes*—secluded almshouse courtyards dating from the 15th century. Wander down a passageway, peer through a half-open door on the street and you'll find them—hidden formal gardens, surrounded by dainty gables and white-painted front doors. Most are still lived in, but if you're discreet you can have a quick look around. The best ones are in the western part of the city around Barrevoetestraat and Tuchthuisstraat.

Frans Hals Museum

Groot Heiligland 62; open Mon–Sat 11–5, Sun 12–5; adm.

Haarlem's star attraction is housed in one of the town's grander *hofjes*, a 17th-century Old Men's Home. The museum isn't devoted entirely to Hals—there's a batch of other Golden Age painters, a wide range of furniture and applied art and an extensive modern collection. The corridors are pervaded by a steady ticking of clocks, and the displays give you some sharp surprises. In a dim 17th-century period room, you'll see an enormous drawing by the 1930s Magic Realist, Pyke Koch. Bright contemporary pieces hang alongside Old Masters or in rooms displaying antique silver. All this gives the museum a quirky liveliness. Don't miss the 18th-century doll's house or the Restoration Workshop. (You stand behind a glass wall and watch painters work painstakingly on the tiny patch of an Old Master that will occupy them for months.) The most intriguing of Frans Hals' works in the museum are the portraits of the *Regents* and *Regentesses of the Old Men's Home*, painted in 1664 when Hals was in his eighties. The story that he was a bitter occupant of the almshouse is not true, but he certainly seems to be taking some sort of revenge with his brush. The Regentesses, in particular, are a sour and terrifying lot. Their expressions range from rosy stupidity to pure evil, and the white faces are thrown into stark relief by the sombre surround. You can see why Van Gogh said that Hals had at least 27 shades of black.

Teylers Museum

Spaarne 16; open Tues–Sat 10–5, Sun 12–5, winter until 4; adm.

The Netherlands' oldest purpose-built museum first opened its doors in 1784. It's the best sort of small museum—one based on the taste of an erudite, eccentric private collector, in this case the 18th-century merchant Pieter Teyler van der Hulst. A succession of astute directors have, in making new acquisitions, skilfully developed the diverse themes of Teyler's original collection. You'll find a fascinating hoard of old scientific instruments and machines, fossils, paintings and drawings (including some by Michelangelo and Rembrandt). Much of the collection is housed in beautiful wooden display cases in the original 18th-century museum building. The superb drawing collection is in a modern wing, that has been added with taste and discretion.

Provinciehuis Noord-Holland

Guided tours by arrangement, contact the VVV.

Slightly out of the centre of town, the Provinciehuis Noord-Holland (North Holland Provincial Government Building) is certainly worth the 20–30-minute walk. It was built as a home and private art gallery by an eccentric Amsterdam banker in 1796, and during its chequered history has been a palace to Louis Bonaparte and a museum. It's a sumptuous neoclassical building with exquisite stucco work, gorgeously moulded ceilings and patterned parquet flooring, whose rooms abound with marble statues and period furniture.

Haarlem © (023–)   **Where to Stay**

Most visitors to Haarlem stay either in Amsterdam or in Zandvoort on the coast (*see* p.154), as the local hotel selection is not exciting.

Golden Tulip Lion d'Or, Kruisweg 34, 2011 LC, © 532 1750, @ 532 9543 (*moderate*). Solid 19th-century building near the city centre, with comfortable rooms.

Carillon, Grote Markt 27, © 531 0591, @ 531 4909 (*inexpensive*). Old-fashioned hotel with friendly staff, in the shadow of St Bavo's.

Haarlem © (023–)   **Eating Out**

The street behind St Bavo's, at the far end of the market, is a good place to look for restaurants and cafés—though you really need go no further than the wood panelling and hanging lampshades of the beautifully restored **Stations Restaurant** (on Platform 2). For a treat there is also **De Componist**, Korte Veerstraat 1, © 532 8853 (*expensive*), a stylish restaurant that is rapidly gaining the reputation of being one of the best in the country. Up-and-coming star chef Michel Lambermon turns out such tasty Franco-Dutch fare as marinated salmon with tomato bouillon and samphire. **Café Brinkmann**, Grote Markt 9–13, © 532 3111 (*moderate*) is an elegant Art Deco establishment overlooking St Bavo's.

In the cheaper range, De Karmeliet, Spekstraat 6, © 531 4426 (*inexpensive*) provides a cheery stopover for a simple snack or sandwich, and **In den Uiver**, Rivier Fischmarkt 13, © 532 5399 (*inexpensive*) is a cosy *proeflokaal* for an invigorating Dutch *jenever*.

Gouda

Gouda (*pronounced with an aspirated guttural G, 'HGowda'*) is not all cheese and ersatz medieval markets. There's a thriving crafts industry, an imaginative historical museum and, in the longest church in the Netherlands, stained glass so beautiful that even the iconoclasts left it alone.

The first-known mention of Gouda was in a deed in 1139, though the area was settled long before that. The city got its charter from Count Floris V in 1272, and by 1400 was the fifth biggest in the land. During the 15th century Gouda prospered on the beer trade, then diversified into making pipes and ceramics—by 1750 about half the population was employed in the pottery trade. It wasn't until the mid-19th century that candlemaking took over as the dominant local industry.

Gouda is 29km (18 miles) southwest of Amsterdam. The easiest way to get there is **by train** from Centraal Station. The journey takes about 50mins and it's a 15min walk from Gouda Station to the market square. Trains average two an hour and a day return costs *f*29.25. The main tourist sights are clustered around the market square and are just a few minutes' walk apart.

Tourist Information

Gouda: VVV, Markt 24, ✆ (0182) 513 666; open Mon–Sat 9–5 (also open Sunday afternoons in summer).

Festivals and When to Go

In mid-December Gouda holds a candle festival. All electric lights in the market square are switched off. The Stadhuis windows and surrounding houses are decorated with candles, and an enormous Christmas tree is lit up. Well worth a special trip.

Church and Market

An exuberantly Gothic **Stadhuis**, built in 1450 (*open Mon–Fri 9am–noon and 2–4pm, Sat 11–3, 11–4 in the summer*) is plonked right in the middle of the market square. With its pixie-capped spires, bright red shutters and cheerful carillon, it can't be missed. It's one of the most popular places in the country for weddings (in Holland you can plight your troth in any town you like) and couples are churned through every few minutes. Nip in between ceremonies for a look at the carved fireplaces and 17th-century tapestries. Remember to walk up the left-hand side of the double staircase at the entrance—criminals used to descend the one on the right on their way to the gallows, and it's considered bad luck to use it.

Behind the Stadhuis is the solid, square **Waag** (public weighing house), built in 1668. An enormous gable stone shows cheeses being weighed. Nowadays the Waag is a **Cheese Museum** (*open April–Oct Tues–Sun 1–5, Thurs 10–5; adm*), comprising mainly interactive computer installations that tell you all you ever wanted to know about cheese, and a lot more besides. Downstairs, on one of the original scales, an attendant weighs young visitors. Anyone weighing under 40 Dutch pounds gets in free.

Every Thursday morning during the summer, farmers and porters dress in traditional costume, and everyone goes through the rituals of an old market beside the Waag, mainly for the benefit of tourists. The *real* cheese-trading takes place a few hours earlier, at 9am, and has more of the appearance of a boot sale. A handful of farmers gather around the market square to sell their wares from the backs of cars, slapping hands with customers to seal the deal.

St Janskerk/Grotekerk (St John's Church/the Great Church; *open Mar–Oct Mon–Sat 9–5; Nov–Feb Mon–Sat 10–4; adm*), just off the market square, is the pride of the town. Earlier churches on the site seem to have been singled out by divine wrath; after three successive buildings had been destroyed by fire or lightning, the present cruciform basilica was begun in 1552. Soft soil precluded any towering Gothic spire, so the building spread horizontally and became the longest church in the Netherlands (123m/403ft). The church is famous for its 70 16th-century stained glass windows, the most detailed and richly coloured of which are by the brothers Dirck and Wouter Crabeth. Not only did the glass survive the scourges of the iconoclasts, but the Reformed Church added some of its own. Rather than scenes from lives of the saints, these depicted moments of historic glory—like the Relief of Leiden with its famous portrait of William of Orange. During the Second World War the windows were taken out and stored, and so survive beautifully intact.

Around Het Catharina Gasthuis

On the lane behind St Janskerk (helpfully called Achter de Kerk—'Behind the Church') is the tall red-brick **Lazaruspoortje** (Lazarus Gate) with a relief showing poor, pustule-ridden Lazarus and the rich man who will never make it to the bosom of Abraham (Luke 16:19–31). This 17th-century entrance to a Lepers' Hospice was transferred here in the 1960s to serve as the back entrance to **Het Catharina Gasthuis** (St Catherine's Hospital, now a municipal museum; *open Mon–Sat 10–5, Sun noon–5; adm; ticket also valid for De Moriaan Museum*), an intriguing collection of 14th–17th-century buildings. You can see a reconstructed 19th-century apothecary's shop (very much in demand as a period film set) and a medieval surgeon's room, a torture chamber and a lunatics' cell; there's a frightening similarity between the instruments used in each. The torture chamber sports an ingenious designer execution block. The victim was strapped down spreadeagled, there are holes for the blood to run through and a spike to display the head on afterwards. The museum also has a good collection of paintings from the French Barbizon school and from the Hague School (*see* p.48) and a fine collection of medieval silver (especially the ornate 15th-century *Chalice of Jacoba of Bavaria*).

Five minutes' walk down the canal from the Catharina Gasthuis, you'll find **De Moriaan** ('The Blackamoor') at Westhaven 29, a 17th-century merchant's house and tobacco shop named after the carving over the door (*open Mon–Fri 10–5, Sat 10–12.30 and 1.30–5, Sun 12–5*). It has a vast collection of pipes, tiles and pottery. The **Goudse Librije**, Gouda Library, Spieringstraat 1, off the square behind the Catharina Gasthuis (*open Mon–Fri 2–4; adm free*) was used as an orphanage from the 17th century up to the 1940s. Now it houses a collection of 16th–19th-century books, some of which you can take down off the shelves and leaf through.

Arts and Crafts

Gouda bustles with craft industry. It's famous for its candles, and claims to produce 85 per cent of Holland's 'Delft' china. At **Het Tin en Keramiek Huis**, Lange Groenendaal 73 (*open Tues–Sat 10–5; adm free*) you can see award-winning designers paint the blue and white Delft patterns on to jugs and plates. Gouda also has its own ceramic style, which use richer colours, is far more beautiful and considerably more expensive. At Peperstraat 76, you can watch the luxuriously moustachioed Adrie Moerings make **clay pipes** in the traditional way (*open Mon–Fri 9–5, Sat 11–5; adm free*). Try to persuade him to make a *doorroker*. This pipe has a plain bowl, but as you use it, a pattern begins to emerge in the clay. At **De Roode Leeuw**, the windmill at Vest 65 (*open Thurs 9–2, Sat 9–4; adm*), you'll meet Marcel Koop, a real rosy-cheeked, flour-covered miller. In the early 1980s he gave up his job as an engineer to renovate the 17th-century windmill. Now it's the only working mill in the Netherlands also lived in by the miller. You can climb almost to the top, accompanied by the deep organic grumbling of the grindstones. And, of course, there's **cheese**. As well as the Thursday market, there are excursions and short bicycle rides to nearby dairy farms where you can follow the whole cheesemaking process from cow to bulging yellow cartwheel (*contact the VVV for details of which farms are open*).

Gouda is not overblessed with alluring hotels. You could consult the VVV for B&B possibilities, or try **De Utrechtsche Dom**, Geuzenstraat 6, 2801 XV, ☎ 528 833, ✎ 549 534 (*inexpensive*), a simple, but clean hotel, centrally situated, just a block or two behind St Jans.

De Zalm Markt 34, ☎ 525 345 (*expensive*). The Dutch royals are known to drop by this 400-year-old inn when they're in town, to enjoy such dishes as Gelderland chicken fillets, stuffed with smoked ham, mushrooms and olives and served with tomato-and-sage sauce.

De Zes Sterren, Achter de Kerk 14, ☎ 516 095 (*expensive*). Authentic Old Dutch interior, complete with tiled stove and a clutter of antiques, in the basement of the Catharina Gasthuis. The menu comprises recipes researched from old Dutch cookbooks. Try *tailoor*—mushrooms with herbs and a poached egg—or *camallien*, grilled suckling pig with a bitter cinnamon-wine sauce.

Goudsche Salon, Wijdstraat 13, ☎ 512 330 (*cheap*). Friendly local café where you can sit and browse through magazines at the large central reading table, or order a filling lunch.

Het Goudse Winkeltje, Achter de Kerk 9a, ☎ 527 874 (*cheap*). Busy café just behind the Grotekerk that sells delicious pancakes and sandwiches.

Van den Berg, Lange Groenedaal 32, ☎ 529 975 (*cheap*). The place to go to savour the local speciality: sweet, sticky Gouda waffles.

Around the Green Heart

Hélène Müller was passionate about art. Her husband, Anton Kröller was equally passionate about nature. She was heiress to a blast-furnace industry; he married the boss's daughter. Together they developed the family firm into a prosperous multinational and used their fortune to realize a dream. Between 1909 and 1914 Anton bought up tracts of wild land near Arnhem. Hélène built up a superb and inspired collection of late 19th- and early 20th-century art. They restocked the land with game, planted copses, built a lodge to live in and a museum for the paintings.

Today the **Kröller-Müller Museum**, set in the vast and varied landscape of **De Hoge Veluwe** national park, is one of the most delightful places to visit in the Netherlands. The estate now covers 5,500 hectares (13,000 acres) of land, the art collection is still growing and there really is something for everyone. You can picnic in forests or lie about on dunes, gallop through the fens on horseback or cycle sedately along leafy lanes. You can bird-watch, look for wild boar or nestle in animal hides waiting for red deer. The airy, intimate museum is a pleasure to walk around, and the collection is one of the best in the country. The sculpture park could detain you for hours and the lodge is unstuffy and well preserved. There are all the cafés, restaurants and children's playgrounds you could wish for, without the horrid ambience of a theme park or tourist trap.

On the outskirts of the park is Paleis Het Loo, a royal residence for three centuries, now open to public view. The villages around the park are good bases for longer stays and quick bites. **Bronkhorst**, just east of the park's borders, is especially worth a visit. It is known as the smallest town in the Netherlands, with just over 160 inhabitants—a pretty place with cobbled streets, an old inn, a church, a handful of farm houses and, curiously, the **Dickens Museum** (Onderstraat 2; *open April–Oct daily 10–5 and Nov–Easter Sat and Sun from 11–5; adm free*) which comprises a roomful of Charles Dickens curiosa.

Getting There and Around

The easiest way to get to and about **De Hoge Veluwe** and the surrounding villages is **by car**. You can drive about in the park, and abandon the car where you wish. Take the A1 to Apeldoorn or the A2 and A12 to Arnhem. There are gates to the park at the villages of Otterlo, Schaarsbergen and Hoenderloo. The journey takes about 1½ hours.

The nearest **railway stations** are at Arnhem and Apeldoorn. The journey from Amsterdam to **Arnhem** takes around 1½ hours and costs ƒ43 return. Trains leave twice an hour. Take bus 107 from Arnhem station for the park. There are about two trains an hour from Amsterdam to **Apeldoorn**. Journey time is one hour and tickets cost ƒ40 return. Bus 110 takes you in to the park, and bus 126 or 104 runs direct from Apeldoorn station to **Paleis Het Loo**.

Once in De Hoge Veluwe park you can get about on the (free) white **bicycles** (*see next page*).

The Midlands

Getting to surrounding villages by public transport is trickier. **Buses** 102 and 104 run from Appeldoorn to the stop 'De Echoput' near **Hoog Soeren** every half-hour, but then it's a half-hour's walk into the village. **Bronkhorst** is best reached by bus 52 from Zutphen, but again it's a 20min walk from the bus stop into the village.

Tourist Information

De Hoge Veluwe: Information is available from the Visitors' Centre (Hoenderloo Gate), © (0318) 59162; open daily Nov–March 9–5.30; April 8–8, May–Aug 8–10, or VVV tourist offices in the area.

De Hoge Veluwe National Park

Open daily Nov–March 9–5.30, April 8–8, May–Aug 8am–10pm; adm f14 per adult, f7 per child, f8 per car—includes admission to museum and sculpture park. From May to Sept no cars are allowed in parts of the park.

De Hoge Veluwe national park is a curious amalgam of drifting sand dunes, watery fens, thick cultivated forests and open heathland. Mrs Kröller-Müller loved autumn colours—so you'll find forests of oak, birch, beech and rowan trees as well as the older plantations of pine and junipers. In the summer there are gloriously coloured thickets of rhododendrons and purple heather covers the heath in August and September. Anton Kröller filled the park with magnificently antlered red deer, moufflons (a curly horned wild sheep from Sardinia), wild boar, roe deer and even kangaroos. All, except the poor roos, survive in multitudes and have such violent fun in the rutting season (*Sept–Oct*) that you're confined to your car in some parts of the park.

There are marked walks throughout the area, though you don't have to keep to the paths. The Visitors' Centre can put you in touch with a local stables if you'd like to hire a horse, or you can pick up a bicycle (*free, no deposit necessary*) from the shelter in the central square. The **Museonder** (*open daily 10–5; adm incl in park entrance*) is an intriguing underground museum, with exhibits on life below the earth's surface including the living roots of a giant tree.

Kröller-Müller Museum and Sculpture Park

Museum open April–Oct, Tues–Sun 10–5; Nov–Mar Tues–Sun 1–5; sculpture park open April–Nov Tues–Sun 10–4.30, Sun 11–4.30.

The Kröller-Müller Museum and Sculpture Park are now state-owned. A collection of exceptional quality is growing around the core of Hélène Kröller-Müller's bequest. It's a far more pleasant place to see **Van Goghs** than the crowded museum in Amsterdam—and Mrs Kröller-Müller had nearly 300 of the painter's works: a version of *The Potato Eaters*, fine self-portraits and landscapes, and some of his best drawings. You'll find good examples of Braque, Picasso and the rather neglected Cubist, Fernand Léger, colourful stippled Pointillist paintings by Seurat, and a touching study of an ageing clown by Renoir—in fact most major movements and artists of the last hundred years are represented. Before you leave have a look for Dutch artist Jan Toorop's eerie fairytale drawings and a dreamy pink and green screen by the French Symbolist painter, Odilon Redon.

Out in the **Sculpture Park** you'll find pieces not only by old familiars like Rodin, Henry Moore and Barbara Hepworth, but also exciting work by a number of contemporary artists. The Park reflects Hélène Kröller-Müller's vision of the way art, nature and architecture can interrelate. The long, low, stone and glass museum blends perfectly into the surrounding landscape. In the pond outside, Marta Pan's enormous, curvaceous, abstract white *Swan* is gently blown here and there by the wind. In a little hollow, over a hill, rusty iron sheets seem to grow up from the soil. Boulders hang suspended in rope hammocks between the trees; giant, seed-shaped balls of clay, slate igloos and odd tent-like structures are scattered about open grass patches. A frail needle of aluminium pipes and steel wire towers up 27m (92ft) into the sky, higher than most of the nearby trees. Anyone under the age of 12 makes a beeline for Jean Dubuffet's *Jardin d'Email* (1972–3). From the outside it's a tall white wall, but once you climb the narrow stairs you're in a big, bumpy white landscape cut up by irregular black lines. Bemused adults sit around the edges, while children tear about, trip over the mounds and bang their heads. (*At present being restored; should be finished in the course of 2000.*)

Jachthuis St Hubertus

Open April–Oct, guided tours every half-hour 10.30–12.30 and 2–4.30; Dec–March 2–3; closed Jan.

Before leaving De Hoge Veluwe, you should try and pay a quick visit to the **Jachthuis St Hubertus** (St Hubert Hunting Lodge). The Kröller-Müller's family home and its artificial lake were built in 1914 by H. P. Berlage, the father of modern Dutch architecture (*see* p.51). It's a compact brick building with an ugly, incongruous tower. Inside, however, the house has a cosy 'lived-in' atmosphere—as well as some superb Art Deco furniture. Coloured bricks and brightly glazed tiles are everywhere. The motif of hunting runs throughout the interior design representing the story of when a stag appeared to St Hubuertus bearing a crucifix. Even the floor plan is in the shap of antlers. St Hubert is now the patron saint of hunters. Monstrous carp swim about in the lake and devour anything you drop in with a nightmarish 'plop'.

Paleis Het Loo

Open Tues–Sun 10–5; adm.

Adjoining the national park is the **Koninklijke Domeinen** (Royal Estate) and the magnificent Baroque **Paleis Het Loo** (Het Loo Palace). Built in 1685 as a hunting lodge for *stadhouder* William III (of 'William and Mary' fame), the palace was used as a royal residence until 1962. Nowadays it is open to the public. Visitors can wander through a succession of lavishly decorated state rooms and boudoirs. Each is done up using furniture that reflects the taste of one the of royal occupants, in sequence from the 17th century to the 1930s. But most splendid of all are the **gardens**, laid out again in the 1980s following the 17th-century plans by Daniël Marot, who also originally designed the palace interior. The best vantage point from which to view the exquisite formal layout is from the roof of the palace. After that, you can descend to stroll among rose bushes, brush against fragrant herbs and wander through the gazebo.

Outside the Park

Herberg de Gouden Leeuw, Bovenstraat 2, 7226 LM Bronkhorst, ✆ (0575) 451 231, ✉ 452 566, *oechies@worldonline.nl* (*moderate–inexpensive*). Charming 17th-century country inn in the Netherlands' smallest village. The oak floors and open hearth of the public lounge are very much in period.

Hotel Hoog Soeren, Hoog Soeren 15, 7346 AB Hoog Soeren, ✆ (055) 519 1231, ✉ 519 1450 (*inexpensive*). Quiet family hotel set in the trees of a small village on the edge of the Hoge Veluwe, convenient for the park and surrounding sights. The rooms are clean and simple, and there's a good café/restaurant downstairs.

Het Roode Koper, Jonkheer Dr J. C. Sandbergweg 82, 3852 PV Ermelo, ✆ (0577) 407 393, ✉ 407 561 (*moderate*). Unpretentious, family-owned country-house hotel. A romantic 1910 villa, tastefully filled with antiques and equipped with pool, tennis court and a large garden. A gem—and good value for money.

Carnegie's Cottage, Onderlangs 35, 6731 BK Otterlo, ✆ (0318) 591 220, ✉ 592 093 (*cheap; breakfast extra*). A cosy white cottage with just 12 guest rooms, set all on its own up a dirt road in the woods. The management is friendly, the rooms have a comfortable, homey feel, and there's an excellent little restaurant.

Paleis Het Loo and De Hoge Veluwe Park ✆ (0318–)

The Museum Café, Paleis Het Loo, ✆ 591 657 (*cheap*). Light snacks and cakes in the old orangerie, with a terrace that catches the sun.

Koperen Kop, Paleis Het Loo, ✆ 591 289 (*moderate*). Fuller meals in a grander setting.

The Kröller-Müller Museum Café, Kröller-Müller Museum, Hoge Veluwe, ✆ 591 041 (*cheap*). Good salads and a large terrace on the edges of the Sculpture Park.

De Hoge Veluwe is also the perfect place for a **picnic**. You can pick up supplies in Apeldoorn or Arnhem.

Outside the Park

Café-Restaurant Hoog Soeren, Hotel Hoog Soeren, Hoog Soeren 15, just off the N344 west of Apeldoorn, ✆ (055) 519 1231 (*cheap*). In a leafy village convenient for the park and Apenheul. Pleasant Old Dutch-style family restaurant complete with open hearth and hunting trophies, good for a game lunch.

Het Jachthuis, Hoog Soeren 55, ✆ (055) 519 1397 (*expensive*). Slightly stuffy atmosphere, but really excellent cuisine with game specialities in season.

De Gouden Leeuw, Bovenstraat 2, Bronkhorst, just off the N48 to the east of the park, ✆ (0575) 451 231 (*moderate*). Stylish restaurant in a 17th-century inn, where a young chef comes up with good Franco-Dutch cuisine and imaginative salads.

Keukenhof

Open late March–late May, daily 8–7.30; adm exp.

In spring, the fields between Haarlem and Leiden glow with the colours of millions of tulips and other bulbs, and attract nearly that number of tourists. Coachloads pour out of Amsterdam, to return traumatized by the sight of great cutting machines churning through the bulbfields scrunching up the flowers. (Most plants are grown for the bulb rather than the bloom, and a swift blade to the stalk makes the bulb subdivide.) The Amsterdam Tourist Board (*see* p.63) and various agencies around town can help with organized tours, but it's a far better idea to go on your own by train or car. The town to head for is **Lisse**, and the garden to see is the **Keukenhof**.

The Keukenhof (literally 'Kitchen Garden') was, in the 15th century, the herb and vegetable patch of the Countess Jacoba van Beieren. Whatever she grew there enabled her to get through four husbands (including a Duke of Gloucester and a Dauphin of France) before her own death at the age of 35. In 1949 a group of Dutch bulb-growers took over the land as a shop window for the bulb industry. It turned out to have a much wider appeal. Today there are some 30ha (74 acres) of nearly 7 million plants and a further 5000sq m (54,000sq ft) of flowers under glass. The best time to go is from mid to late April, when tulips, daffodils, narcissi and hyacinths are all flowering at once.

Tulip Mania

Tulips—homely, suburban and pure—have become a national cliché along with clogs, canals and windmills. Yet behind these apparently innocent and colourful blooms lurks a past of envy, greed and intemperance that is almost unparalleled in Dutch history.

Tulips were first spotted in Adrianople, Turkey, by Dutch diplomats at the Ottoman court. In the early 17th century the flowers made a spring début in some of French and Dutch society's best gardens. Soon, Johan van Hooghelande, a Leiden botanist, had found out how to vary the colour and shape of the blooms. Connoisseurs queued up, money pouches bulging, for the latest varieties and by the 1620s the tulip was *the* flower of fashionable aristocracy. This alchemical combination of scientific research, visual allure and the chance of profit—three great Dutch enthusiasms—incited the Great Tulip Mania. At first, the bulbs were seen as exotic rarities. The Calvinist Church even regarded them as dangerous—perhaps because the flamed petals reminded them of the ribbons, ruffs and other vanities that ministers railed against from the pulpits. The bulbs were swapped and grown by a handful of aristocratic connoisseurs who, as was their wont, imposed a strict hierarchy on the tulip world. The noblest were the roses (red and pink on white), then came the violets (lilac and purples on white) and finally *bizarden* (red or violet on yellow). Humble plain colours barely merited an estate. It was the irregular, flamed and striped varieties, like the red and white Semper

Augustus and the Viceroy, that mattered. (The democratically minded Dutch, however, preferred to call their nobler varieties 'Admiral' or 'General' followed by the name of the grower.)

Gradually *hoi polloi* began to edge in on the scene. Tulips were easily reproducible for a wider market. Delftware, an imitation of expensive Chinese porcelain, was already decorating more modest homes. The Flemish carpet industry had its foundations in copying Turkish rugs. Tulips copied themselves, so by the mid-1630s weavers, black-smiths and bakers were able to buy the bulbs at village fairs. The fashion spread and a tulip fever gripped the nation. Prices took off, then went into orbit. An Admiral de Maan that sold for *f*15 in 1634 went for *f*175 three years later. At the height of the boom an *f*800 Scipio changed hands after a few weeks for *f*2,200. People went to any lengths for a prized bulb. One farmer met the *f*2,500 demanded for a single Viceroy by payment in kind: two *last* of wheat, four of rye, four fat oxen, eight pigs, a dozen sheep, two oxheads of wine, four tons of butter, 1,000 pounds of cheese, a bed, a suit of fine clothes and a silver beaker.

The rocketing prices were fuelled not only by demand, but by the growth of a futures market. In 1634 one bright dealer had the idea of buying in the winter for future delivery, and then selling to a new buyer before he actually possessed the stock. Soon deals were being done on negotiable pieces of paper, with the time of delivery as an expiry date. A quick turnover meant a quick paper profit. Money hungry dealers were selling bulbs they didn't yet possess, for amounts they couldn't ever possibly raise. As the delivery date drew closer, the danger that you would actually have to pay up increased, but so did the possibility of making an intoxicating profit as prices rose, even by the hour. At the bottom of the pile, and in danger of ending up with a heap of worthless bulbs if the market collapsed, were the growers. (The actual tulips would be the last thing on the mind of a merchant facing bankruptcy and trying to settle his paper debts.)

And collapse it did. By 1636 this *windhandel* (literally 'trading in the wind') was beginning to worry the city magistrates and outrage the Church. Whether it was the rumour of intervention that caused the panic, or the panic that caused the intervention, is unclear. But on 2 or 3 February 1637 a warning whisper shot round Haarlem and dealers went all-out to sell. Prices plummeted, the bubble burst and the magistrates had to intervene with special legislation to rescue the innocent growers from the debris of bankrupts. It wasn't until the spring of 1638 that the market found a normal level, but the passion for tulips was there to stay. As the scandal subsided they quietly assumed their place alongside clogs, cheese and blue and white china as part of the nation's iconography.

Eating Out

The cafés around the Keukenhof are crowded and fairly unexciting. You'd be well advised to pack yourself a picnic.

Amsterdamse Bos

You can get to the Amsterdam Woods (open 24 hours; adm free) by bus—nos. 170, 171, 172—but a quainter way to go is by antique tram. On Sundays, and some other afternoons from March–September, a variety of old trams run from Haarlemmermeer Station in west Amsterdam. There's one every 20 minutes (but contact the VVV for full details).

You don't have to go too far afield from Amsterdam for a healthy bit of greenery and a dose of fresh air. The wilds of the Amsterdamse Bos are only a tram ride away from the centre of town. The Amsterdamse Bos was created in the 1930s, providing jobs for hundreds of unemployed needed to produce it, and a new recreation space for the ever expanding city. The **Bos Museum**, Koenenkade 56, in the northeast corner of the Bos (*open daily 10–5; adm free*) tells the story of how it all happened. There is plenty to do here, whether you want to laze around or be a little more energetic. You can go for secluded walks, cycle (there are bikes for hire at the main gate), go boating on one of the vast stretches of water, or visit the buffalo reserve. There are lots of places to picnic, or you can have a pancake amongst the live peacocks on the terrace of the **Boerderij Meerzicht** (*open summer months 10–7*), an old farmhouse near the museum. The Bos is the ideal place to go if children are getting small-space fatigue.

Beaches

Amsterdam's Beach

Canal water can be pretty poisonous, so if the weather is hot and you feel like an outdoor swim, you can join the flocks of Amsterdammers heading for the beaches of Zandvoort.

Getting There and Around

Trains to Zandvoort from Haarlem run every 15 minutes, and the trip takes 15 minutes.

Bus connections (No.90 to Den Haag) Haarlem/Katwijk/Noordwijk/Leiden.

Tourist Information

Zandvoort; Schoolplein 1, © (023) 571 7947; open Tues–Fri 10–12.30 and 1.30–4.30, Sat 10–3.30.

Katwijk; Vuurbaakplein 11, © (071) 407 5444, @ (071) 407 6342; open Jan–April Mon–Fri 9–5, Sat 9–1; April–July Mon–Sat 9–6; July–Sept Mon–Sat 9–6, Sun 11–1; Sept–Jan Mon–Fri 9–5, Sat 9–1.

Although **Zandvoort** is just beyond Haarlem (another 15 minutes on the train) it has achieved the honorary status of being 'Amsterdam's beach'. It's a crowded and commercial resort, though if you wander farther up the coast you'll find a nudists' beach, a gay beach and lots of quieter spots among the dunes. On hot summer's nights Zandvoort is the scene of trendy Ibiza-style beach-party clubbing.

Following the N206 south, you pass through bulb fields (making slabs of bright colour in early spring) to the dune reserve of **Noordwijkerhout** (free access). Marked paths wind through stubby forests and scrubby coastal grassland to the windswept North Sea coast. It's a great place for walking and cycling, and outside weekends can even achieve a measure of romantic loneliness.

The resort of **Noordwijk** on the other hand is hardly more than a tacky little town that cowers behind a ghastly row of high-rise hotels. **Katwijk**, a little farther on, is a mild improvement; then, after a wild and open area of rolling dunes and marshy lakes, you reach the resort of **Scheveningen** (*see* above, p.193). Located between Katwijk and Noordwijk is the sprawling European Space Research and Technology Centre, the nerve centre of the European Space Agency. Attached to it is a **Space Expo** (Bus 32 from Leiden or 90 from Haarlem or The Hague; *open Tues–Sun 10–5; adm*), which has exhibitions on the history of space travel and what life is like for astronauts (including a cut-away space suit and a suction loo). Eerie music and blue light permeate the large hall, giving it the atmosphere of a James Bond set. Unfortunately, the presentation of the exhibition is a little dull and there are surprisingly few buttons to push or levers to pull (*though at the time of going to press the Space Expo was due for a revamp*).

Noordwijk © (071–)   **Where to Stay**

Hotel Edelman, Koningin Astrid Boulevard 48, 2202 BE, © 361 3124, ✉ 361 0773 (*moderate–inexpensive*). The Hotel Edelman is an old-fashioned place just outside Noordwijk that gives visitors a good idea of how attractive the resort must have been before crass developmers moved in and spoiled it. Many of the rooms have wooden balconies with a sea view, and, if asked nicely, the proprietor Mr Edelman will do his John Cleese impersonation.

Noordwijk © (071–)   **Eating Out**

Noordwijk can hardly be described as gourmet territory by anyones standards. The coastal towns have rows of barely distinguishable beachfront cafés and pancake houses, and there's a passable pizzeria at the northern entrance to the Noordwijkerhout reserve. It's not all bad, however. One exception is **Latour**, Konigin Astridboulevard 5, Noordwijk, © 365 1239 (*lunch moderate, dinner expensive*). Here, a piano tinkles in the background as you savour such delights as *coquilles St Jacques*, smoked salmon and sweetbreads, in classically stylish surrounds, and with a view of the sea to boot.

The East Coast

In distinction to places such as Noordwijk, the coasts, canals and waterways north of Amsterdam make ideal day-trip destinations from the city. Even more so if you are travelling by bicycle. Provided you have suffcient puff to pedal, you can easily combine a cycling trip to Broek-in-Waterland, a friendly and likeable place, with a visit to one of the Meer towns, such as Marken, in a day. If you don't like crowds, try to avoid the area during high season as tourists can get pretty thick on the ground.

Well-signposted cycle paths criss-cross the whole area.

Broek-in-Waterland: Bus 110/111 runs from Amsterdam Centraal Station.

Zaanse Schans: Take a train from Amsterdam to Koog Zaandijk, then an 8-minute walk; or bus 88 from Zaandam station. You can hire **bicycles** at the entrance to Zaanse Schans for *f*9 per half-day.

Bergen: Take the train to Alkmaar, then bus 160/162 to Bergen. Buses go every half-hour.

Broek op Langedijk: Take the train to Alkmaar then bus 155, every half-hour.

Museum Broeker Veiling: Take a train to Alkmaar, then bus 155 to Broek op Langedijk.

Tourist Information

Zaanse Schans: Visitors' Centre, Schansend 7, © (075) 616 8218 (at the entrance); open daily 8.30–5 (8.30–6 in summer).

Bergen aan Zee: VVV, Van der Wijckplein 8, © (072) 581 2400.

Broek-in-Waterland

Heading northeast out of Amsterdam, through a gentle landscape of fields and waterways, you come to the village of **Broek-in-Waterland,** a cluster of pretty wooden houses surrounded by canals and small lakes. Set in leafy gardens, some of these cottages date back 300 years and have become hot property amongst design-conscious moneyed Amsterdammers. At the heart of the hamlet is a 16th-century church that holds the grave of one Neeltje Pater, a whizz 18th-century businesswoman who built up a fleet of 16 merchant ships, and had a nest-egg of eight million guilders stashed away in the Bank of England.

Zaanse Schans

Free access and free entry, though individual sights have own opening times and fees; parking f15 for two hours.

A few kilometres west, outside the town of Zaandam, you'll find the **Zaanse Schans**, resplendent with twelve working windmills. This cluster of green wooden houses dating from the 17th and 18th centuries was put up in the 1950s, to help convey the impression of what a village in the area was like at a time when more than 1,000 windmills ground away at various activities along the river Zaan. Though it throngs with tourists, the Zaanse Schans somehow manages to preserve some charm, and a visit to one or two of the mills is fascinating—one grinds mustard, another produces cooking oil, in a third a man makes paint from natural pigments (highly popular with Amsterdam artists). There's also a working dairy, a clog maker and a pewterer. You can see the first ever Albert Heijn grocery store (which grew into the nation's biggest chain of supermakets), and visit the Clock Museum, where a timepiece from 1520 thunks away in one corner, while in another a 31-bell carillon tinkles out folk tunes. At the entrance to the village, the **Zaans Museum** (*open Tues–Sat 10–5, Sun noon–5; adm*) offers an excellent multimedia presentation on the history of the district, which brands itself 'the oldest industrial area in Europe'.

The Western Coast

West of Zaandam, you come to the **Noord-Holland Duinreservaat** (*North Holland Dune reserve; free access*), one of the most beautiful stretches of coast in the country, and a far better destination on a hot summer's day than Zandvoort, 'Amsterdam's beach' farther south. In places the dunes are like rugged little mountains, at times they waft down into meadows. The north of the reserve is thick with forest, the beaches are long, sandy and often quite deserted. **Egmond aan Zee** gets very overrun—the towns to head for as a base are **Castricum aan Zee** and **Bergen aan Zee**.

At **Broek op Langedijk**, about 10km northeast of Bergen (just north of Alkmaar), is one of Holland's most curious museums. The **Museum Broeker Veiling** (Museumweg 2, Broek op Langedijk; *open April–Oct Mon–Fri 10–5, Sat and Sun 12–5; adm; with boat trip adm exp*) is a sail-in auction house dating back to the turn of the last (i.e. 19th–20th) century. Barges laden with fruit and vegetables would follow a canal into the middle of one of a number of auction halls, and moor there while the sale took place. Visitors can join in a Dutch auction in a *Jugendstil* hall, see a collection of old barges, and take a boat trip themselves out into the 'Realm of a Thousand Islands', a waterland nature reserve.

Where to Stay

Hotels along the coast tend, alas, to be pretty grotty, or soulless monstrosities. But if you want to spend an evening beside the seaside, and not head straight back to Amsterdam, one exception is **Villa de Horizon**, C. F. Zeilerboulevard 1, 1865 BB Bergen aan Zee, ℗ (072) 589 6868 (*inexpensive*), a friendly, family-run pension perched all alone on its own dune overlooking the beach. Rooms are furnished in a modern though not tacky style and most have balconies with sea views.

Eating Out

Broek-in-Waterland ℗ (020–)

De Witte Swaen, Dorpsstraat 11, ℗ 403 1525 (*cheap*). Old-fashioned pancake parlour in a traditional Broek-in-Waterland building, with a sunny terrace.

Zaanse Schans ℗ (075–)

There's a busy pancake restaurant just near the entrance, or you could treat yourelf to **De Hoop Op d'Swarte Walvis**, Kalverringdijk 15 , ℗ 616 5629 (*expensive*). One of the region's top restaurants, housed in a complex of three historic buildings in the Zaanse Schans village. You can taste soup made with mustard ground at the windmill nearby, or lash out with veal served with creamy spinach, polenta, turnips and a laurel-leaf gravy.

The Dunes ℗ (072–)

Cheap 'n' cheerful eats are to be found in the beach pavilion restaurants at Egmond aan Zee (**de Uitkijk** is the most recommendable), but for something a little more special head to **De Kleine Prins**, Oude Prinsweg 29, Bergen, ℗ 589 6969 (*expensive–moderate*), where you can tuck into such delights as grilled rabbit with calvados sauce.

Muiden and Muidenslot

First stop out along the A1, at the mouth of the river Vecht, is the village of **Muiden**—hardly more than a cluster of dinky gabled houses along the waterfront. But on the village outskirts is the **Muiderslot** (*guided tours only, every half-hour, duration one hour; open April–Oct, Mon–Fri 10–5, last tour at 4, Sat and Sun 1–4, last tour at 3; Nov–May Sat and Sun only; adm*), a stumpy castle that stands firmly fixed in the national psyche for two reasons. It was here in 1296 (a date almost as familiar to Dutch schoolchildren as 1066 is to British) that Count Floris of Holland was imprisoned and murdered. Over three centuries later, the castle was the focus of the Muiderkring (Muiden Circle), the country's most famous ever literary circle, centring on the poet P. C. Hooft.

Tesselschade

One rough night, towards the end of the 16th century, a small trading ship ran aground on one of the treacherous sandbanks around the island of Texel off the coast of North Holland. The young Dutch merchant and man of letters, Roemer Visscher, was one of the few survivors. That very night his wife (snug in their house on the Engelsekaai in Amsterdam) gave birth to a daughter. Although she was christened Maria, her father felt compelled to mark the coincidence and celebrate his survival by burdening her with the sobriquet 'Tesselschade' (literally Tessel/Texel-damage, but with gentler connotations of mischief).

Despite her nickname (and an accident involving a spark from a blacksmith's anvil) Tesselschade went on to become the one-eyed doyenne of Amsterdam salon culture. Her father made sure that Maria and her sister Anne got a sound classical education (a younger daughter, Geertruid, seemed content with embroidery) and that they picked up all the subsidiary skills required to sparkle in erudite society. By the time she was a young woman the handsome (if slightly imperfect) Tesselschade could supply fluent translations of the most complex Latin, Greek or Italian texts, was an accomplished poetess, would entertain delightfully on harpsichord, lute and viol and had a singing voice of high repute. When some of the older Chambers of Rhetoric (medieval literary societies) joined forces in 1630, it was Tesselschade who won the competition to write a poem celebrating the union.

In the first two decades of the 17th century, the house on the Engelsekaai became Amsterdam's foremost literary and philosophical salon. When their father died, the daughters were snapped up by the poet Pieter Cornelisz. Hooft to join his famous literary circle at Muiden Castle, where they held court until their respective marriages. The list of Tesselschade's suitors had read like a *Who's Who* of Dutch letters—men like Vondel, Bredero, Constantijn Huygens and P. C. Hooft plied her with eulogistic verses. But she finally married a sea captain from Alkmaar. Anne fulfilled her merchant family's social ambitions by marrying a minor nobleman. Tesselschade returned to Amsterdam as a widow in 1640 to resume her position as a literary *Grande Dame* and when she died in 1649, Huygens compared her to the sun. Yet despite their obvious attributes and the frantic praises heaped upon them, the sisters never appear in any of the group portraits of the Muiden circle, and seem to have been regarded as prodigious ornaments. It took a 19th-century painter, J. C. Kruseman, to give the Visscher sisters pride of place among the male luminaries of the Muidenkring and today (if the painting's not in storage in the cellars) you can see the portrait hanging in the Rijksmuseum.

For 'castle' in Holland you can usually read 'stately home'. But Muiderslot is very much in the moated, turreted, impenetrable stone-wall mould. Most of the building dates back to the 13th and 14th centuries, though inside it has been restored in a style which rather effectively recreates an atmosphere that would have been more familiar to members of the Muiderkring. You can see the chamber where Floris met his fate, and the desk at which P. C. Hooft wrote his poems, standing up. The rooms are filled with such curiosities as a 'money table' (you detected counterfeit coins by clinking them on the limestone top), and a family box-bed (children in drawers underneath, parents shut into a wardrobe above, with a cord to pull that opened a vent when it all got a bit too pongy). Keep an eye open for a painting in which human figures have cabbages for heads—done a good 400 years before Magritte came up with the idea.

Eating Out

Muiden ℂ (0294–)

Graf Floris V, Herengracht 72, ℂ 261 296 (*cheap*). Traditional café in the village, where you can get savoury and sweet pancakes, and simple meals.

Volendam and Edam

Edging farther along the coast, you come to the somewhat larger town of **Volendam**. People flock here from all over the world to ogle and photograph locals in traditional dress—men in fez-like black hats and wide lapels, women in pointy lace caps and long aprons. But there is real life in Volendam too—quaint, empty side streets lined with gabled houses, the occasional real fishing boat with a catch for sale, and even its own pop music style, '*palingbeat*' (eel beat), which emerged in the late 1980s. If you come in midwinter, you might find the harbour frozen over, the townsfolk turned out to skate, and barely a visitor in sight.

Now almost a suburb of Volendam, **Edam** is perhaps best known to outsiders because it gives its name to the round, rubbery cheese that the Dutch export in large quantities. Yet despite a tacky and utterly fake **cheese market** (*held on Wednesday mornings in summer*), Edam escapes the worst toy-town excesses, and is perhaps the most pleasant and atmospheric of all the towns on this stretch of coast. Founded in the 12th century, Edam enjoyed its high point in the 16th and 17th centuries, and still bears the architectural imprint of that time. The imperious Gothic **Grote Kerk** on the edge of the town centre was largely rebuilt in the 1620s, after it had been struck by lightning, and contains some beautiful stained glass—rare in the iconoclast-ravaged north. The slender, solitary **Speeltoren** (built 1561) was also once part of a church, demolished in the 19th century. In 1970, its original six-bell carillon was augmented by another 29 bells—so many that some had to hang outside, and the tower nearly fell over from the weight two years later.

The richly decorated **Kaaswaag** on the Kaasmarkt still weighs out Edamer cheese at the statutory 1000 or 1600 grams, though as far as décor goes it's upstaged by the ornate 18th-century **Stadhuis** on nearby Damplein. Next door to the Stadhuis, in a step-gabled house that dates back to 1550, is the **Edams Museum** (*open mid-April–Oct Tues–Sat 10–4.30, Sun 1.30–4.30; adm*), restored as a period merchant house but most famous for its floating cellar floor, supposedly built by a sea captain who just couldn't get to sleep on solid land.

Where to Stay

All these little towns are mainly day-trip destinations from Amsterdam, but two hotels are worth special recommendation.

Volendam ✆ (0299–)

Hotel Spaander, Haven 15–19, 1131 EP, ✆ 363 595, ✉ 369 615, *spaander@ tref.nl* (*inexpensive*). Legendary hotel that is a testament to Volendam's long history of attracting tourist hordes—Renoir and Picasso were apparently once guests. Rooms range from standard to luxury and décor mixes traditional cosiness with Best Western modern, and the hotel can boast a fitness centre, large pool and Turkish bath.

Edam ✆ (0299–)

De Fortuna, Spuistraat 3–7, 1135 AV, ✆ 371 671, ✉ 371 469, *fortuna@ fortuna-edam.nl* (*inexpensive*). Family-run hotel occupying five 17th-century houses and two garden houses. Some rooms open directly on to the garden terrace. The décor has a traditional Dutch touch that manages to avoid kitsch.

Eating Out

Restaurants in this area cater almost exclusively to tourists, and are barely distinguishable from each other. Those overlooking the little harbour at **Markum** have the best views. All serve the usual range of pancakes, apple pie, mussels, fish dishes, and meat with salad and chips. One notable exception is in Edam, at the **De Fortuna** hotel (*see* above; *moderate*). Dinky step-gabled building belonging to a family-run hotel—heavy beams, soft lighting and superb food. Try the home-smoked lamb with mint and rocket couscous.

Rotterdam

Rotterdam

Centraal Station

Nederlandse
Architectuurinstituut

NIEUWE BINNENWEG

ROCHUSSENSTRAAT

'S. GRAVENDIJKWAL

WIJTEMAWEG

Delfshaven

Coolhaven

ROCHUSSENSTRAAT

Coolhaven

Oude Kerk

De Dubbelde
Palmboom

Coolhaven

Euromast

PIETER DE HOOCHWEG

VOORHAVEN

VOORHAVEN

WILLEM

Delfshaven

HOFFSTRAAT

BUYTEWECHSTRAAT

Parkhaven

Pa

SCHIEHAVEN

St. Jobshaven

Schiehaven

For over 25 years Rotterdam, on the delta of the river Maas, has topped the list of the world's largest ports. Unlike anywhere else in the Netherlands, Rotterdam has the skyline, pace and aggressive edge of a big city. Locals dub it 'Manhattan-on-the-Maas'.

Old Rotterdam was all but flattened by bombs early in the Second World War. The imagination and sense of adventure that the authorities brought to rebuilding their city has resulted in some bravura feats of modern architecture. As you step out of Rotterdam Centraal Station, you are confronted by the tallest office block in the Netherlands—a shard of black glass 150m high, belonging to an insurance company. The shapes, angles and colours of the buildings beyond it grow increasingly weird. But Rotterdammers take to this innovation with gusto, even giving some of the odder buildings nicknames. 'Rotterdam,' they say, 'will never be finished.' But there is another side to the city. Recently, the few patches of historic dockland that survived the bombing have been restored and injected with new life, largely in the form of cafés and restaurants. These romantic little harbours, coupled with some excellent museums, make Rotterdam worth at least a day or two of your time.

History

Towards the end of the 13th century, three people settled beside the river Rotte (part of the Maas delta) and built a dyke to reclaim some of the boggy land that stretched out around them. They paid a rent to Count Floris V of 12 chickens a year. Soon a mildly prosperous settlement grew up, relying on fishing, farming and trade with passing ships to trickle gold into the coffers. By 1328 Rotterdam had its own sheriff, and in 1340 the town was granted a charter by Count William IV. Rotterdam became the port serving the textile towns of Delft and Leiden and trade flourished—even through an English embargo. Canny Rotterdammers named a dockside tavern 'Calais', so that visiting captains could stop off for a drink and quite honestly record that they had been to Calais.

At the end of the 16th century, after suffering catastrophic floods and the privations of the Eighty Years' War, Rotterdam was quick to recover—European trade was shifting its focus from the Baltic to the North Sea. In 1585, when the Duke of Parma seized Antwerp, refugee merchants fleeing to Rotterdam brought secrets of the new spice routes and trade burgeoned as never before. But during the 17th-century Golden Age, Amsterdam (the seat of the Dutch East India Company) took over as the larger and more prosperous port, and Rotterdam went into decline. An 18th-century British trade embargo (Holland had become embroiled in the war between Britain and France) made the situation even worse. The 1,800 ships that visited Rotterdam annually had, by 1799, dropped to just 140. The city fathers' Luddite attitude towards steamships and the railways didn't help the local economy either.

But improving trade relations with Britain, and the growth of the Ruhr industrial area (to which Rotterdam is connected by inland waterways), gave the port a much-needed boost in the late 19th century. Expansion and excavation of the port gave access to even the largest ocean-going ships and laid the foundations for the massive harbour of today. Rotterdam became an important passenger port, especially for emigrants to the Americas. Between 1880 and 1940 around a million people passed through Rotterdam on the way to the USA, many of them Jews fleeing persecution in Eastern Europe. As an important international harbour, Rotterdam was a prime target for German bombers, and was razed to the ground on 14 May 1940. During the Nazi occupation Allied bombers had a go at the harbour facilities, and occasionally hit the town by mistake. But within a few years of the war the port was back to its normal capacity, and was one of the first in Europe to respond to the new demands of containerization. Today it has one of the most advanced technological support systems in the world.

Getting There

Rotterdam is 45 miles (72km) south of Amsterdam along the A4 and A13, and 18 miles (28km) from the Hague. Train journeys from Amsterdam's Centraal Station (there are four to five and hour) take 60 minutes.

Getting Around

If the weather is good, and you take time to stop off in cafés along the way, it is perfectly possible, even pleasant, to **walk** from Blaak in the east, through old docklands and along the Maas to the Euromast. After that it's a dull ten-minute walk to Delfshaven.

If you don't feel like legging it, the most convenient form of public transport is the **metro**. There are four lines running roughly east to west, and two going south from Centraal Station. Lines going in a similar direction stop at the same stations for most of their length, only fanning out in the distant suburbs—so the metro is easy to negotiate. There's also an efficient network of **trams** and **buses**. *Strippenkaarten* (*see* p.8) are valid, and you can get **information** from the national information line on ✆ (0900) 9292.

Should you want a close-up view of the world's largest port, you can go on a **harbour tour**. Spido Havenrondvaarten (situated at Leuvehoofd on the Leuvehaven, ✆ (010) 275 9988) offers a variety of boat tours starting from ƒ 16.50.

Bicycle hire: Rijwiel Shop, Stationsplein 1, ✆ (010) 412 6220.

Taxis: ✆ (010) 462 6060.

Tourist Information

The main branch of the VVV tourist office is at Coolsingel 57, ✆ (010) 402 3200; open Mon–Thurs 9.30–6, Fri 9.30–7, Sat 9.30–5, Sun 10–4. Not only can staff supply maps and the usual information, but they can suggest walking routes for people interested in modern architecture.

Festivals

The **Rotterdam Film Festival**, held in late January and early February, screens the pick of the latest art movies as well as commercial hits. In August, the **Heineken Jazz Festival** fills cafés (and sometimes streets) with eager fans of popular jazz and improvised music. There is also a two-month-long **Summer Festival** in July and August, which involves a wide variety of outdoor events and street entertainment.

Boymans-Van Beuningen Museum

Museumpark 18–20; open Tues–Sat 10–5, Sun 11–5; adm.

Amsterdam and The Hague both cornered royal art collections for the foundation of their showpiece museums. Not only did Rotterdam lack the advantages of royal patronage, it had to contend with a series of philistine city councillors, who turned down offers of at least two magnificent private collections. Yet today the Boymans-Van Beuningen Museum can stand shoulder to shoulder with the Rijksmuseum and the Mauritshuis as one of the finest collections of art and design in the country.

It was Frans Jacob Otto Boijmans who, in 1841, finally persuaded the council to accept his collection, provided they could find suitable accommodation for it. The eccentric hotchpotch of paintings, drawings and porcelain, which Boijmans had previously been unable to sell at auction or unload on the Utrecht city council, was housed in the Schielandshuis (*see* below), and much of it was lost when the building burnt down in 1864. But the museum's second major benefactor, the industrialist Daniel George van Beuningen (1877–1955), donated a treasury of masterpieces, including *Child in a Landscape*, the only **Titian** in any Dutch collection. Successive museum directors championed modern art and design. In 1903 the museum acquired *Lane of Poplars near Nuenen*, the first **Van Gogh** ever to appear in a public collection. More recently, director Wim Beeren has established the museum's reputation in the art world by commissioning work from the likes of Joseph Beuys, Andy Warhol, Bruce Nauman and Claes Oldenburg. Today, the 'Boymans' is housed in a building designed in 1935 and extended in the 1970s. Navigating through the warrens of rooms, arranged around two courtyards, can be utterly bewildering, but it is a pleasure getting lost. A **floorplan** (available free at the ticket office) is essential.

Downstairs, in the west wing, you'll find **decorative art and design**, ranging from a 16th-century Nautilus cup that belonged to the Czar of Russia (an iridescent shell covered with silver-gilt and rubies) to an Olivetti calculator. There is an especially good collection of 20th-century chairs, and also glass and ceramics. The **Print Room** in the east wing reveals just part of a rich store that includes work by Dürer, Bellini and Rembrandt. The two floors of the southern extension are devoted to **modern art**. Here highlights include Degas' *Little Dancer, fourteen years old*, a delightful sculpture in bronze, muslin and satin; work by Pyke Koch and other Dutch Magic Realists (*see* p.49); and a world-class collection of Dali, Magritte and other surrealists, much of it from the collection of English eccentric (and alleged illegitimate son of Edward VII), Edward James.

But the cream of the museum's collection is on the first floor of the west wing. Here you'll find a wealth of canvases by the likes of **Rubens**, **Frans Hals** and **Rembrandt** (including a touching portrait of his son Titus). Famous images, such as **Breughel**'s *Tower of Babel* and **Hieronymus Bosch**'s *The Vagabond*, hang alongside lesser-known but nonetheless exquisite pieces like **Bartholomeus van der Helst**'s intimate, 17th-century *Portrait of Abraham del Court and Maria de Keerssegieter*, in which Maria wears a breathtakingly beautiful silver satin dress. The Boymans is renowned for the quality of its temporary exhibitions, and has a large museum shop, well stocked with art books and designer knick-knacks.

Around the Museumpark

Adjoining the Boymans-Van Beuningen Museum, the Museumpark is really no more than a vast, rather barren city square. At the southern end are the blank slabs of the **Kunsthal Rotterdam** (Weestzeedijk 341; *open Tues–Sat 10–5, Sun 11–5; adm*), a giant exhibition space built in 1992. Here you are sure to catch some travelling blockbuster—anything from African sculpture to classic cars. Beside a pond at the northern end of the square is the **Nederlands Architectuurinstituut** (Netherlands Architecture Institute, Museumpark 25; *open Tues–Sat 10–5, Sun 11–5; adm*), which was designed by local architect Jo Coenen in 1993. A glass box, apparently suspended from scaffolding and with an arcaded offshoot that lights up in different colours at night, this is a zany home for the nation's architectural archive. There is no permanent display, but the institute holds temporary exhibitions on architectural themes.

Het Schielandshuis

Korte Hoogstraat 31; open Tues–Sat 10–5, Sun 11–5; adm.

Built between 1662 and 1665 as government offices for the surrounding province of Schieland, the pristine white Schielandshuis is a beautiful example of the poise and proportion of Restrained Dutch Classicism. Though the building burnt down in 1864 (by which time it was already in use as a museum), the façade survived, and the rest was carefully restored. Today it houses a Historical Museum, most noted for the ***Atlas van Stolk***. In 1835, the timber merchant Abraham van Stolk began to compile an 'historical atlas' of prints that depicted events in Dutch history and which portrayed his own life and times. The tens of thousands of prints he collected came into the possession of the Rotterdam municipality in 1967. Only a tiny fragment of the *Atlas* goes on show at any one time, on the ground floor, usually in the form of an exhibition arranged around a specific theme. Also on the ground floor is a series of exceptional Baroque- and Rococo-style rooms, taken from mansions around Rotterdam and reassembled in the Schielandshuis. Upstairs you'll find displays on the history of Rotterdam (including some intriguing old children's toys) and a small collection of costumes, featuring not only little sequinned numbers from the 1920s, but hippie and flower-child garments too.

The Eastern Docklands

Blaak

Emerging from the space-age metro station at Blaak, you are confronted with two of Rotterdam's most photographed modern buildings, an apartment block nicknamed 'the Pencil' (for reasons that are quite evident), and the **Blaakse Bos** (Blaak Forest). The 'forest' comprises a thicket of cube-shaped apartments, up-ended on one corner and perched on tall stalks. Designed by Piet Blom in 1984, these curious homes are all occupied except one, which you can visit: the **Kijk-Kubus** (Show-Cube, Overblaak 70; *open March–Dec daily 11–5; Jan–Feb Fri–Sun 11–5; adm*). It is surprisingly ordinary inside. Sticking up incongruously in these modern surrounds is the Gothic tower of the **Grote of St Laurenskerk**, Grote Kerkplein 3 (*open Tues–Sat 10–4, but closed Thurs in winter and sometimes closed for conferences; adm free*). Built between 1449 and 1525, the church is a lonely survivor of

Second World War bombs, and contains three organs by the Danish Marcussen company—the oldest dating back to 1540. There's a coffee corner at the back of the nave, where you can sit, sip a hot drink, and possibly be deafened by a blast from the main organ, which is one of the biggest in Europe.

Across the busy marketplace behind the church you'll find the **Nationaal Schoolmuseum** (Nieuwemarkt 1a; *open Tues–Sat 10–5, Sun 1–5; adm, children under 16 free*), a series of classrooms down the ages, starting in the 12th century, all reconstructed using authentic furniture. By 1910 school slates have given way to exercise books and by 1960 communal tables have replaced long wooden desks, and there is a TV set in the corner. In a 1930s classroom, a message chalked up on the blackboard invites you to sit down and try your hand at using a dip-pen.

Oude Haven

Stretching out on the other side of the Blaakse Bos is the Oude Haven (Old Harbour), the first of a series of docks that were the predecessors of today's busy port. Nowadays the Oude Haven is filled with boats of the **Openlucht Binnenvaart Museum** (*open access; adm free*), workaday vessels that have plied the inland waterways over the centuries. The old warehouses that surrounded the docks have gone, but as you wander from Oude Haven to Scheepmakershaven ('Shipbuilders' Harbour') and Wijnhaven ('Wine Harbour') these colourful, much-used old boats stand in startling contrast against a backdrop of angular modern architecture. There is even a whiff of tar and diesel in the air. At Wijnhaven you'll find the floating museum of **Schepen uit Verre Landen** (Ships from Far Countries, Wijnhaven 20a; *open Tues–Fri 10–4, Sat and Sun 12–5; adm*). Inside is a fascinating collection of craft, from painted sampans to tiny reed rafts from the Andes, and a fishing boat on which 16 Vietnamese refugees were found floating on the ocean in 1981.

Maritiem Museum Prins Hendrik

Leuvenhaven 1; open Tues–Sat 10–5, Sun 11–5; adm.

Models and paintings of ships abound in the Maritime Museum. Unless your interest is passionate, you could skim through the first two floors stopping off only at the **Schatkamer** (Treasury), where the choicest examples are kept. After that, displays become more varied and interesting, with lots of hands-on exhibits for children. In a reconstructed warehouse office you can open drawers and sniff the aromas of a variety of cargoes—from cinnamon to bananas and peanuts. You can peer out at Rotterdam through a submarine periscope (accompanied by appropriate sound effects), and push buttons to guess at the speed of the wind that a machine blows in your face.

Grown-ups might prefer the old sea charts and navigation instruments—Lucas Waghenaar's *Spieghel der Zeevaert* (1584), the first printed maritime atlas, is on show—and there's an informative display on the history of the port of Rotterdam. But by far the most riveting part of the museum is moored in the harbour outside: the 19th-century warship *Buffel*. The ship has been perfectly restored, from the rows of enamel basins in the crew's washroom to the polished mahogany and leather of the captain's cabin. You can see the shining, pumping engines and drop in on the ship's jail, situated in the bow just behind the battering ram.

Along the Maas

The Boompjes (literally 'little trees') was once a tree-lined promenade along the river Maas. Today it is a wall of high-rise blocks skirted by speeding traffic and dotted with nervous-looking pedestrians. Despite this, it does offer a fine view of the bridges over the river—the bright red **Willemsbrug** (built in the 1980s), and the spectacular white **Erasmusbrug**, a 410m-long suspension bridge hanging from a single 139m-high pylon. It is nicknamed 'the swan' by those who like it. Those who don't refer to is rather unkindly as the 'washing-up brush'. The Erasmusbrug opened in 1996 but was forced to close again a few weeks later because the cables flapped alarmingly in the first strong wind. Across the water you can see the twin towers of the former headquarters of the **Holland-Amerika Lijn**, the company that ferried so many people across the Atlantic to a new life in the USA. (Nowadays the building is a hotel.)

A little further down the river, around Veerhaven, old Rotterdam reasserts itself. The quays are lined with turn-of-the-century buildings, there is the occasional flourish of greenery, and smart yachts moored in the docks. In a 100-year-old building beside the harbour, the **Museum voor Volkenkunde** (Ethnological Museum, Willemskade 25; *open Tues–Sat 10–5, Sun 11–5; adm*) offers three floors of changing exhibitions devoted to the the cultures of distant lands. Nearby, through a small park, is Rotterdam's post-office tower, the **Euromast** (Parkhaven 20; *open April–Sept daily 10–7; Oct–March 10–5; July and Aug until 10.30pm; adm exp*). A lift takes you up 92m to the viewing platform, then you have to hold on to your hat as—amidst much roaring and dry-ice smoke—the **Space Adventure** capsule will shoot you up to the top of the tower, all of 185m above the ground, for a view that extends to the North Sea.

Delfshaven

The most appealing of all Rotterdam's historic harbours is Delfshaven, which manged to get through the Second World War relatively unscathed. Delfshaven was once a separate town, made rich by *genever* distilleries and as the main port serving the textile factories and potteries at Delft. The narrow harbour (it's more like a canal) runs past an old windmill, once used to grind grain for the distilleries, and is edged with dainty gabled buildings, mostly dating from the 17th century. Nowadays they house art galleries, antiques shops and a string of cafés and restaurants, giving Delfshaven a sedate, leisurely air that makes it seem quite detached from the rest of Rotterdam.

In **De Dubbelde Palmboom** (Voorhaven 12; *open Tues–Fri 10–5, Sat and Sun 11–5; adm*), a converted 19th-century warehouse, you can see a number of exhibits on working life in the area. These range from an Iron Age farmstead to a reconstruction of the interior of a worker's cottage built early this century. A few minutes' walk further up the harbour is the **Oude Kerk** (*open Sat 2–5; adm free*). This is the church where, on the 21 July 1620, the Pilgrim Fathers spent their last night on Dutch soil, praying for safe conduct and sleeping on the pews. The next morning they embarked on the *Speedwell* for Plymouth, where they changed ships for the *Mayflower*.

If things continue as they have done then the centre of Rotterdam is well on the way to becoming one enormous shopping mall. It was one of the first inner-city areas in Europe ever to be pedestrianized and ambitious plans are already being implemented to link up existing shops with brand new buildings to create what has been described as a 'shopping environment', canopied by glass and full of eager Euro-shoppers. If this is how you enjoy spending your money, head for **Beurs metro station** but if you prefer more of an individual approach, try **Nieuwe Binnenstraat**, where you'll find magic mushrooms, plenty of music, designer furniture, and a branch of the Witte Tandenwinkel (which has more varieties of toothbrush than you could possibly imagine). You can find some adventurous **art galleries** on Witte de Withstraat, and antiques shops in Delfshaven. Every Tuesday and Saturday browsers can enjoy the good **antiques and fleamarket** on Grotemarkt and Hoogstraat, near the Blaak metro station.

Rotterdam ✆ (010–)　　　　　　　　　　　　　　　　**Where to Stay**

Bilderberg Parkhotel, Westersingel 70, 3015 LB, ✆ 436 3611, ✉ 436 4212 (*expensive*). The Bilderberg Parkhotel is a gracious turn-of-the-century mansion with a giant metallic annexe. It can be found just around the corner from the Boymans-Van Beuningen Museum. Staff are super-friendly and the rooms are modern and comfortable. From ƒ305.

Hotel Central, Kruiskade 12, 3012 EH, ✆ 414 0744, ✉ 412 5325 (*inexpensive*). This is just what it says. In the heart of the shopping district, and with a faded air of the 1970s.

Hotel New York, Koninginnenhoofd 1, 3072 AD, ✆ 439 0500, ✉ 484 2701 (*moderate–inexpensive: from ƒ160 to ƒ275 with river view*). The Hotel New York is a trendy and stylish hotel housed in the converted headquarters of the Holland-Amerika Lijn. Rooms are furnished in a hip modern style and have great views across the harbour.

Hotel Van Walsum, Mathenesserlaan 199–201, 3014 HC, ✆ 436 3275, ✉ 436 4410 (*inexpensive; price incl. breakfast*). The Hotel Van Walsum is a real gem being one of those family-run hotels managed by people who actually take a pride in what they're doing. In a 19th-century building just a short walk from the Museumpark, and offering excellent value for money. (Be sure to check out the restored 1890s loo on the 3rd floor.)

Alexander Hotel, Pieter de Hoochweg 115a/b, 3024 BG, ✆ 476 5277, ✉ 425 4201 (*inexpensive*). Simple hotel with friendly management and a restaurant downstairs. Near Delfshaven.

Hotel Baan, Rochussenstraat 345, 3023 DH, ✆ 477 0555, ✉ 476 9450 (*cheap*). A comfortable family-run hotel on the waterside near Delfshaven.

Youth Hostel, Rochussenstraat 107–9, 3015 EH, ✆ 436 5763, ✉ 436 5569 (*from ƒ32.25 p.p. for a bed in a dorm including breakfast*).

Parkheuvel, Heuvellaan 21, ✆ 436 0766 (*expensive*). Modern restaurant with a view over the Maas, a classic ambience and a reputation almost unrivalled by any in the land. Imagine scallops with acorn bread and truffles; langoustines and sole with sun-dried tomatoes and grilled artichoke. Or don't even attempt to imagine, just try it.

De Engel, Eendrachtsweg 19, ✆ 413 8256 (*expensive*). Owned and operated by a chef whose favourite movie is *The Cook, the Thief, his Wife and her Lover*. Sumptuous décor in a patrician mansion, and a menu that depends on what's fresh and special in the market that day. Delicious dishes that rely more on good ingredients and subtle combinations of flavour than on fancy sauces.

Parkzicht, Kievitslaan 25, ✆ 436 8888 (*moderate*). A pavilion in the middle of a park beside the Maas. On one side is a bar and brasserie where you can have light meals, or just a drink. On the other is a pricier candlelit restaurant where pigeon cooked with goose liver is more the order of the day.

Eten, Nieuwe Binnenweg 153, ✆ 436 4474 (*moderate*). An interior design that manages to be both hyper-modern and cosy, painted in deep blues, greens and browns, with a sweeping, curved leather bench and a plethora of fish sculptures. Fish dishes are indeed a speciality. Start with excellent seafood tapas, then try brill steamed with asparagus and thinly layered with duck liver.

De Tijd Geest, Oost Wijnstraat 14, ✆ 233 1311 (*moderate*). Popular lunchtime spot overlooking the Oude Haven (though it's open for dinner too). Formal décor under the high ceilings of a 19th-century building—with the occasional startling flash of fake cheetah-skin upholstery. Join Rotterdam business folk for such dishes as duck breast with lavender honey and shiitake mushrooms.

Eethuisje de Parel, Voorhaven 54b, ✆ 476 5558 (*moderate*). A tiny restaurant beside the harbour at Delfshaven. Oddball décor—as if Dali had been let loose in an aquarium, though the food is less bizarre. Try the smoked pork chops with mushrooms, or duck with forest berries.

Henkes, Voorhaven 17, ✆ 425 5596 (*moderate*). An enormous *grand café*, with an interior that 100 years ago belonged to a Brussels insurance office. Tasty fare with a traditional Dutch touch, such as brown bean soup with smoked eel, or halibut with leeks and home-ground mustard.

Loos, Westplein 1, ✆ 411 7723 (*moderate*). Big, noisy, perennially popular brasserie. A lively, slightly artsy Rotterdam crowd tuck in to such delights as sea bass wrapped in Chinese greens and served with stir-fried veg and hazelnut sauce.

Wester Paviljoen, Nieuwe Binnenweg 136, ✆ 436 2322 (*cheap*). 'Brown café' writ large, with a young friendly crowd. Dishes such as lasagne or rabbit casserole are uneventful, but good value for money.

Cambrinus, Blaak 4, ✆ 414 6702 (*cheap*). In the shade of the Blaakse Bos. You can sit inside on plush, comfy chairs in winter or join the crowds on the large, waterside terrace in good weather. There are tasty *hapjes* (snacks to accompany your drink) and fuller meals, such as squid stir-fried with chickpeas, green beans and bamboo shoots.

The **Rotterdam Philharmonic Orchestra**, as well as any visiting artiste of note in the classical music world, plays at **De Doelen** concert hall, Schouwburgplein 50, ✆ 217 1717. Rotterdam also boasts one of the best modern dance troupes in the country, Scapino Ballet, which performs at the **Rotterdamse Schouwburg**, Schouwburgplein 25, ✆ 411 8110. Visiting rock stars head for **Ahoy Rotterdam**, Zuiderparkweg 20–30, ✆ 481 2144.

There is a flourishing live music scene centred mainly on **Café Dada**, Westewagenstraat 58, Popular, Westkruiskade 26, and **Rotown**, Nieuwe Binnenweg 19. **Nighttown**, Westkruiskade 26, is the city's trendiest club, and also often features live music, and **Heksenkethel** (underground, entrance opposite Centraal Station) is popular for its retro Seventies vibes. The new, multi-level **Hollywood Music Hall**, Delftestraat 14 and the tropical **Baja Beach Club**, K. Doormanstraat 10–12 are hottest on the disco scene.

Leiden

Leiden

200 metres
200 yards
N

LANGEGRACHT

VEST
Oude
Vest

OOSTDWARS-GRACHT

gracht

Oude Heren-

Blekerspark

MAREDORP

VAN DER WERFSTRAAT

HARLEMMERSTRAAT

OUDE   RIJN   KAASMARKT

PELIKAANSTRAAT

HAVEN

Haven-
plein

De Haven

ZUIDSINGEL

Amker-
park

Singel

Zijl

De Burcht

MIDDELWEG

HOOIGRACHT

GROENE

MIDDELSTEGRACHT

UITERSTEGRACHT

VESTESTRAAT

PANCRASWIJK

HERENGRACHT

LANGESTRAAT

ORANJEGRACHT

OOSTERKERKSTRAAT

STEEG

Katoen-
park

MRKT

Nieuwe

Rijn   NIEUWE RIJN   NIEUWE RIJN

LEVENDAAL

GEREGRACHT

LEVENDAAL

GORTESTRAAT

LEVENDAAL

STRAAT

ÚTKADE

Singel

VENDAAL

175

The plan of a Dutch town is: a bridge, a canal: under an arch into a street: pointed stepped houses; 1620: on brand new garages: a great red brick tower, then a vast church, shut up... Some frescoes on white-washed walls... Flights of cyclists. Immense profusion of highly civilised shops—flower shops, shoes, bicycles, books, everything the more solidly placed wealthy but not frivolous citizen can eat or wear or use: all shining spick & span.

Virginia Woolf, *Diary: May 8, 1935*

Leiden fits the plan perfectly, and even throws in a couple of windmills for good measure. This was Rembrandt's birthplace and home to the Pilgrim Fathers, the site of the most famous battle in Dutch history and of the first tulips grown in Holland. Yet despite its wealthy air and historical resonance, Leiden is no stuffy museum piece. The local university, founded in 1581, is one of the most prestigious in the country and student life gives the town spirit and verve. 'A new harvest of sanskrit!' exclaims the sign on a bookshop window; the 'frescoes on whitewashed walls' are texts by the world's greatest poets; glimpses through canal-house windows reveal the chaos of communal student kitchens; doors of ancient Student Corps' headquarters fly open and tipsy young men tumble out into the night air. Inside, the sounds of carousing continue. In surrounding cafés people are locked in earnest conversation.

Just a few minutes' journey from Amsterdam, Leiden is a popular day-trip destination. But if you spend a night there, when most of the visitors have gone, you're more likely to appreciate the university-town atmosphere. Just visiting the museums could easily consume a day of your time. The Molenmuseum Valk gives a fascinating insight into the innards of a windmill, the collection of Japanese artefacts at the Rijksmuseum voor Volkenkunde is so impressive that people make pilgrimages from Japan to view it, and the Egyptian antiquities at the Rijksmuseum van Oudenheden are of world renown.

History

The locals (known as 'Leijenaars') like to claim that the Leiden grew from the Roman settlement of Lugdunum, but it's safer to pinpoint the town's origin at the appearance of De Burcht (The Stronghold, *see* below) around AD 1000. Around 1050 the powerful Counts of Holland moved into the town, so ensuring Leiden's prosperity for centuries to come. At the beginning of the Eighty Years' War, the Spanish besieged Leiden (1573–4). The starving town was eventually relieved by William the Silent, who broke down the dykes and, to the Spaniards' utter surprise, came sailing across the fields with the Dutch navy. The Spanish made off with such haste that they left their dinner—an enormous pot of stew—still simmering on the fire. It was found by a city marksman (some romantics say a wandering orphan). He carried it back to the hungry Leijenaars who were already laying into the white bread and herring that the navy had brought. Every year, on 3 October, the town celebrates the anniversary of its relief with festive public consumption of bread, herring and *hutspot* ('hotch-potch'). As a reward for their endurance William offered the people of Leiden either eternal relief from taxation, or Holland's first university. With characteristic far-sightedness they chose the latter.

Leiden went on to become a prosperous wool-trading town, but towards the end of the 18th century the trade (and the city) went into decline as the industrial revolution passed Holland by and British towns cornered the wool market. It was the university that helped the town keep its head above water—and it still does. Although Leiden's suburban sprawl now links up with the industries and larger cities of the Randstad, it is the university and its associated research institutes that drive Leiden's economy.

Getting There

Leiden is only half an hour by train from Amsterdam's Centraal Station. One leaves every 15–20 minutes. By car, it's 25 miles (40km) along the A4.

Getting Around

All the main tourist sites are within easy walking distance of the centre and the railway station. They are all very well signposted, and there are helpful maps dotted all over the city centre (look for the **i** sign). *Strippenkarten* (*see* p.8) are valid on public transport here too, though Leiden's buses tend to skirt the historic core of the city and are of limited use to tourists. For **information** on public transport, telephone the national information line on ✆ (0900) 9292.

Bicycle rental: Behind the station, ✆ (071) 512 0068; *f*8 per day. You'll need to leave *f*100 deposit and have proof of identification.

Taxi: ✆ (071) 521 2144 or 512 3300.

Boat trips: Rederij Sleutelstad (dep. Beestenmarkt, ✆ (071) 513 4938) offer trips through the city's canals (mid-April–mid-Sept); Schuitje Vaart (dep. Stille Mare, ✆ (071) 512 0394) does the same, but in smaller boats (May–Sept).

Tourist Information

The VVV tourist office is right near the railway station at Stationsplein 210, ✆ (0900) 222 2333, ✉ (071) 512 5318; open Mon–Fri 9–5.30, Sat 9–4; *www.tref.nl/3355/sport/vvv.htm*. Here you can pick up a map and advice on routes of walks around the town.

Festivals

Most of Leiden erupts in a city-wide party on **3 October** (as it has done for over 400 years) to celebrate the relief of its siege in 1574. Traditional white bread, herring and *hutspot* (*see* above) are served, and celebrations in restaurants and cafés spill out into the street.

Rijksmuseum voor Volkenkunde

National Museum of Ethnology, Steenstraat 1; open Tues–Fri 10–5, Sat and Sun 12–
–5; adm. Until 2001 the museum will be undergoing extensive renovation, and only a
small part of the collection will be on view at any one time. Adm will be only f3.50
during the renovation period.

You have barely stepped off the train when you come across one of Leiden's weighty museums. In a converted 19th-century hospital beside what was once part of the city moat, you'll find Javanese puppets, Bornean ear-jewellery made from the beaks of hornbills, a Greenlander's Sunday best, and other riches from around the world.

But the real attraction is the **Siebold Collection** of Japanese art and artefacts. In 1825, Philipp von Siebold went to Japan as a doctor, under the auspices of the Dutch government. He had instructions to collect as much information as he could about what was then a relatively unknown culture. Siebold came back laden with 6,000 objects, ranging from fans to enormous 17th-century statues of Buddha. This stash forms the core of what has become one of the most noted representations of traditional Japanese culture in the world. There are rooms set out ready for a tea ceremony, cabinets of beautiful lacquerware, suits of Samurai armour and ceremonial swords. The display of prints boasts work by Utagawa Hiroshige (1797–1858), including the well-known *Sudden Shower over the Bridge of Atake*. Keep an eye open for the 17th-century clocks. At that time the Japanese divided the daylight hours into six equal periods, named after animals in the Chinese astrological chart. The length of these periods varied according to season. The mechanisms of these first clocks were copied from western models, but a clockmaker had to visit every month to adjust them to follow seasonal fluctuations.

Molenmuseum de Valk

2ᵉ Binnenvestgracht 1a, open Tues–Sat 10–5, Sun 1–5; adm.

A restored 18th-century grain mill, 'De Valk' offers a rare inside view of how windmills work. You can potter about the lower storeys, where the last miller lived until the turn of this century. Then leave the cosily furnished rooms to clamber past millstones and flour chutes to the grinding cogs, seven storeys high. On the way you can step out on to the reefing stage (the platform that runs around the middle of the windmill) for a view over the city.

De Lakenhal

Oude Singel 32, open Tues–Fri 10–5, Sat and Sun 12–5; adm.

'The Cloth Hall' was built in 1640 as the administrative centre of Leiden's prosperous cloth industry. In 1874 it was converted into a municipal museum. Much of the original interior wall panelling and stucco work is intact, and there are good collections of silver and furniture. But the star attractions are the paintings. Look out especially for Lucas van Leyden's fine and delicately coloured triptych, *The Last Judgement* (1572); works by the young Rembrandt and his studio-mate Jan Levens; Gerard Dou's tiny, intense oils (which established a Leiden style); and the lecherous abandon of Jan Steen's *Amorous Couple* (1660). There's a painting depicting the brave Burgemeester van der Werff who, at the height of the siege, offered his own body as food to the faltering citizens. They refused but were fired by his courage to hold out even longer. (In the painting they look well-fed and a little embarrassed by the offer.)

Museum Boerhaave

Lange St Agnietenstraat 10, open Tues–Sat 10–5, Sun 12–5; adm.

The idea of a museum of scientific and surgical instruments might not have you immediately reaching for your wallet, but this one is worth every cent of the entry fee. First off, on the ground floor, is a reconstruction of a wooden Anatomy Theatre—a mini-colosseum with steep rakes of spectators' seats surrounding a central operating table. It was in theatres like this that Rembrandt's *Anatomy Lesson of Professor Tulp*, and countless other paintings of the genre, were set. Next, you wander through five centuries' worth of medical instruments and scientific paraphernalia. There's a 17th-century painting depicting God as a doctor (complete with a urine specimen jar), and the world's first herbarium—a book of pressed herbs, all still intact, put together by one Leohart Rauwolf in 1560. Next comes a range of beautifully crafted early microscopes, one of the first ever pendulum clocks, and astronomy globes and instruments galore. Look out for the 19th-century Zander equipment, such as the 'Apparatus for Massaging the Chest and Back'—an eccentric contraption made of cast iron, with all sorts of cogs, belts and rubber hammers. You can also see a prototype heart-lung machine, and one of the first commercially produced electron microscopes. Along the way there are models of machines to play with, and everything is given clear labelling in English.

Hofjes

Beside the Boerhaave museum is a green door with 'Zion' elaborately scripted on the jamb. Through it you'll find a pretty garden courtyard surrounded by dainty houses. This is the **Groot Sionshof**, a court of almshouses built for elderly married couples in 1668. There are many such *hofjes* around Leiden, hidden behind unassuming doors. On your wanderings, pop in for a glimpse of the rather grand 18th-century **Coninckshofje** (Oude Veste 15); **St Stevenshof** (Haarlemmerstraat 48–50), founded in 1487; and the **Groeneveldstichting** (Oude Veste 41), built for the widows of clergy in 1882. All are still private residences, but provided you respect that you are usually welcome to look around quietly. Though if you see a sign reading '*Verboden Toegang Art. 461*', bear in mind that means 'Trespassers will be Prosecuted'.

Around the Stadhuis

Leiden's **Stadhuis** (City Hall) was built in 1597, though the unattractive brick pile you see today dates back to the 1930s, rebuilt after the old Stadhuis had been razed. All that was left was the front façade (which you can still see, in Breestraat). At one corner of the City Hall stands a sturdy 17th-century **Waag** (Weighing House), once the focus of an enormous market place: many of the street names in the area still end with '*markt*', from Kaasmarkt (cheese) to Aalmarkt (eels) and Beestenmarkt (cattle), giving you an idea of just how large the market was. A walk through the elegant classicist buildings that once accommodated the fish market brings you to **De Burcht** (The Stronghold). The dumpy fortress was built around AD 1000 on a mound between two branches of the Rhine to protect a small settlement of fishermen and farmers from marauding Vikings, fractious local lords and the fickle water levels. You can still march around its sturdy battlements and look out over the whole city.

Rijksmuseum Van Oudenheden

National Museum of Antiquities, Rapenburg 28; open Tues–Sat 10–5, Sun 12–5; adm.

The country's leading archaeological museum houses the entire 1st century AD *Temple of Taffeh* donated in 1960 by the Egyptian government to the Dutch in gratitude for their contribution to UNESCO excavations in Abyssinia. The squat stone building is in the museum foyer (it was a condition of the gift that no one should pay to see it) and overhead lighting simulates the passage of the sun (a second stipulation). The museum has a thrillingly gruesome collection of mummies (including one of a crocodile), and good stores of Greek and Roman antiquities. Star exhibits are the *Tomb Statues of Maya and Merit*. Maya was Director of the Treasury to Tutankhamun; his wife was a priestess. Although the statues arrived in Holland in 1832, their provenance was obscure, and it was only in 1986 that the tomb was rediscovered (a CD-ROM tells the story).

The University

Founded in 1581, the University of Leiden now spreads throughout the city, rather in the manner of Oxbridge colleges. But the focus of university life is the **Academiegebouw**, Rapenburg 73, one of the oldest parts of the unversity. Once a nunnery, it has for centuries been used as an exam hall. Inside, up a spiral wooden staircase, you'll find the 'Sweat Box'—the room where anxious candidates sat before exams and later awaited their results. The room is now hermetically sealed to protect the generations of signatures they left behind them on the walls. There is also a small **Academic History Museum** (*open Wed, Thurs, Fri 1–5; adm free*) with displays of mortar boards, gowns and students' bric-a-brac down the ages.

Hortus Botanicus

Open April–Sept Mon–Sat 9–5, Sun 10–5; Oct–Mar Mon–Fri 9–5, Sun 10–5; adm.

The part of the university most worth visiting is its Botanical Garden. Planted in 1594, it is one of the oldest botanical gardens in Europe. A 17th-century traveller described the Hortus as 'ravishing in rare curiosities', and it is here that the botanist Clusius planted the first tulip bulbs in Holland. They had come from Turkey via an embassy garden in Switzerland, where Clusius had spotted them. Unfortunately, the professor never saw his plants bloom: they were stolen one night before spring came. Today, Clusius' garden has once again been laid out in its original form. Later, when you have inhaled the perfume of scores of roses, visited the 350-year-old laburnum, and grown tired of the elegantly laid-out shrubberies, you can push your way through hothouses of sticky exotica, past signs warning you to 'Beware of the Butterflies' to the massive Victoria Amazonia lily, reputed to be able to support the weight of three men on its pads, and which flowers but one night a year.

Pieterskerk and Pilgrims

The 15th-century **Pieterskerk** (*open daily 1.30–4*) is in the heart of the student quarter. The church was originally called St Pieters, but was stripped of its saintly title, and any other papist ornamentation, during the Reformation. By far the most interesting thing to see in the plain, cavernous church is a mummified body. It was found, dried out by the draught, in a secret room under the pulpit and now lies in the church with its ankles neatly crossed and its head on a pillow. No one knows how it got there, or even how old it is. Some suspect murder, or a priest's secret lover; others mutter darkly about Nazis and the Occupation.

Pieterskerk's other attractions include the tomb of Jan Steen, the 17th-century Dutch painter. Rembrandt's parents are also buried at Pieterskerk, though their graves are unmarked. Very little remains in Leiden to remind you of the painter's early years in the town. (A plaque on the side of a 1960s block of flats in Weddesteeg, halfway between the railway station and the university, marks the spot where he was born.)

In the church, you can also see a chart tracing ex-President George Bush's family tree, showing his descent from the Pilgrim Fathers. From 1609 to 1620 a group of Puritans, finding the religious atmosphere in Holland more congenial than in England, settled in Leiden with their preacher, John Robinson. **Jan Pesijnshofje** (Pieterskerkhof 21), a late 17th-century almshouse near the church, now marks the site where Robinson lived and preached. The congregation felt the need for an even freer climate, so in 1620 they boarded the *Mayflower* and set sail for the New World. Robinson stayed behind and is buried in the Pieterskerk.

Naturalis

Darwinweg 2, ℭ (071) 568 7600; open Tues–Sun noon–6pm, adm.

Naturalis is the National Museum of Natural History, situated just behind Leiden station. The entrance building was originally put up in the 17th century as a *pesthuis* (hospital for sufferers from the plague). Nowadays a covered walkway transports you past a couple of life-size rhinos to a modern high-rise that's been hollowed out and filled with tiers of dinosaur skeletons, minerals, stuffed animals, preserved fish and thousands of plants and neatly ranged insects. No mangy bears and faded parrots here: everything is in top-top better-than-real-life condition, and interestingly presented. There are intriguing displays on environment and the planet, and a wealth of multimedia facilities—though it's a new museum and as yet much of the labelling and all of the multimedia is in Dutch only.

Shopping

Haarlemmerstraat is the main shopping drag, with branches of all the Dutch high street stores. But you'll find well-stocked bookshops, junk shops and quirkier boutiques around the top end of Nieuwe Rijn and in the alleys around the Pieterskerk.

Leiden ℭ (071–)   ***Where to Stay***

Golden Tulip Leiden, Schipholweg 3, 2316 XB, ℭ 522 1121, ✆ 522 6675 (*expensive*). Smart business persons' hotel just a bleeper's pip from the railway station.

Mayflower, Beestenmarkt 2, 2312 CC, ℭ 514 2641, ✆ 512 8516 (*moderate–inexpensive, price includes breakfast*). Overlooking the newly renovated Beestenmarkt square, though with a slightly eerie, furniture-warehouse atmosphere.

Nieuw Minerva, Boommarkt 23, 2312 EA, ℭ 512 6358, ✆ 514 2674 (*inexpensive; includes breakfast*). Long having worn the mantle of Leiden's best bet for lower budgets, it is now tired—especially when it comes to furnishings and service. But it does have an attractive canalside location.

De Doelen, Rapenburg 2, 2311 EV, ✆ 512 0527, ✉ 512 8453 (*inexpensive; includes breakfast*). Converted from a grand canal house. The rooms are tastefully furnished and the public areas still bear traces of sumptuous décor. Good value.

The Rose, Beestenmarkt 14, 2312 CC, ✆ 514 6630, ✉ 521 7096 (*inexpensive; includes breakfast*). Small hotel above a café, overlooking the Beestenmarkt and a canal. Friendly owners, though the rooms are spartan, and could be cold in winter.

Pension In de Goede Hoek, Diefsteeg 19a, 2311 TS, ✆ 512 1031 (*cheap*). Cosy little pension in the heart of student land.

Youth Hostel, Lange Scheistraat 9, 2312 CR, ✆ 512 8457, ✉ 512 8763 (*f23.50 for dormitory room, f5 sheet hire*).

Leiden ✆ *(071–)*　　　　　　　　　　　　　　　　　　　　**Eating Out**

The best place for cafés and restaurants is around **Pieterskerkhof** and **Hooglandskerk**.

Fabers, Kloksteeg 13, ✆ 512 4012 (*expensive*). Cool service, *haute cuisine* and a good price to quality ratio.

Malle Jan, Nieuwsteeg 11, ✆ 512 3888 (*moderate*). Lively brasserie offering good, substantial Franco-Dutch favourites, with lots of salad and potatoes.

Het Panacee, Rapenburg 97, ✆ 566 1494 (*moderate*). Realm of the deans and professors. Tuck into such dishes as venison with forest mushrooms and honey-truffle sauce.

Scarlatti, Stille Mare 4, ✆ 512 2114 (*moderate*). Friendly café atmosphere, candlelight and excellent cooking.

De Brandery, Middelweg 7, ✆ 513 3728 (*moderate*). Multi-tiered restaurant made with galleries rescued from an old church, but with a curious Wild West bordello atmosphere. Good hearty cooking.

Koetshuis, Burgsteeg 13, ✆ 512 1688 (*moderate*). A converted 17th-century carriage house at the foot of the Burcht. Serves good light lunches.

Mangerie de Koekop, Lange Mare 60, ✆ 514 1937 (*moderate*). Fresh décor, Lloyd's loom chairs and tasty vegetarian options on the menu.

Lunchroom Snijders, Botermarkt 15, ✆ 512 2583 (*inexpensive*). Behind a richly carved 19th-century shop front, through a tempting patisserie, is a room with a gently fading 1930s atmosphere. Good for a quick sandwich or gooey cake.

Annie's Verjaardag Brasserie, Oude Rijn 1a, ✆ 512 5737 (*inexpensive*). Snacks, soups and sandwiches during the day, and more substantial fare in the evenings.

De Waterlijn, Prinsessekade, ✆ 512 1279 (*inexpensive*). Floating, angular, modern glass-walled café with a view up the canal to a windmill. Apple pie and light meals.

Entertainment and Nightlife

Student cafés are the best places to meet up with people, and to find out about the club scene. **Barrerra** (cnr Kloksteeg and Rapenburg) is a good place to start, night and day, and **Leidseplein** (cnr Diefsteeg and Pieterskerkgracht) also has a friendly crowd. The current music and dance hotspot is **LVC**, next to the post office on Breestraat.

The Hague and Delft

The Hague (Den Haag)

Sealife Centre

Museum Beelden aan Zee

HARTEVEL STR

RENBAANSTRAAT

STRAND WEG

Scheveningen

JURRIAN KOKSTRAAT

HAVENKADE BADHUISKADE

SCHEVENING

STADHOUDERSLAAN

PRINSESSEGRACHT

KAZERNESTRAAT

Het Paleis

LANGE VOORHOUT

LANGE VOORHOUT

KORTE VOORHOUT

KON. JULIANAPLEIN

Central Station

PARKSTRAAT

NOORDEINDE

Museum Bredius

LANGE VIVERBERG

Haags Historisch Museum

HERENGRACHT

Paleis Noordeinde

Hof-vijver

Mauritshuis

Gevangen Poort

Ridderzaal

RIJNSTRAAT

MOLENSTRAAT

PRINSESTR

PIPESTR

HOOGSTR

KORTE VLIVERBERG

HOFSTR

BUITEN-HOF

Binnen-hof

Schildergalerij Prins Willem V

GRAVEN STR

ACHTEROM

Passage

SPUI

Grote Kerk

DAGELIJSKE GROENMARKT

SPUISTRAAT

MARKTSTRAAT

KALVERMARKT

WESTEINDE

JAN HENDRIKSTR

GROTE

N

LANGE LOMBARDSTR

PRINSEGRACHT

250 metres

250 yards

Kurhaus

i Tourist Office

ZWOLSE

STRAAT

PERBAANSTRAAT

750 metres
800 yards

N

Nieuwe
Scheveningse
Bosjes

Westbroek
Park

SCHEVENINGSEWEG

HARTINGKADE

● **Madurodam**

Hubertuspark

Scheveningse

Bosjes

seon/Omniversum/
meente Museum

Huis ten Bosch 🏛

Haagse-

Bos

CARNEG
PLEIN

🏛 🏛 **Museum Mesdag**

Vredespaleis

LAAN VAN MEERDERVOORT

ZEESTRAAT

**Panorama
Mesdag**

i Tourist
Office

Centraal
Station

See Inset Map

STATIONSWEG

Station HS

185

A 17th-century travel guide describes The Hague as 'the fairest village in the world, both for the pompous buildings, and for the largeness thereof'. Two centuries later Matthew Arnold wrote: 'I never saw a city where the well-to-do classes seem to have given the whole place so much of their own air of wealth, finished cleanliness and comfort; but I never saw one, either, in which my heart would so have sunk at the thought of living.' And early this century, Aldous Huxley observed that The Hague 'tries to be elegant and only succeeds in being respectable and middle class'. Little has changed. People still call The Hague 'the largest village in Europe' and the many ex-colonials who have retired here have generated another nickname: 'the widow of Indonesia'.

The wide boulevards and graceful architecture do speak of quiet, established wealth, and Amsterdammers, in particular, complain that The Hague is a stuffy domain of diplomats, civil servants and businessmen. (Though Amsterdam is the capital of the Netherlands, The Hague is the centre of government and the chosen seat of the present queen.) It may not be the place you would go to bop until dawn or throng singing through the streets, but the spotless architecture, acres of greenery and inimitable museums give it an atmosphere of tranquil refinement which is rather alluring. The Hague offers the bonus of the seaside resort of Scheveningen, on its northwestern perimeter, and the town of Delft to the south. Most of the main sites in the city are centrally situated, though if you really want to appreciate all The Hague has to offer, you'll need more than a day.

History

Around the year 1230, Floris IV, Count of Holland, built himself a country cottage beside a pond in the North Sea dunes. His son William II, who was elected King of the Romans and Emperor of Germany in 1247, thinking that a grander hunting lodge better befitted his status, began to put up a small palace on the site. The settlement that grew up around it was known as 's-Gravenhage (the Count's Hedge), and this is still The Hague's official name. Over the centuries, successive counts added to the original buildings and put up new palaces. They progressed from being mere counts to becoming *stadhouders* and eventually kings of Holland (*see* **History** pp.25–38). The Hague became their official seat and, after 1578, the meeting place of the States General, the predecessor of the present-day Dutch parliament. Yet the counts and their successors contrived to keep The Hague detached from the strife of day-to-day politics. Great battles were fought at Leiden, Breda and Utrecht. Assemblies were held and treaties signed at Brussels and Bruges. Amsterdam swept to glory and heady riches on the back of the Dutch East India Company during the Golden Age. The Hague remained serenely apart from the fray, and was officially classed as a 'village' well into the 19th century. But all the time it was gaining importance as an administrative and judicial centre.

In 1511 the highest court of Holland was established here, and by the 17th century The Hague had become such a vortex of intrigue among foreign diplomats that it was called 'the whispering gallery of Europe'.

In 1899 the Permanent Court of Arbitration (later to become the International Court of Justice) was established in The Hague, giving this long tradition a mark of respectability. But in the meantime, the 'village' had suffered a sharp blow to its pride. During the French occupation (1806–13), King Louis Napoleon had lingered in The Hague just a few months, before deciding to move his capital to Amsterdam. After the French had withdrawn from the Netherlands, Amsterdam retained this status—although the new Dutch king, William I, moved the seat of parliament back to The Hague. Rivalry between the two cities remains intense. As recently as 1953 there was a massive attempt to have The Hague reclassified as the Dutch capital, and the public wrangling was finally resolved only after an appeal to original documents signed by King William I. But each city still regards the other as in some way second-best.

Getting There

Trains take 50 minutes. There are about four an hour. The Hague has two railway stations: Den Haag HS (Hollands Spoor) and Den Haag CS (Centraal Station). There are frequent tram and rail links between the two, but the CS is the more convenient.

Getting Around

You can use your *strippenkaart* (*see* p.8) on any buses and trams in The Hague, or buy a *dagkaart* (day card) from the VVV tourist office. The national information number for public transport is ✆ (0900) 9292. Most of the tourist sites are within very easy walking distance of each other, though you will probably prefer to hop on to Tram 8 for the Panorama Mesdag and the Museon. Tram 9 takes you via Madurodam to Scheveningen, and Tram 1 will trundle you through the Scheveningense Bosjes to the sea.

Bicycle hire: Beside Station Hollands Spoor, ✆ (070) 389 0830.
Taxi: ✆ (070) 390 7722 or ✆ 364 2828.

Tourist Information

The VVV tourist office (open Mon–Sat 9–5.30, in July and Aug also Sun 10–5, ✆ (0900) 340 3505) is on Koning Julianaplein, just outside Centraal Station. Staff can supply you with maps and information about tours and public transport.

Festivals

The Hague knows how to let its hair down with some lively summer festivals. In June there's a 10-day long Indonesian market, the **Pasar Malam Besar**; the **International Kite Festival** at Scheveningen; and a two-day **international horse show** on the Lange Voorhout, a large green square in the middle of town. The **North Sea Jazz Festival**, held annually in The Hague in mid-July, is one of the world's most important celebrations of jazz.

Binnenhof

Guided tours of the Binnenhof and Houses of Parliament Mon–Sat 10–4; adm; © (070) 364 6144 to book in advance. All tours start at the Ridderzaal, but after that itinerary varies according to which house is in session. Try to get on a tour that visits the old, rather than the new chambers.

The count's courtyard, the **Binnenhof**, remains the centre of town, though now it's an amalgam of architectural styles. On the third Tuesday in September, Queen Beatrix sweeps into the courtyard in a gold carriage to open parliament. The ceremony takes place under the high oak vaulting and delicate turrets of the **Ridderzaal** (the 'Hall of Knights') in the centre of the Binnenhof. The Ridderzaal, the oldest building in the complex, was built to host the early Counts of Holland's hunting parties. Later it served as a court. High up in the rafters of the barrel-vaulted roof are small carved heads. The judges encouraged miscreants and witnesses to tell the truth by warning them that these 'eaves-droppers' listened to all they said and passed it on up to God. By far the best view of the Binnenhof is from the outside—across the **Hofvijver** (Court Pond), a glassy expanse of water with a softly spraying fountain.

The First Chamber of the States General (the equivalent of the British House of Lords or the US Senate) still meets within the Binnenhof complex, in a grand Baroque ball room. The Second Chamber (the effective governing body of the Netherlands) now meets in a modern building around the corner from the Ridderzaal. Completed in 1993, the new chambers are decorated in a way intended to portray the Dutch landscape. This is done with disarming honesty: one wall represents sheets of pouring rain, and the ceiling of the plenary hall is painted to symbolize a low blue-grey sky. A glance at the staff list reveals another, rather charming aspect of life in the Netherlands: the government employs 75 people to clean the house, and only 50 to guard it.

Mauritshuis

Open Tues–Sat 10–5, Sun 11–5; adm.

Next to the parliament buildings, on a corner of the Hofvijver, the Mauritshuis, a grand 17th-century mansion built for a favoured general, is now home to the Royal Collection of paintings once owned by *stadhouders* William IV and William V. High points of three centuries of Dutch and Flemish art cover the walls, stacked one above the other (a fashionable way of displaying pictures in the 18th century); there's hardly an inch of wood-panelling or flock wallpaper to be seen between the gilt frames. It's a heady experience. You can see Rembrandt's first Amsterdam commission, *The Anatomy Lesson of Professor Tulp* (1632)—the corpse, like the painter, had just arrived in Amsterdam from Leiden; and the erudite surgeon was renowned for his advice that patients drink 50 cups of tea a day. There are three of Vermeer's rather minimal œuvre, Frans Hals's manic *Laughing Boy*, Paulus Potter's nightmarish, meticulously finished *Young Bull* (complete with frogs and flies) and works by Rubens and Holbein. There are also nine paintings by the 17th-century innkeeper Jan Steen. His postcard-sized cheekily lascivious *Girl Eating Oysters* alone would make a visit to the museum worthwhile.

Schildergalerij Prins Willem V

Prince William V Gallery, Buitenhof 35, open Tues–Sun 11–4; adm.

In 1773 Prince William V had an art gallery built in his palace, and condescended to allow the general public in for a look on three days a week. This gives the *Schildergalerij* some justification in its claim to be the oldest museum in the Netherlands, though the palm really goes to the Teylers Museum in Haarlem, which was purpose-built in 1784. Today, the better part of the royal collection is housed across the pond in the Mauritshuis. But although the larger museum has creamed off the masterpieces, the *Schildergalerij* has the edge when it comes to atmosphere. There are seldom many people in the long gallery, with its high Louis XVI stucco ceilings and walls plastered with paintings. At times it feels almost as if the prince himself had invited you up to see his collection.

Museum Gevangenpoort

Prison Gate Museum; open Tues–Fri 11–5, Sat and Sun 12–5; guided tours only, on the hour; adm.

Once the gate to the Binnenhof, this solid, step-gabled building served as a prison from 1420 to 1828, though warders seldom managed to outwit The Hague's maidservants, who were notorious for their ability to spring incarcerated lovers and brothers. Nowadays it houses a gory collection of torture instruments, from thumbscrews and whipping benches to a branding iron bearing The Hague's coat of arms. Give it a shudder as you pass by. A tour is of interest only to the morbidly curious.

Museum Bredius

Lange Vijverberg 14, open Tues–Sun 12–5; adm.

Erstwhile director of the Mauritshuis Museum and renowned art scholar Abraham Bredius (1855–1946) managed over the years to build up an impressive private collection of 17th-century Dutch art. He also established a reputation for being stubborn and cantankerous, and had some very public set-tos with his superiors at the museum. He invariably came out on top. Wrapped in furs, Bredius would spend days in chilly archives researching his beloved 17th-century paintings—it is his research that showed a number of works previously attributed to Rembrandt to be by the Master's pupils. The collection that he accumulated for himself is notable not so much for its big names (though there are enough of these) as for the way it reveals the astonishing high quality that existed across the spectrum of Dutch art in the Golden Age.

The Bredius Museum is filled with extraordinarily good paintings by artists most people would not have heard of. Look out for Godfried Schalken's delicately rendered *Lady Playing a Lute*, Willem Drost's poised *Portrait of a Lady* and Aert van der Neer's wintry *Scene on the Ice outside the Town Walls*. You'll also see work by better-known artists: a *Bust of Christ* by Rembrandt; a floral still-life by Simon Verelst (such as the one that sent Samuel Pepys into rhapsodies, *see* p.46) and some exceptional paintings by Jan Steen—including one that until recently was cut in half. It was Bredius who, in the 1920s, realized that the two halves belonged together, but it wasn't until 1996 that the painting was restored to its original state. Bredius donated some 46 paintings to the Rijksmuseum in Amsterdam, loaned another 25 to the Mauritshuis and, when he retired and went to live in Monaco, gave his entire collection to the municipality of The Hague, so that it would remain in the Netherlands. Today the paintings are hung in the intimate domestic setting of an 18th-century patrician mansion, just across the pond from the Mauritshuis.

Haags Historisch Museum

The Hague Historical Museum, Korte Vijverberg 7; open Tues–Fri 11–5, Sat and Sun 12–5; adm.

Completing the circuit of museums around the Hofvijver, the Historisch Museum is housed in the former barracks of the civil guard, built in 1636. Tucked in between countless paintings of views of The Hague and Scheveningen and memorabilia of municipal history are some interesting old doll's houses. The most intriguing is the one that belonged to one Lita Tholen-de Ranitz in 1910. It comes equipped with such state-of-the-art conveniences as running water, central heating, a telephone and even a vacuum cleaner.

Beyond the Binnenhof

The Counts of Holland were incorrigible palace-builders. On Noordeinde you can see the classicist pile of the **Paleis Noordeinde** (restored to the appearance it had in 1640). Paleis Noordeinde is where Queen Beatrix, very much a workaday monarch, clocks in to do her share of the country's administration, and it is not open to the public.

Queen B.

Queen Beatrix of the Netherlands arrives to open an art exhibition. There are only about four police officers in evidence. None of the guests has been screened. There is no ripple of curtsies as she walks up the aisle to her seat. The Dutch do not have to bow before their sovereign...and no one has even thought of taking a pot shot at a Dutch monarch since an assassin hiding behind a pillar did for the first William of Orange in 1584. Queen Beatrix's departure doesn't stop the traffic. A blue limousine, accompanied by just two outriders, glides her away; only to reduce speed to a gentle cruise when it gets stuck behind a bus around the corner. This is a down-to-earth, democratically minded monarchy. Yet it commands a loyalty so fierce that the British royals must glance across the Channel with envy. In Holland you can joke about anything. You can even be quite rude about the Dutch. But make a disparaging remark about 'our Queen', and the room plummets into icy silence.

Queen Beatrix's hands-on approach to running her country has a lot to do with this. Hard work, in a Protestant country, is always a strong plus. Beatrix does her fair share of ribbon-cutting, smiling and waving, but most of her time is spent in an office in The Hague, involving herself directly with government (so much so that a recent headline raised eyebrows with *'Beatrix Bemoeial?'*—'Busybody Beatrix?'). For decades every Dutch government has been run by a coalition. After an election the process of choosing a Prime Minister and cabinet involves much discussion. The Queen is at the heart of it all, a mover and shaker rather than simply the wielder of a rubber stamp.

Yet the Dutch royal family could be Dallas to the Brits' Dynasty. Juliana, the Queen Mother, was embroiled in a Rasputin-like relationship with a faith healer after one of her daughters was born blind. The young princess grew up to marry a penniless Cuban refugee, later divorced him and sold the contents of her house (everything from potpourri holders to priceless works of art) to finance a move to the USA. Another daughter married a Roman Catholic, renounced her Protestant religion and gave up all the trappings of royal life and any claim to the throne.

The present Crown Prince cavorted, clad in orange bermuda shorts, with a victorious Dutch hockey team at the Atlanta Olympics. Such behaviour may cause some muttering and murmurs, but the public remains relatively unobtrusive and unconcerned. The most passionate reaction in the past few decades was saved for when Beatrix married a German: people pelted them with tomatoes at their wedding in Amsterdam. But Prince Claus's charm, fluent Dutch and air of gentle vulnerability has defused even that.

Hollanders are a no-nonsense bunch and appreciate the common touch, and their royal family has it in large measures. Before she got married, Beatrix studied social work, as well as a stint with the Salvation Army, which at the time had its headquarters in Amsterdam's red-light district. The entire royal family arrived in Amsterdam in a bus for the service to celebrate Beatrix and Claus's silver wedding anniversary. A few years ago, on Queen's Day (the Queen's official birthday, when people party on the streets all day and there is a free-for-all fleamarket) Beatrix decided on the spur of the moment to visit Amsterdam. She wandered about the streets of the Jordaan with just a few family and friends. It took a while before somebody actually recognized her. Then a young man in the crowd yelled out: *'Meid, geef me een kus'* (roughly translated: 'Oi, gi's a kiss, old girl').

Beaming, the Queen took hold of his shoulders and obliged.

In the centre of the town, on **Lange Voorhout** is a vast tree-filled square. Part of this was at one time a medieval tournament field. Visitors can see the neat, modest 18th-century **Het Paleis** (Lange Voorhout 74; *open Tues–Sun 11–5; adm*). Het Paleis was once the winter home of Queen Emma (Beatrix's great-grandmother) but now hosts temporary art exhibitions. Behind Het Paleis, on Prinsessegracht, is the **Museum van het Boek** (Museum of the Book, Prinsessegracht 30; *open Tues–Fri 11–5, Sat and Sun 12–5; adm*). In the rich mahogany cases of an 18th-century library you can see such treasures as fragments of a 6th-century bible, a copy of *Le Roman de la Rose* (1370) and the 17th-century *Blaeu Atlas*, one of the earliest and most beautiful ever atlases of the world.

Just south of Paleis Noordeinde is the imposing, rather gloomy **Grote Kerk** (Great Church, © (070) 365 8665; *open by request*). It dates back to 1539, though most of the structure you see today was built a century later, after a fire had destroyed the earlier church. Next door is the elaborately decorated **Oude Stadhuis** (Old City Hall), built in the 17th century, and now a restaurant.

Vredespaleis

Peace Palace, Carnegieplein 2; open May–Oct Mon–Fri 10–5; Nov–April Mon–Fri 10–4; tours 10, 11, 2 and 3; adm.

The 1899 Hague Peace Conference established the Permanent Court of Arbitration—a court with global jurisdiction, still widely respected and considered neutral—but gave it a rather dingy home. In 1903 the American millionaire Andrew Carnegie donated $1.5 million to build a more appropriate palace for the court. Countries from all over the world contributed ironwork, stained glass, statuary and furniture to create a quirky hotchpotch of a building, which you can visit by guided tour only.

Panorama Mesdag and Museum Mesdag

Hendrik Willem Mesdag (1831–1915) was a leading member of the Hague School of painters (*see* p.48). He considered his *Panorama*—painted in the 1880s during a craze for such entertainments—to be his most important work, because it gave 'such an awesome impression of nature'. At the **Panorama Mesdag** (Zeestraat 65; *open daily 10–5; adm*) you walk about under a canvas canopy and look out on all sides, across real sand dunes littered with clogs and empty gin bottles, at a huge, circular view of Scheveningen. The painting is done with such realism that contemporaries accused Mesdag of having projected new-fangled photographs on to the canvas and traced them. Though it was an artistic success, the *Panorama* was a commercial failure, helping drag the Belgian company that funded it into bankruptcy. Eventually it was bought by the artist himself, and is now jointly owned by 33 of his descendants. A few minutes' walk away is the **Museum H. W. Mesdag** (Laan van Meerdervoort 7f; *open Tues–Sun 12–5, adm*), where you can see the artist's own collection of Hague School paintings, as well as works of the related French Barbizon School and a reconstruction of Mesdag's living quarters and studio.

The Gemeente Museum Complex

The superb **Gemeente Museum** (Municipal Museum, Stadhouderslaan 41; *open Tues–Sun 11–5; adm*) was designed in 1935 by the influential architect H. P. Berlage. The spacious tiled interior looks, at first glance, like a bank—or a very upmarket public lavatory. It houses a beautiful collection of glass and silverware, some important 19th-century paintings, superbly reconstructed period rooms and one of the best modern art collections in the country. You'll find lots of familiar names from the first half of the century—Monet, Picasso, Egon Schiele—as well as the pick of modern Dutch artists like Jan Toorop, Pyke Koch and the painters of the COBRA movement, Karel Appel and Constant (*see* p.49). There are a number of early works by Mondriaan—realistic landscapes and bright impressionistic studies—that hint only slightly at the abstract style for which he later became famous (*see* p.48).

The collection of contemporary work gives you the rare impression of a healthy budget being intelligently spent. Don't leave without visiting the **music department**, which displays instruments ranging from exquisitely crafted harpsichords and viols to an Indonesian gamelan.

Adjoining the Gemeente Museum is the **Museon** (Stadhouderslaan 41; *open Tues–Fri 10–5,*

Sat and Sun 12–5; adm), which offers a romp through the world of popular science. Computers, CD-i players and imaginative displays bring to life everything from the Big Bang to contemporary electronics. A passageway leads on to a 1990s version of a panorama, the **Omniversum** (President Kennedylaan 5; *programmes on the hour Tues–Sun 11–5; adm exp; call © (070) 354 7479 or contact VVV for programme details*). Lasers and films (such as *Speed* and *The Future of Time*) are projected on to a dome-shaped screen, sounds explode all about you and special 'sub-woofers' produce bass notes so deep you can only feel them.

On the Edge

A few minutes' ride east of the centre (on Bus 4 or 43), in the thickets of the Haagse Bos, you can peer through the trees at the present Royal residence—the dinky, domed **Huis ten Bosch** ('House in the Woods', built 1654), though it isn't open to the public. Just north of the city centre is the **Scheveningse Bosjes**, an urban forest so rambling that you can quite easily get lost in it. If you make your way across the wilds you'll come to the miniature town of **Madurodam** (*open daily March–Aug 9–8; Sept–Mar 9–5; adm exp*). You can see models of landmarks from all over the Netherlands, little residential canals, football grounds, an airport, railways and a harbour—all on a scale of 1:25. By far the most enjoyable sight, however, is from up on the coffee terrace where you can watch the visitors tramp, Gulliver-like, up and down the paths.

Scheveningen

At its northwestern end, The Hague merges with the fishing port and seaside resort of **Scheveningen**. (Don't worry if you can't pronounce it—only the locals can. During the Second World War Dutch Resistance fighters made suspected German infiltrators say it as a test of their true nationality.) The long, white stretch of sand, lapped by the grey-brown waters of the North Sea, somehow seems in its element on blustery days when tiny figures, buttoned up and bent over, battle against the wind. The pink bodies that stretch out in deckchairs on sunny days look curiously out of place.

Badly bombed during the war and hastily rebuilt, Scheveningen is a tacky resort.. But you will find the **Kurhaus**, a gracious *grande dame* of a hotel, built in 1885 and now a national monument. The kings and queens of Europe have stayed here; Dietrich, Piaf, Chevalier and even the Rolling Stones have played in the concert hall. A little further along the promenade in the only other old building of note in Scheveningen, a pavilion built for King William I in 1826, is **Museum Beelden am See** (Sculptures by the Sea, Harteveltsraat 1; *open Tues–Sun 11–5; adm*). Set in a tranquil hollow in the dunes, it is devoted to sculptures of the human form. Have a look at Igor Mitoraj's mysterious, veiled marble reliefs, then don a sou'wester off the rack and step out on to the terraces to see Arthur Spronken's idiosyncratic portrayal of the Dutch royal family. Nearby the **Sealife Centre** (Strandweg 13; *open daily 10–6, July and August 10–8; adm exp*) is home to creatures of the deep, from shrimps to stingrays. Presentation is imaginative (at one point you walk through an underwater glass tunnel, with sharks swimming above your head), and the centre is a great hit with children.

If you feel like escaping the crowds, **Kijkduin**, a few kilometres up the promenade, is a quieter spot where you can sit undisturbed on the windy dunes and look out over the grey North Sea.

The **Passage** (off Gravenstraat, near the Buitenhof) is a grand neoclassical shopping arcade lined with *chocolateries*, boutiques and specialist shops—including one that sells only teddy bears. There's a branch of the stylish department store, Maison de Bonneterie, near the Oude Stadhuis on Groen Markt. Nearby Hoogstraat and the alleys leading off it are the location of classy clothes shops and antiques stores. There is a traditional **market** around the Grote Kerk on Wednesday afternoons, and an **antiques and book market** on Lange Voorhout on Thurs and Sun in the summer.

The Hague/Scheveningen ✆ (070–)   **Where to Stay**

Hotel Des Indes Inter-Continental, Lange Voorhout 54–56, 2514 EG, ✆ 361 2345, ✉ 361 2350 (*luxury*). Once a splendid patrician mansion, converted into a hotel in the 19th century, the Des Indes has been home to the likes of Mata Hari and Cecil Rhodes. The circular lobby is redolent of the grand old days, a great place for afternoon tea—but the furnishings in some of the rooms show signs of wear that you would not expect in a hotel of this class.

Steinberger Kurhaus Hotel, Gevers Deynootplein 30, 2586 CK Scheveningen, ✆ 416 2636 (*expensive: f380 land side, f430 sea side*). A battle rages inside the stately old seaside hotel between what is left of the original fittings and insensitive (if not downright kitsch) modern décor. Alas the latter usually wins, but the rooms are comfortable, and the staff pleasant.

Carlton Ambassador Hotel, Sophialaan 2, 2514 JP, ✆ 363 0363, ✉ 360 0535 (*luxury*). Quietly plush, ever so tasteful hotel in the embassy district. Rooms are done up in Dutch and English repro antique style.

Parkhotel Den Haag, Molenstraat 53, 2513 BJ, ✆ 362 4371, ✉ 361 4525 (*luxury–expensive; price includes breakfast*). Back-to-back with the Paleis Noordeinde, decorated in soothing pastel shades and with a small enclosed garden.

Paleis Hotel, Molenstraat 26, 2513 BL, ✆ 362 4621, ✉ 361 4533 (*moderate*). In a quiet alley near the Binnenhof, and convenient for sights and shops. Rooms are on the small side, and rather functionally decorated.

Hotel Petit, Groot Hertoginnelaan 42, 2517 EH, ✆ 346 5500, ✉ 346 3257 (*moderate–inexpensive*). In a smart suburb near the Vredespaleis. Bright, airy rooms and personable owners.

Hotel City, Renbaanstraat 1–3, 2586 EW, Scheveningen, ✆ 355 7966, ✉ 354 0503 (*inexpensive*). Scrupulously clean and well-run family hotel just a few minutes' walk from the beach.

Albion, Gevers Deynootweg 118–20, 2586 BP, Scheveningen, ✆ 355 7987, ✉ 355 5970 (*inexpensive*). Good, solid Dutch hospitality in a converted 1930s house a block away from the sea.

Aristo, Stationsweg 164–66, 2515 BS, ✆ 389 0847 (*cheap*). Simply furnished but clean hotel just a short totter from Station Hollands Spoor.

Youth Hostel: Gevers Denooytweg 2, ✆ 354 7003 (*f45 for dorm bed*).

The side streets and canals to the east of Lange Voorhout are well-stocked café and restaurant hunting grounds. The Hague is renowned for the quality of its Indonesian restaurants.

Le Restaurant, Hotel Des Indes, Lange Voorhout 54–56, ✆ 361 2345 (*expensive*). A small restaurant opening on to the sumptuous circular lobby of the hotel. Service is impeccable and the cuisine a skilful combination of the best of Dutch and French traditions, with a touch of Indonesian exoticism. Try the guinea fowl with a secret Des Indes sauce (there are vanilla and cardamom in there somewhere).

Da Roberto, Noordeinde 196, ✆ 346 4977 (*expensive*). Top-class Italian restaurant, under the personal eye of owner-chef Roberto de Luca. He uses trad ingredients in imaginative ways: lasagne with pigeon and spinach, or polenta with snails. There's an excellent list of Italian wines.

Greve, Torenstraat 138, ✆ 360 3919 (*moderate*). Long trestle tables, boards of steaming home-made bread, and friendly service. Go for the chicken soup, thick with vegetables, and then one of the daily specials.

Bogor, Van Swietenstraat 2, ✆ 346 1628 (*moderate*). Excellent Indonesian cooking in an elegant *Jugendstil* house.

The Raffles, Noordeinde 196, ✆ 345 8587 (*moderate*). An Indonesian restaurant that dares to be a little different, with a cook who doesn't feel bound to produce the usual Indonesian fare, but experiments within the tradition.

Le Haricot Vert, Molenstraat 9a, ✆ 365 2278 (*moderate*). Intimate, candlelit restaurant in a 17th-century house that once accommodated palace flunkies. French-inspired cuisine with a robust Dutch hand.

Tampat Senang, Laan van Meerdervoort 6, ✆ 363 6787 (*moderate*). Elaborate décor, fine Indonesian food and, from time to time, a live gamelan orchestra.

Bengel, Hooikade 2, ✆ 364 2898 (*moderate*). Cherubs, chandeliers and push drapes everywhere. A relaxed, arty crowd tuck in to such dishes as lamb with grapes, garlic and thyme.

De Dageraad, Hooikade 4, ✆ 364 5666 (*cheap*). Plain pine décor, but inspired vegetarian cuisine. There's a wide selection of cheese fondues (including cider and Calvados, and beer, mustard and garlic) as well as some special seasonal and regional set menus with such adventurous combinations as goat's cheese with dates and orange sauce.

Schlemmer, Lange Houtstraat, ✆ 360 9000 (*cheap*). A 19th-century officers' mess, still sporting grand fireplaces, Schlemmer has both café and restaurant sections. The atmosphere in both is informal and friendly. Dawdle over a coffee, or enjoy duck bouillion, or omelette with mascarpone and grilled aubergine.

Broeders, Buitenhof 19, ✆ 356 2900 (*cheap*). Buzzing, trendy Grand Café in the city centre. The pastas and salads make a good quick lunch.

De Posthoorn, Lange Voorhout 39a, ✆ 346 2338 (*cheap*). Serves light snacks and sandwiches and has a pleasant terrace overlooking the tree-lined marketplace.

Achterommetje, Achterom 71, © 364 5876 (*cheap*). Friendly place in an alley behind the Passage shopping arcade in the city centre. They play jazz, sell good, healthy, home-cooked food and delicious cakes.

't Syndicaat, Nieuwe Molstraat 10, © 360 0053 (*open 5pm–8pm Mon, Wed and Fri only; cheap*). Vegetarian eating-house in a small alternative arts complex. Menus vary according to what's in the market.

The Hague/Scheveningen © (070–)　　　　　　***Entertainment and Nightlife***

The Hague has a rich cultural life. The city orchestra, **Het Residentie Orkest**, is almost as good as the Royal Concertgebouw. Its home is the **Dr Anton Philipszaal**, Spuiplein 150, © 360 9810, which offers a varying programme of classical music.

The national modern dance company, the renowned **Nederlands Danstheater**, can be found performing next door, at the **Lucent Danstheater**, Spui 152, © 360 4930, and you'll find drama (sometimes in English) at the **Koninklijke Schouwburg**, Korte Voorhout 3, © 346 9450.

The Hague's most famous cultural event, the **North Sea Jazz Festival**, is held annually over a weekend in mid-July at the city's Congres Centrum (information from the VVV, *see* above).

There's a vibrant live music scene centered on **Paard**, Prinsengracht 12, © 360 1618, Syndicaat, Nieuwe Molstraat 10, © 360 0053, and **Backstage**, Lange Houtstraat 9, © 364 8464, all of which have dance floors and party nights.

Boko Bar, Nieuwe Schoolstraat 1, © 362 1614 is a friendly place to begin an exploration of The Hague's relatively small **gay** scene.

Delft

> *Delft has as many bridges as there are days in the year and a like number of canals and streets with boats passing up and down.*
>
> William Crowne, on visiting Delft with the
> Duke of Arundel in December 1636

Though overrun by tourists in season, of all the towns on the Randstad Delft manages to preserve its ambience of age. You might not be able to count as many bridges and canals as did the rather excitable Will Crowne, but get up early before the crowds descend and you might suddenly glimpse an alley, a skyline, a stretch of façades that could come right out of the View of Delft by the city's most famous son, the painter Johannes Vermeer (*c.* 1632–75).

Established early in the 11th century, Delft soon became a prosperous weaving and brewing town. By the end of the 16th century it held such control over the surrounding land traffic and waterways, and was so well fortified, that William the Silent (*see* p.29) chose it as his HQ during the Dutch revolt against Spain. He was assassinated here in 1584, and so resides in Delft for ever more, in a tomb that has become the Dutch royal family mausoleum. In 1645, an exploding arsenal destroyed much of the medieval town, but a massive rebuilding programme soon restored its former glory. It was around this time that De Porceleyne Fles started making and exporting the blue and white earthenware that was to make the town famous.

Getting There

Delft is part of The Hague's urban network; tram journeys take 20 and 15mins respectively. There are also train connections between The Hague CS and Delft.

Getting Around

Most sights are within **walking** distance, ranged around the Markt. To reach the Markt from Delft station, cross the Westsingelgracht and Oude Delft canals and turn left at Koornmarkt.

There are **tram** connections to The Hague, and your *strippenkaart* (*see* p.8) is valid on public transport.

Tourist Information

VVV, Markt 85, ✆ (015) 212 6100; open April–Oct Mon–Fri 9–6, Sat 9–5, Sun 10–3; Nov–March Mon–Fri 9–5.30, Sat 9–5, closed Sun.

The Markt

Facing each other proudly across the market square are the Stadhuis and the Nieuwe Kerk. In between come rows of cafés, restaurants, souvenir shops selling tacky ersatz Delftware, and—on Thursdays—a busy general market. Of the medieval **Stadhuis** only the 13th-century tower remains. The surrounding solid grey stone building, with its scarlet shutters and fussy cornice, was put up in 1618 by leading Renaissance architect Hendrick de Keyser (*see* p.50), after a fire had destroyed the original city hall. The late-Gothic **Nieuwe Kerk** (*open April–Oct Mon–Sat 9–6; Nov–March Mon–Fri 11–4; adm free*) took more than a century to build, between 1383 and 1510. Even then the stonemasons could not down chisels, because the church was badly damaged by the fire that swept Delft in 1536 and by the arsenal explosion a hundred years later. It wasn't until 1872 that the flamboyant architect P. J. H. Cuypers (*see* pp.51 and 67–8) shot the tower up to its present 109 metres. Inside the church is the sumptuous black marble and alabaster tomb of William of Orange, together with a carving of the prince and, nearby, his small dog, which pined to death after William was assassinated. A stone slab in the floor marks the entrance to the royal mausoleum, where all but a few Dutch monarchs have been buried ever since.

Oude Delft

A walk along the Oude Delft canal, lined with elegant patrician mansions, provides a charming impression of the old city. At one end the tower of the **Oude Kerk** (*open Mon–Sat 9–6; adm free*) seems to tilt in four directions simultaneously—with a two-metre tilt to the east and one metre to the north. The tower houses a 9,000kg carillon that, understandably, is rung only on special occasions. The church was begun in the 13th century, though much of its austere interior dates from 200 years later. Inside you'll find the graves of Vermeer, and famous Dutch admirals Martin Tromp and Piet Hein.

Across the way from the church, off a quiet courtyard, is the Prinsenhof Museum (*open Tues–Sat 10–5, Sun 1–5; adm*). The former cloister houses the Delft historical museum—stocked with pottery, silver, tapestries and royal portraits—but is more famous as the spot where William of Orange was assassinated by Catholic fanatic Balthasar Geraerts. You can still see the bullet holes the murderer left behind in the wall of the stairwell. Across the courtyard is the Nusantara Museum (*open Tues–Sat 10–5, Sun 1–5; adm*), which has a colourful and fascinating collection of costumes and artefacts from the Dutch East Indies—much of it booty brought back during the 17th century by members of the Dutch East India Company. Further up the canal, just beyond the Prinsenhof, is the **Museum Lambert van Meerten** (*open Tues–Sat 10–5, Sun 1–5; adm*), which offers a fine opportunity to view a canal house from inside. As well as finely furnished rooms, you'll find a vast collection of Delft tiles and ceramics from around the world.

Further Afield

South of the Markt, along the Koornmarkt, is the **Koninklijke Legeran Wapenmuseum** (Royal Army and Weapon Museum; *open Mon–Fri 10–5, Sat and Sun noon–5pm; adm*) which has swords, guns and other implements of warfare and traces the history of Dutch battles up to the 20th century. But if it's porcelain rather than pistols you're after, then head farther south to **De Porceleyn Fles** (Rotterdamseweg 196, ✆ *(015) 256 0234, Mon–Sat 9–5; adm*), the famous **Delftware** factory, where you can see the blue and white ceramics being hand-painted, and buy the real thing rather than the repro tack sold in most souvenir shops.

Delft ✆ (015–)   **Where to Stay**

Delft Museum Hotel, Oude Delft 189, 2611 HD, ✆ 214 0930, ▧ 214 0935 (*moderate*). Eleven beautifully restored canalside houses, converted into a comfortable hotel. Antiques and contemporary art in the lounge areas, with quietly tasteful more modern furniture in the rooms.

De Plantaan, Doelenplein 10, 2611 BP, ✆ 212 6046, ▧ 215 7327 (*inexpensive*). Pleasantly run hotel with somewhat wacky design—some rooms sporting eccentric *trompe l'œil*. There's a good restaurant downstairs too.

Les Compagnons, Markt 61–65, ✆ 214 0102 (*cheap*). Clean, simple family-run pension in the heart of town. If there's no room at the inn, and you can afford the price hike, ask the same family about their three- and four-star hotels nearby, but make sure you specify this branch if you want the cheap one.

Delft ✆ (015–)   **Eating Out**

Explore the side streets between Koornmarkt, Oude Delft and Phoenixstraat for the cosiest cafés and best eats.

Le Vieux Jean, Heilige Geestkerkhof 3, ✆ 213 0433 (*moderate*). Long-time family-run favourite (soon to celebrate its 25th anniversary). Son Robert-Jan Polman is giving new vim and verve to his parents' traditionally good cooking by slipping the odd bit of curry in with the langoustines, or adding figs to the duck with red wine sauce.

De Prinsenkelder, Schoolstraat 11, ✆ 212 1860 (*moderate*). Rich Franco-Dutch cuisine in the cellar of the Prinsenhof cloisters.

Kleyweg's Stads-Koffiehuis, Oude Delft 133, ✆ 212 4625 (*cheap*). Good coffee, crispy pancakes, a relaxed neighbourhood-café atmosphere, and a view on to the prettiest canal in town.

Utrecht

to Hilversum

200 metres
200 yards

N

VOORSTRAAT

DRIFT

LANGE JANS STR

Stadsschouwburg

Janskerk

HOOGT

Museum Voor Het
Kruideniersbedrijf

MINREBRODER
STRAAT

GANZEN-
MARKT

ACHTER

KROMME NIEUWE GRACHT

MALIE

Stadhuis

OUDKERKHOF

STRAAT

PIETERSKERKHOF

CHOORSTRAAT

VISMARKT

Dom

Groot
Paushuize

LEPELENBURG

SINGEL

SERVET
STR

Dom-
plein

TRANS KROMME NIEUWE GRACHT

Domtoren

JELSTR

Maartens
Brug

BOTERSTR

Museum van Speelklok
tot Pierement/Buurkerk

KORTE NIEUW
STRAAT

HERENSTRAAT

Malie Brug

Spoorweg
(Railway)
Museum

OUDEGRACHT

HAVERSTAAT

LANGE

NIEUWE

Museum
Catharijne-
convent

GRACHT

SCHALKWIJKSTR

SPRINGWEG

NIEUW

St
Catharijne-
kerk

ZUILENSTR

to Rietveld-
Schröder House

STRAAT

Servaas
Park

LANGE SMEE STRAAT

TOLSTEEGZIJDE

Stadsbuitengracht

AGNIETENSTRAAT

Centraal
Museum

A12

NICOLAAS
STR

Nicolaikerk

Anyone who arrives in Utrecht by train might be forgiven for thinking that half the city is a shopping mall. One of the Netherlands' most unfortunate 1960s architectural aberrations, a gigantic shoppers' warren (24ha in extent, with over 200 shops trailing along five kilometres of passageways, if you really want to know), sprawls around the station. It can take a determined ten-minute walk to reach the outside world.

But the ordeal is worth it. 'Amsterdam,' say the locals, 'was built by man, Utrecht by God himself.' The old centre of Utrecht is one of the most alluring in the land: spruce and stately, yet at the same time low-key and romantic—graced with two long canals and a network of side streets; rows of chic and quirky shops, a handful of top-rate museums, and an impressive Gothic spire to navigate by.

History

The Romans were encamped at this strategic crossing over the river Rhine as long ago as AD 48, in a fort named *Trajectum ad Rhenum* (later shortened to 'de Trecht'). Next came the newly Christianized Franks, who set up a church in 620. The zealous British missionary monk Willibrordus lost little time in heading south from his usual stamping ground in Friesland to be installed as the first Bishop of Utrecht in 695—it was a position that, over the next few centuries, was to become one of the most powerful in the Low Countries. In the Middle Ages four churches were built at the points of an enormous cross, with the present Dom at the centre, in an attempt to make 'de Trecht' into a northern New Jerusalem. The city thronged with monks and canons, nuns and novices, curates and ecclesiastical hangers-on. Bald pates abounded, and barbers must have earned a pretty penny. But outside this holy city—'Uut-Trecht'—a thriving red-light quarter grew and, curiously, the name of this quarter has stuck.

Meanwhile, the river Rhine shifted naturally, and split to form the Lek and the Waal—leaving Utrecht with a trickle named the Leidse Rijn. As a religious metropolis the city grew ever more prosperous. It was granted its charter as early as 1122. The Bishops of Utrecht, together with their neighbours the Counts of Holland, were involved in the wheeling, dealing and waging of war that led to the eventual unification of the Netherlands, and it was the Union of Utrecht, signed in 1579, that first united the Seven Provinces against Spain (see p.30). Legend has it that two years earlier a Boadicean local woman, Katrijn van de Leemput, drove the Spaniards out of Utrecht almost single handed, then returned with a pick and her willing ad-hoc army to demolish their fort. She is commemorated by a fountain outside the Vredenburg Music Centre.

Ironically, it was the Union of Utrecht that marked the beginning of the city's slide from prominence, for the new Union was Protestant, and Utrecht's might had rested on the Roman Catholic church. In 1580 the monasteries were seized and Catholic worship forbidden. In the 17th century, while the rest of the country embarked on its Golden Age, Utrecht declined into genteel provincialism, though there was a brief flash of glory in 1810, when King Louis Bonaparte (see p.34) temporarily chose the city for his residence. The 20th century saw great expansion and industrialization, and Utrecht is still the seat of one of the most important bishops in the Netherlands—but it remains, essentially, a charming provincial town, somewhat enlivened by the presence of a university, founded in 1815.

Getting There

Trains leave Amsterdam's Centraal Station for Utrecht four times an hour, and the journey takes just over 30mins. If you arrive at the railway station, follow the unobtrusive 'Centrum' signs to escape the shopping mall. Utrecht is about half an hour's drive from Amsterdam on the A2. If you arrive by car, bear in mind that the inner part of the city is a pedestrianized zone. There is ample parking beneath the aforementioned shopping mall (follow signs to Hoog Catharijne or Vredenburg).

Getting Around

Utrecht's main sights are reachable on foot, though all but the bounciest will be in need of a little sit-down by the time they've made it out to the Centraal Museum. For the Railway Museum and Rietveld-Schröder House you will need some sort of mechanization, but buses are plentiful, and your *strippenkaart* (*see* p.8) is valid here too. You can hire pedalos from **Canalbike**, on the Oudegracht opposite the Stadhuis.

Tourist Information

VVV, Vredenburg 90 (follow the signs through the shopping mall), ✆ (0900) 414 1414; open Mon–Fri 9–6, Sat 9–5.

Festivals

Utrecht's main festivals are cultural ones. There's a lively festival of **modern dance** and a **jazz festival** in April, and an experimental art festival in May. The city has a strong international reputation for Old Music—the **Festival Oude Muziek**, held in late August/early September, is world-renowned. The **Nederlands Filmfestival**, held in late September, is beginning to rival the Rotterdam Film Festival in reputation. The VVV can help with information on all of these.

Along the Oudegracht

The Oudegracht—a sunken canal, unique in the Netherlands—has run through the heart of Utrecht for more than 700 years. As the water level dropped over the centuries, the resourceful burghers responded by building a second sidewalk below street level, and digging cellars in the former canal walls. Today, many of these cellars are restaurants or cafés. The shops here along the Oudegracht and in its surrounding squares and alleys sell designer clothes, antiques and knick-knacks, and curiosities from all over the world. Many of the streets are pedestrian-only, and—unlike so many other Dutch cities—care has been taken not to destroy old gables with hideous new shop fronts.

Just east of Oudegracht you can take a step in shopping nostalgia at the **Museum Voor Het Kruideniersbedrijf** (Grocer's Museum, Hoogt 6; *open Tues–Sat 12.30–4.30; adm free*), a reconstructed 1873 grocer's store complete with old-fashioned scales, open barrels of beans and rice, and rows of old tins and cartons. Following Oudegracht south, you pass the rather worse-for-wear neoclassical **Stadhuis**. Down an alley across the way, situated in a medieval church, is one of the delights of Utrecht, the **National Museum van Speelklok tot Pierement** (National Music Box and Barrel Organ Museum; *open Tues–Sat 10–5, Sun 12–5; adm*), a vast collection of automated musical instruments ranging from the 15th to the

20th centuries. You can wander about part of the museum alone, but would be strongly advised to wait for a tour (*also in English, duration 1hr, on the hour, but frequency according to demand at busy times, price incl in adm*), which not only shows you the full collection, but allows you to experience the twangs, tinkles and airy blasts of some of the machines in action—from a furry bunny that wiggles its ears in time to the music, through pianolas to a machine that plays three violins simultaneously.

Around the Dom

Bishop Hendrik van Vianden laid the first stone of Utrecht's **Dom** (cathedral) in 1254. An earlier cathedral had been razed to the ground, and its replacement was to be in the very latest French Gothic style—including a 112m-high tower that rises in three magnificent stages, and is topped by an octagonal filigreed cone. The tower was completed only in 1382, and building went on until 1517. But in 1674 a hurricane hit Utrecht, completely demolishing the nave. This was never rebuilt, so today only chancel and tower remain, separated by an open space. You can climb the **tower** (*open Mon–Sat 10–5, Sun 12–5, guided tours only, on the hour, last tour 4pm; adm*) for a view that reputedly includes Rotterdam and Amsterdam on a clear day, or pop in to the remaining building (*open May–Sept Mon–Fri 10–5, Sat 10–3.30, Sun 2–4; Oct–April, Mon–Fri 11–4, Sat 10–3.30, Sun 2–4; adm free*) for an idea of how vast and glorious the cathedral must once have been. Behind the chancel is a 15th-century cloister with a formal herb garden (divided into squares for medicinal, kitchen and dyeing plants), which was replanted in the 1960s. Have a look at one of the Gothic arches in the southwestern corner of the cloister—a jokey stonemason has carved ropes around the Gothic tracery, apparently holding the delicate stonework together.

Domplein, the square beside the cathedral, has an appealing Parisian air, and just to the east (near the corner of Kromme Nieuwegracht) you can see the **Groot Paushuize**, an elegantly simple red-brick building put up as a residence for the only-ever Dutch pope, Hadrian VI, in 1517. But Hadrian died less than a year after he had been elevated to the papacy, and never saw his Utrecht home. Today it is used for private functions and houses part of the university.

A short walk south of the Dom brings you to the **Museum Catharijneconvent** (Nieuwegracht 63; *open Tues–Fri 10–5, Sat and Sun 11–5; adm*), housed in a late-medieval convent. The museum offers an overview of Dutch religious art, with beautiful medieval manuscripts, richly embroidered vestments, carved altarpieces, and 16th- and 17th-century paintings by the likes of Rembrandt, Frans Hals and Saenredam. You can see the sobering influence of the Reformation on art (though there's also a painting of a pope that turns upside down to become a portrait of the devil), and the museum is known for excellent temporary exhibitions.

The Centraal Museum

Agnietenstraat 1; open Tues–Sun 11–5; adm.

Substantially renovated and extended in 1999, the Centraal Museum occupies a number of buildings around a large garden (to which visitors have access). You walk through underpasses and up spiral stairways, travel in glass-box lifts to Gothic chapels and large halls, explore cellars and suddenly discover attics. The collection is vast and varied, the presentation modern and imaginative, and the layout mind-boggling—though it's a pleasure to get lost. In the depths of one part of the building, accompanied by a whiff of creosote, is the skeleton of a wooden boat, dating from around AD 997. A long former stables building contains parallel exhibitions of fashion, interior design and contemporary art, arranged not chronologically, but along a spectrum from sober to extravagant. You begin with such exhibits as minimalist lampshades, geometric abstract paintings, a 1930s tennis frock and a white 1818 housecoat, and work your way to a neo-Gothic cabinet, a dramatic 3-D 'assemblage' on the wall, and an atomic-bomb silhouette overcoat by hot new Dutch designers Viktor and Rolf.

In the main building you can see part of the museum's extraordinary collection of **Golden Age** art—including Jan van Bronkhorst's beautifully pensive *Young Woman* (1655), and famed artists of the Utrecht School (*see* p.41) such as Van Scorel, Bloemaert and Terbrugghen—as well as modern and contemporary Dutch painting. There are some particularly good pieces by Pyke Koch and Charley Toorop (*see* p.49), as well as by present-day artist Marlene Dumas. For a small fee, and after a short wait, you can order up anything from the museum's depot for a private view. Across the way, an entire wing is devoted to *De Stijl* architect and designer Gerrit Rietveld (*see* pp.48–9), including a reconstruction of his studio and an apartment interior, and lots of original Rietveld furniture.

On the Outskirts

Two more museums lure you further afield. To the east of the centre, just beyond the former city wall, is the **Nederland Spoorwegmuseum** (National Railway Museum, Maliebaan Station; bus 3 from Centraal Station; *open Tues–Fri 10–5, Sat and Sun 11.30–5; adm*). A converted 19th-century train station holds a shiny collection of over 60 old locomotives, trams and carriages, from the earliest days of steam and horse-drawn trams, to sleek electric trains.

A little farther east is the **Rietveld Schröder House** (Prins Hendriklaan 50, ✆ (030) 236 2310; bus 4 to De Hoogstraat; *open Wed–Sat 11–5, Sun 12–5, guided tours only, booking recommended, tours Wed–Sat 11, 11.30, 12.15, 1.45, 3.30, Sun 12.30, 1, 1.45, 2.45, 3.30; adm*), a highpoint of *De Stijl* architecture, designed by Gerrit Rietveld in 1924 for Mrs Truus Schröder, who lived there until her death in 1985. The house preserves original features, including bold yellow, red and blue colours, lamps and furniture designed by Rietveld, and an upper floor that is almost entirely subdivided by moving screens.

Shopping

The area to head to for designer boutiques, quirky speciality shops, antiques and interiors stores is along the Oudegracht to Vismarkt, the alleys to the west of Vismarkt, and around the Dom.

There's a small **flower market** at the top end of the Oudegracht on Saturdays, and on Fridays the farmers come to town to sell **organic produce** in front of the Vredenburg.

Utrecht ✆ *(030–)*   ***Where to Stay***

Most of Utrecht's hotels are functional, unexciting places aimed at the trade-fair market. But there are a few exceptions.

Malie Hotel, Maliestraat 2, 3581 SL, ✆ 231 6424, ✉ 234 0661, *info@malie hotel.nl* (*moderate*). Converted from a 19th-century town house in a quiet part of town, fairly convenient for the centre. The rooms are modern, and the staff charming.

Ouwi, F. C. Donderstraat 12–14, 3572 JH, ☎ 271 6303, 🖷 271 4619 (*inexpensive*). Cared-for family hotel, with simple, clean rooms and a small terrace, a little way from the centre.

Smits Utrecht, Vredenburg 14, 3511 BA, ☎ 233 1232, 🖷 232 8451, *smits@ smits.nl* (*expensive–moderate*). Most pleasant of the standardized hotels, and certainly the best positioned, directly opposite the Vredenburg Music Centre.

There's a privately run B&B service that arranges rooms in family homes around town: Booking Office, Egelantierstraat 25, 3551 GB, ☎ (06) 504 34884, 🖷 (030) 2448764, *amitie@xs4all.nl* (*double rooms cheap*).

Utrecht ☎ (030–)   **Eating Out**

Winkel van Sinkel, Oudegracht 158, ☎ 230 3030 (*cheap*). Busy, trendy, cavernous café built as a department store in the 1830s, and serving as a bank for most of the 20th century. The gigantic, cast-iron caryatids propping up the front portico were made in England, and were so heavy that they caused the canal wall beneath them to collapse. Pastas, salads and dishes of the day.

De Soepterrine, Zakkendragerssteeg 40, ☎ 231 7005 (*cheap*). Busy soup-kitchen down an alley near the Vredenburg Music Centre. Mouthwatering home-made soups include not only Dutch favourites, but exotica from Mexico or Japan. There's good bread, and a variety of salads too. Soups around ƒ8.

Stadskasteel Oudaen, Oudegracht 99, ☎ 231 1864 (*moderate–cheap*). Grand old canalside mansion now converted into a large café with its own brewery. There are hearty meat-chips-and-salad meals downstairs to accompany your beer, and a smarter restaurant upstairs.

Het Grachtenhuys, Nieuwegracht 33, ☎ 231 7494 (*moderate*). Popular restaurant in a gracious old canal house. Good ingredients and careful, unfussy preparation make for an excellent meal. Good vegetarian options.

Sot-l'y-laisse, Zadelstraat 20, ☎ 232 1573 (*expensive*). Tiny, 'you're at a dinner party really' restaurant, with excellent cuisine. There's no menu, you choose your wine and set a limit to the number of courses you want, then just sit back and enjoy what comes—very much in a rich Franco-Dutch culinary tradition. Booking is advisable, as there are only 16 places.

Utrecht ☎ (030–)   **Entertainment and Nightlife**

Utrecht's students strike a lively note at cafés around the centre—during the week more than over weekends. Larger cafés such as **Winkel van Sinkel** and **Oudaen** (*see* above) are gathering spots for all ages. Hottest dance spot at the time of writing is Club Risk, late night at Winkel van Sinkel (latest info on *www.nachtwinkel.nl*).

The **Vredenburg Muziek Centre** (Vredenburgpassage 77, ☎ (030) 231 4544 for box office, ☎ 231 3144 for information) is the venue for most of the important classical music concerts in town.

Historically, Dutch is the same language as German, a descendant of the language spoken by West Germanic tribes and the Salic Franks. Even today there are many similarities of sentence structure and vocabulary between the two languages. But Dutch doesn't have the gloss and edge of German. It's a softer language that seems to have grown out of the bogs and polders. Dutch is not an easy language to grapple with. However, to a short-term visitor to Amsterdam this need present no problem, as nearly everyone you meet will speak such good English that you could almost consider it to be the city's second language. The list of words and phrases below will help the polite and adventurous who wish to master everyday courtesies, interpret the menu, or disentangle themselves from sticky situations.

Pronunciation

Pronunciation is a question of tackling some rather difficult vowel sounds. Happily, spelling is phonetic, so once you've learned the sounds you'll be able to make a pretty accurate stab at pronouncing anything you read. The stress in Dutch, as in English, generally falls on the first syllable of a word.

Consonants

Most consonants are pronounced the same as in English. However, *ps*, *ts* and *ks* aren't aspirated (i.e. they're pronounced without the accompanying puff of air). Say *ch* and *g* as in the Scottish 'loch' (*g* is more strongly voiced in northern parts of the country). Good luck in getting your tongue around the combined *s* and *ch* sounds in words like *schip* (ship), *school* (school) or *schrijter* (writer). You have a choice for *r* —you can roll it at the back of your mouth or trill it behind your teeth, but you must *always* pronounce it. Say *w* halfway between the English 'w' and 'v', except before *r*, when you pronounce it 'v'. The Dutch *v* is closer to English 'f'. Say *j* as English 'y'; *sj* as English 'sh' and *tj* as English 'ch'.

Vowels

Pronounce the basic *a, e, i, o, u* sounds the same as you would in English, but *much shorter* (*a* as in 'hard', but shorter). Say *ie* as in 'neat', *oo* as in 'boat' and *oe* as in 'pool', but make all the sounds shorter. *aa* is like the 'a' in 'cat', but longer and *ee* is similar to the vowel sound in 'hail'. Say *eu* to rhyme with 'err', but round your lips tightly, and say *uu* as English *oo* in 'hoot'. The combination *ij* is a distinct letter in the Dutch alphabet, and is

Language

pronounced 'ay', whether it begins a word like *ijs* (ice/ice-cream), or comes in the middle, as in *wijn* (wine). The stretch of water north of Centraal Station is Het IJ, 'het ay'. The diphthong *ui* is a killer. In getting their tongues around the streetname Spui, Americans usually come up with 'Spew-ee' and the Brits manage 'Spow'. The Dutch sound is closer to the way a French person would say *œil*. If that leaves you none the wiser, try running together 'er-ee', but with no hint of an 'r' sound.

do you speak English?	*spreekt u Engels?*	where	*waar*
I don't understand	*Ik begrijp het niet*	what	*wat*
could you speak	*kunt u wat lang-*	when	*waneer*
more slowly?	*zamer spreken?*	which	*welk*
hello/goodbye	*dag*	who	*wie*
hi	*hoi* (grating to	why	*waarom*
	some ears)	where is the lavatory?	*waar is het toilet?*
'bye	*doei* (grating)	may I	*mag ik*
goodbye	*tot ziens*	can you	*kunt u*
see you later	*tot straks*	how much is	*hoeveel kost*
good morning/	*goede morgen/*	this/that?	*dit/dat?*
afternoon/night	*middag/nacht*	expensive	*duur*
good evening	*goedenavond*	cheap	*goedkoop*
yes/no/maybe	*ja/nee/misschien*	can you help me?	*kunt u mij*
please	*alstublieft*		*helpen?*
thank you/thanks	*dank u wel/bedankt*	I'm hungry/thirsty	*ik heb honger/dorst*
don't mention it	*niets te danken*	I'm in a hurry	*ik heb haast*
there is/there are	*er is/er zijn*	I'm lost	*ik ben verdwaald*
there isn't/aren't	*er is/zijn geen*	call a doctor quickly	*roep vlug een*
I have	*ik heb*		*dokter*
I don't have any	*ik heb geen*	call the police/	*roep de politie/*
I'd like	*ik wil graag*	an ambulance	*een ambulance*
we'd like	*wij willen graag*	entrance/exit	*ingang/uitgang*
I like it	*ik vind het leuk*	push/pull	*duwen/trekken*
I don't like it	*ik vind het*	open/closed	*open/gesloten*
	niet leuk		*(dicht)*

Meeting People

how do you do?	(say your name and	fine, thanks	*heel goed, dank je*
	surname clearly)	and you?	*en u/jij?*
how are you?	*hoe maakt u het?*	my name is...	*mijn naam is...*
very well, thank you	*uitstekend, dank u*	what are you having?	*wat neem je?*

Hotel

single room	*eenpersoonskamer*
double room	*tweepersoonskamer*
with private bath/shower/toilet	*met privé bad/douche/toilet*
may I see the room?	*mag ik de kamer zien?*
did anyone telephone for me?	*heeft er iemand voor mij gebeld?*
may I see the manager, please?	*mag ik de directeur spreken, alstublieft?*

Transport

airport	*luchthaven/vliegveld*	car	*auto*
customs	*douane*	bicycle	*fiets/rijwiel*
railway station	*trein station*	ticket	*kaartje*
platform	*perron*	occupied/reserved	*bezet/gereserveerd*
platform five	*spoor vijf*	where can I get a taxi?	*waar kan ik een taxi*
			krijgen?

what's the fare to...?	wat kost het naar...?	single/return	enkeltje/retourtje
take me to this address	breng me naar dit adres	change (trains)	overstappen
I want to go to...	ik wil naar...	when does the next/ first/last train leave?	wanner vertrek de volgende/eerste/ laatste trein?
how can I get to...?	hoe kom ik bij...?		
where is...?	waar is...?	how long does it take?	hoe lang duurt het?
the ticket office	het loket	near/far	dichtbij/ver weg
I'd like a ticket to...	ik wil graag een kaartje naar...	left/right/ straight ahead	links/rechts/ vooruit

Numbers

nought	nul	seventy	zeventig
one/two/three	een/twee/drie	eighty	tachtig
four/five/six	vier/vijf/zes	ninety	negentig
seven/eight/nine	zeven/acht/negen	hundred	honderd
ten/eleven/twelve	tien/elf/twaalf	two hundred and twenty	tweehonderd- twintig
thirteen, fourteen etc.	dertien/veertien etc.	thousand	duizend
twenty	twintig	million	een miljoen
twenty-one	eenentwintig	first/1st	eerste/1e
twenty-two	tweeëntwintig (etc.)	second/2nd	tweede/2e
thirty	dertig	third/3rd	derde/3e
forty	veertig	fourth/4th	vierde/4e
fifty	vijftig	eighth/8th	achtste/8e
sixty	zestig		

Time

what time is it?	hoe laat is het?	tomorrow	morgen
one o'clock	een uur	morning/afternoon	morgen/middag
a quarter past one	kwart over een	evening/night	avond/nacht
half past one	half twee [sic]	Monday	maandag
a quarter to two	kwart voor twee	Tuesday	dinsdag
ten to/past three	tien voor/over drie	Wednesday	woensdag
twenty past five	tien voor half zes	Thursday	donderdag
twenty-five to eight	vijf over half acht	Friday	vrijdag
I'll come at 2 o'clock	ik kom om twee uur	Saturday/Sunday	zaterdag/zondag
today	vandaag	day/week/month	dag/week/maand
yesterday	gisteren	year	jaar

Menu Guide

may I see the menu/wine list?	mag ik de spijskaart/wijnkaart zien?
bon appétit	eet smakelijk
it tastes good/bad	het smaakt lekker/niet lekker
may I have the bill, please?	mag ik de rekening, alstublieft?
waiter/waitress	ober/serveerster
service	bediening
starter	voorgerecht
soup	soep
main course	hoofdgerecht
dish of the day	dagschotel
dessert	nagerecht

Drinks

a beer, please	*een pils, alstublieft*	fizzy mineral water	*spa rood* (brand)
a bottle of wine	*een fles wijn*	still mineral water	*spa blauw*
red/white	*rode/witte*	coffee (with milk)	*koffie (verkeerd)*
sweet/dry	*zoete/droge*	tea	*thee*
fresh orange juice	*jus d'orange*	(with milk/lemon)	*(met melk/citroen)*
tomato juice	*tomatensap*		

Dutch Specialities

amandelbroodje	sweet roll with almond-paste filling
appelgebak	world-famous apple pie
appelmoes	apple sauce (with everything)
belegd broodje	bread roll with variety of fillings
bitterbal	ball of meat purée covered in breadcrumbs and deep fried
blinde vink	slice of veal rolled around stuffing
boerenomelet	omelette with vegetables and bacon
drie-in-de-pan	fluffy pancake with currants
erwtensoep	thick pea soup with sausages in it
frikandel	meatballs
hete bliksem	potatoes, bacon and apples cooked in butter, salt and sugar
Hollandse nieuwe	freshly caught filleted herring
hutspot	hotchpotch, i.e. hotpot (beef and vegetable stew)
kroket	croquette (with any filling imaginable)
pannekoek	pancake
poffertjes	mini doughnut-like pancakes
rolpens	fried slices of beef and tripe with apple
speculaas	spiced almond biscuit
uitsmijter	bread, ham and fried eggs (and variations)
vla	custard, served with everything that doesn't have *appelmoes* (q.v.)
Vlaamse karbonade	braised beef and onions—usually with beer
wentelteefje	bread fried in egg batter, then sprinkled with cinnamon and sugar

Main page references are in **bold**. Page references to maps are in *italics*.

Index

Why pay more?

Amsterdam

from
£30
single

- Flights from London Luton and Liverpool
- All our fares are flexible – flights can be changed for just £10 plus any difference in fare!
- Our one way fares allow you to return when you like, and unlike other airlines we don't require any minimum stay to get the cheapest prices!
- **Save £5 on all return flight booked online**

easyJet.com
the web's favourite airline